55

D0788673

The Ethics and
Mores of Race

The Ethics and Mores of Race

Equality after the History of Philosophy

Naomi Zack

ROWMAN & LITTLEFIELD PUBLISHERS, INC.
Lanham • Boulder • New York • Toronto • Plymouth, UK

Published by Rowman & Littlefield Publishers, Inc.
A wholly owned subsidiary of The Rowman & Littlefield Publishing Group, Inc.
4501 Forbes Boulevard, Suite 200, Lanham, Maryland 20706
http://www.rowmanlittlefield.com

Estover Road, Plymouth PL6 7PY, United Kingdom

British Library Cataloguing in Publication Information Available

Library of Congress Cataloging-in-Publication Data

Zack, Naomi, 1944–
    The ethics and mores of race : equality after the history of philosophy / Naomi Zack.
        p. cm.
    Includes bibliographical references (p.   ) and index.
    ISBN 978-1-4422-1125-4 (cloth : alk. paper) — ISBN 978-1-4422-1127-8 (ebook)
    1. Racism—Moral and ethical aspects—United States. 2. Race discrimination—United States. 3. Social ethics—United States. 4. United States—Social life and customs. 5. Racism. 6. Race discrimination. 7. Social ethics. 8. Manners and customs. I. Title.
    HT1523.Z33 2011
    177'.5—dc22   2011007583

∞™ The paper used in this publication meets the minimum requirements of American National Standard for Information Sciences—Permanence of Paper for Printed Library Materials, ANSI/NISO Z39.48-1992.

Printed in the United States of America

To my first grandchild, Cloé Milan Mahon
(b. December 28, 2010)

Men occasionally stumble over the truth, but most of them pick themselves up and hurry off as if nothing ever happened.

—Winston Churchill

Not thine the labour to complete, and yet thou art not free to cease!

—*The Talmud*

Contents

Acknowledgments

$\mathcal{A}$fter almost twenty years of thinking, speaking, and writing about the epistemology, ontology, and philosophy of science of race and mixed race, in May 2009 I decided to write a book about race relations and racism. My monograph *Ethics for Disaster* had just been published, but still in a moral frame of mind I began to think about how ethics, as understood by philosophers, could intersect with race and racism. This inquiry led me through key moments in the history of moral and political philosophy in a process of discovery that almost seemed to have a plot. It was a project requiring that I find the end for myself before seeking sustained discussion. Nevertheless, I had good support and assistance along the way, from several sources.

First, I thank Jason Hill (DePaul University) for his interest in the project in terms of his own normative work in cosmopolitanism. We do not agree on where cosmopolitanism fits into the architectonic of an ethics of race, but this makes his engagement with my work interesting. Jason Jordan (University of Oregon) read the first five chapters of an earlier manuscript, and his points of disagreement with my leftish liberatory perspective were interesting spurs toward greater precision. Jordan's historical erudition of ancient and medieval philosophy was very useful in several places (he also helped correct page proofs). I am also grateful to George Theodoulou for editorial promptings in my preparation of "Requirements for an Ethics of Race," an overview of the present book, published in *Global Dialogue* (volume 12, number 2, summer/autumn 2010—Race and Racisms. www.worlddialogue.org).

Thanks to Jeffry Gauthier and his students and colleagues at the Department of Philosophy at the University of Portland. The paper I gave there, "The Need for an Ethics of Race," in May 2010, was a productive opportunity for me to "try out" the first four chapters while the work was in progress.

My participation in the Roland Altherr Memorial Symposium and Lecture at Haverford College in November 2010 was one of my most enjoyable academic experiences—ever. Joel Yurdin organized my visit and both he and his colleagues took up my ideas, alongside the seniors who had selected me as their philosophical interlocutor for the year, and read most of the manuscript before I arrived. The philosophers at Haverford surprised me in finding an ethics of race a novel idea, and their willingness to step into this first comprehensive attempt at the subject was very encouraging.

Once again, I am grateful to have worked on a book with Jon Sisk at Rowman & Littlefield. Jon remains as decisive and steady at the helm as he has been since I first published with the press in 1995. I also thank Darcy Evans, acquisitions editor, for her editorial assistance, and Kellie Hagan, production editor, who oversaw the manuscript transition to a book. Both Darcy and Kellie have been conscientious, skillful, and attentive. Jeremy Rehwald's noninvasive and highly professional copyediting helped streamline the process and I appreciate his contribution also.

I'm afraid that there are almost certainly many remaining mistakes, but they are all mine.

—Naomi Zack, Eugene, Oregon

Introduction

Ethics, Mores, and Race

In The Moral Life of Children, child psychologist Robert Coles relates how he tried to understand the courageous behavior of black children who were the first to desegregate schools in the US South during the 1960s. At first, Coles used clinical terminology to describe six-year-old Ruby Bridges, who day after day had braved a gauntlet of jeering white adults to enter her new school. But his wife told him, "You are making her sound as if she ought to be on her way to a child guidance clinic, but she is walking into a school building— and no matter the threats, she is holding her head up high, even smiling at her obscene hecklers." Coles believed that his wife had made a judgment that Ruby Bridges had character. Ruby's comportment compared to that of her adult hecklers dramatizes the difference between ethics and mores.[1] Character is a matter of ethics; the defense of racial segregation is also a matter of ethics, but it is strongly motivated by mores.

It is difficult to make ethical judgments about racial matters in contemporary US society. People may have strong ethical intuitions in single concrete cases, but there is no general ethical system in common reference. As Coles's example illustrates, real life can serve up disturbing expressions of mores. The biggest problem with mores as a source of opinions and values is that conflicts between different mores very easily reduce to conflicts between the people who belong to the groups that generate the mores. The language of professionals can neutralize high emotion, but here, too, at the expense of ethical judgments. Ethical judgments are risky in the absence of a recognized general ethical system because they may seem to be mere opinions with the potential to ignite fresh conflict. Philosophy has something to offer here, the potential to provide general intellectual support for ethical judgments concerning race.

Philosophers now use the terms 'ethical'/'ethics' and 'moral'/'morals' synonymously.[2] But the public restricts the words ethical/ethics to behavior in civic or work life, whereas moral/morals are reserved for private life. For example, Americans talk about ethics in business, medicine, and politics, and philosophy obliges this discourse with 'applied ethics' for these fields and others, yielding "professional ethics." But in ordinary life, individuals who misbehave sexually or abuse drugs are criticized for their morals. Those who take good care of their families and obey the rules of their religion are considered "morally good," or even just "good" or "moral." Those undeserving of such approval, on account of their deliberate actions, are "immoral," whereas those who are oblivious to moral values and rules are "amoral."

"Ethics" derives from the Greek *ethos*, pertaining to the spirit or character of a people. "Moral" comes from the Latin *mores*, pertaining to the vital customs necessary to sustain a people.[3] This distinction between spirit and practice is relaxed when ethics and morals are used interchangeably by philosophers. But the distinction is supported by the close connection between the mores of different American groups and what they think of as their morals, in contrast to their relegation of more formal matters of principle and character to official life.

Part of the difference between ethics and mores is a distinction between individual and group. Philosophers have concentrated on the hearts, minds, and actions of individuals, whereas ethos/mores and the morality arising from them are group based. Individual perspectives can accommodate greater abstraction than group perspectives. In their rhetorical address to individuals as readers,[4] Western philosophers have been able to construct abstract and ideal ethical systems, requiring for their validation only the comprehension and agreement of individuals, who do not have to be in the same place and time as either one another or the philosopher being read. Moral systems in society, by contrast, are closely tied to understanding and agreement within groups, occurring at the same time, often defined by place. Mores and morals are thus concretely historical, compared to ethics. Mores need not be ethical and ethics does not require a foundation in mores.

Both mores and ethics are *normative*: the common subject is right action and the nature of the good. Philosophers work with the moral systems constructed within their discipline—virtue ethics, deontology, and consequentialism. They call 'moral theory' that discourse which compares and contrasts moral systems and analyzes the value terms ('good,' 'right') used within moral systems. The substance of philosophical work in ethics is theoretical inquiry. The public continually demonstrates that its morals do not come from this or that abstract system, but from religion, tradition, and family. Its inquiries into morals are more likely to involve recourse to role models, memorials, and retelling of group histories than to abstract or theoretical considerations.

Philosophers hold that disputes over moral systems and their applications can be resolved by reasoning and orderly argument, through the recognition of incompatible beginning premises, or via analyses of the meanings of moral terms. Disputes or struggles among those with different mores-based morals are not matters of orderly argument, so much as contending constellations of affect, competition for recognition, and material group interests. In the absence of agreement, resolution lies in the outcome of social contest or overt conflict, with war as the extreme. An agreement to disagree and keep on disagreeing is a rule of discourse in ethics. Hope that one's side will win, but with a prior agreement to accept defeat, is a rule for settling disputes about mores.

Toleration within the same society of different moral perspectives arising from mores is one of the meanings of social, political, or cultural "pluralism." But the theoretical model of pluralism, in which pluralism is put forth as a democratic ideal, often fails to capture the strife in the reality of continually competing groups. Moreover, pluralism is often described as though the views and practices of all striving groups have equal merit. For example, in an April 2010 poll of the views of Tea Party Movement members, whose membership is 89 percent white and 1 percent African American, it was found that they were more likely than other Americans to believe that "too much was made of the problems of African-Americans."[5] That a question of whether "too much" is being made of a particular group's problems is considered a valid question for polling reduces any ethical issues involved in attitudes and behavior toward that group to mere matters of opinion. The neglected ethical question is whether African Americans have problems based on their racial identities and whether it is morally obligatory for others to pay attention to those problems.

Ethics and mores are frequently in conflict. Practical applications of professional ethics or an ethical policy such as school desegregation may occur as interventions in practices taken for granted. Ethical actions can break with mores, as individuals and small groups make a fresh normative start. We can say now that racial segregation is part of American mores, even though it is held to be unethical, not only philosophically but in the official, formal public domain to which ethics are relegated by nonphilosophers. But this has been true only after the civil rights movements successfully challenged the practice of segregation on ethical grounds. It has been taken for granted over the history of Western philosophy, beginning with Socrates, that ethics will diverge from mores. However, the public views ethical actions that are opposed to existing mores as heroic, strange, or morally bad, depending on the context, how well the issues are understood, and how strong the opposition. (For example, whistle-blowing is considered heroic, animal rights activism, strange, and atheism, bad.)

Overall, there remains a big rhetorical and social distance between philosophical and formal ethical treatments of race, on the one hand, and what race means in practice and how ordinary people think about it, on the other. This is mainly a normative distance between race theorists' judgments that some practices and beliefs are unethical, and the acceptance or approval of those same beliefs and actions in private, social, and official life. For example, most race theorists consider the ongoing practice of *white privilege*, or the way white people continue to benefit from race-based advantages in comparison to non-whites, to be unethical. However, in private and social life, white privilege is taken for granted and the subject is difficult to broach in noncontroversial ways in formal or official contexts, and apparently impossible to explain.[6] In real life, including the most formal public contexts, there is no recognized ethics of race, and to a large extent even theorists of race advance the mores of the groups to which they belong or with which they have the most sympathy. The absence of an ethics of race and the practice of mores contribute to a failure to regard issues of race in ethical terms.

The historical and contemporary reality of race in the United States encompasses race relations (interactions between different racial groups and their members), laws concerning members of different racial groups, the mores of these groups, and individual identities based on group membership. This reality is mostly a matter of mores. It is difficult to render theoretical judgments about race ethically persuasive and obligatory when such judgments conflict with the mores of either the white majority or different nonwhite groups. What may be genuine ethical judgments about race often sound like attacks on existing mores because the common ground on which they can be expressed and understood, as ethical judgments concerning race, does not yet exist. Whites object to what could be ethical judgments that identify racism; nonwhites object to what could be ethical judgments about racial identities and loyalties. Just to say this is a simplification because racial discourse is shaped by distinctive, varied contexts and multiple meanings. Even the word "race" is ambiguous, sometimes referring to skin color, other times to skin color and group history, sometimes to biology and genealogy, other times to culture by itself or culture combined with the other factors. Exponentially more complicated than this American situation is the global reality and history of race.

Mores were not the original ground for racial liberation or social justice in American society. Ethics used to be the primary tool against white oppression. Martin Luther King spoke ethically in expressing his dream about a future in which a person's character would be considered more important in assessment of human worth than the color of her skin. And before King, nineteenth-century abolitionists spoke from ethical principles when they inveighed against slavery. The view that slavery was a "moral wrong"—in the public's sense of an ethical wrong—based on fundamental principles of human worth and core human equality, was put forth not only by abolitionists but by some slave owners, such as Thomas Jefferson.[7] Abolitionists could talk about race relations on the same ethical ground that allowed them to talk about harms to whites. Emerson wrote: "I think we must get rid of slavery or we must get rid of freedom. . . . If you put a chain around the neck of a slave, the other end fastens itself around your own."[8]

Not everyone in the nineteenth century made it to that high ground. Mark Twain's character, Huckleberry Finn, for example, thought it was immoral for him to help his friend, Jim, escape from slavery. Huck solved his dilemma of conscience by vowing to eschew "morality," which he thought was coextensive with the mores of his slave-owning community.[9] He was not thinking ethically (or morally in the philosophical sense). After the Civil War, generations of white Americans preserved their social superiority based on race through mores of segregation, overt legal discrimination, economic exploitation, and institutionalized terrorism against the free descendants of slaves, as well as Native Americans and Chinese immigrants. These white mores, now considered racist, were accepted as ways of life. They had no ethical support but were justified by social and speculative, pseudoscientific ideas of white superiority and nonwhite inferiority. Matching the dominance of mores based on white racial life and identities, nonwhites did not endure their oppression as abstract ethical individuals. They created lifeways in reaction, for survival, and as resistance, which became their distinctive group mores. W. E. B. Du Bois famously argued for the retention of ideas of race that included cultural aspirations, so that American blacks could realize their full destiny as a "race."[10] In the officially and formally egalitarian, democratic, but not yet fully racially just US society that endures today, the historical legacy of race remains a contest of mores, defended by disparate moral rhetoric (arising from the contesting mores).

Today, almost all of contemporary public and scholarly discussion about race expresses conflicts in morals that are closely tied to mores. The national conversation about race is superficial compared to a scholarly tradition that is largely carried on within the intellectually segregated subject of race, usually by nonwhites. Thus, in the academy, "race" is practiced in distinctive subfields in the humanities and social sciences, mainly by small minorities of nonwhite scholars. In the media, white announcers, even or especially on public radio, tend to introduce discussions of race with preambles about how it is not often talked about. Indeed, the more it is talked about, the more fervently it is described as something arcane. This rendering of talk about race as "exotic" in the public auditorium supports the segregation and devaluation of the nonwhite subjects of discourse.

There are black and Hispanic radio and television programs, but all the rest are just radio and television, not white radio and television. However, it would be highly problematic if everyone referred to mainstream radio and television as "white radio and television" because that would imply that it was for whites only. The symbols of American segregation have advanced from explicit markers of facilities according to whether they are for white or nonwhite use to markers only for nonwhite interest. No one could or would want to stop nonwhites from consuming the mass media. But it is assumed that only nonwhites would find black, Hispanic, or Korean radio and television more interesting than radio and television. The history that has resulted in blacks having more interest in some topics than whites is the same history that constrains whites from putting a white label on entertainment that is mainly of interest to them because it iconographically (i.e., white actors playing white people) represents them. Knowledge of this history of segregation results in feelings of guilt and shame for many whites, so they do not easily discuss or explicitly mention this history, even when it is directly relevant to a present situation. But most blacks are neither ashamed of this history nor do they have reason to feel guilty about it, so they talk about it more easily, especially among themselves and other people of color. This moral structure perpetuates a general sense that race is something that belongs only to nonwhites, and that general sense is a matter of both white and nonwhite mores. Race in early twenty-first-century America is stuck in mores.

Would the familiar subjects discussed in the scholarship of race, chief among them, racism, appear differently if they were integrated with insights from ethics and moral philosophy? What if it were agreed beforehand that ethical insights derived independently of race were to provide standards for conclusions about race? Would this solve long-standing contentions in race debates, such as questions about the nature of racism, the existence of white privilege, and whether human racial categories ought to be eliminated? Would those ethical answers put the subject of race on the intellectual map in a more accessible place for white, in addition to nonwhite, intellectuals? The answers to these questions could depend on the ethical system(s) accepted beforehand. Independently of the subject of race, philosophers have little consensus about competing ethical systems, so the philosophical results of 'integrating' race into the rest of philosophical ethical/moral discourse would likely be inconclusive. Still, we might be able to see what different ethical/moral systems and traditions could contribute to the subject of race at this time. In the process, certain moral impasses concerning race—in that sense pertaining to mores—might be broken up for one or more of several reasons: their ethical treatments could be more compelling than conflicting stances based on mores; the perceived importance of standing disagreements might be diminished because they turn out not to be ethical matters; different sides might approach the same issue with different facts and meanings, yielding their disagreement more of a misunderstanding than a contradictory clash; different views may be compatible in ethical terms; some conflicts might resolve in favor of one side or the other. Despite ongoing disagreements, explicitly ethical treatments of race would move the discussion ahead, as well as make the subject of ethics more inclusive.

But of course, before the discussion concerning race can be moved ahead in this way, ethics itself, as distinct from mores, has to be an attractive enterprise with basic assumptions and methods that all principled parties can accept. For the public, this is a matter of conscience, social change, and rhetoric. For philosophers and those in other humanistic disciplines who address race, what could begin as a fruitful theoretical issue might quickly encounter skepticism about the possibility of using Western philosophical ethics for racial liberatory purposes.[11] Beginning with Plato, Western moral philosophy seems to have been elitist on exactly those grounds that later came to be the grounds of modern race, with its attendant white racial supremacy. So why should intellectuals who are people of color make use of a system of thought that was used to exclude people of color from the goods of human life?

The answer is that the system of thought cannot be appropriated just exegetically but requires a critical reading, an inquiry in search of philosophical egalitarianism. Along the way, it should be possible to show how certain theoretical gaps or omissions enabled professional moral philosophers to propound elevated and seemingly egalitarian theories that were compatible with inequality and injustice in the world. The inquiry here is not a matter of pointing out hypocrisy or other kinds of disconnections between theory and practice, but discovering the inadequacies of some otherwise good moral theories.

The trajectory of this book is to garner intellectual support for an ethics of race through an inquiry into the history of moral philosophy. I cannot promise an ethics of race, itself, because the diversity of racial experience and history is too great to admit of one ethics of race. But a critical and historical examination of ethics as a philosophical subject does yield *requirements* for an ethics of race. Beginning with a general and vague presumption of human equality, several moments in the history of moral philosophy contribute to these requirements, although it is often because their inegalitarian presumptions are now so blatant.

Any ethics, of anything, is indebted to Plato for his break with mores and to Aristotle for his development of a psychological technology for character construction, even though both legitimized elitisms that later supported false and racist racial taxonomies (chapter 1). Cosmopolitanism provides a cautionary requirement of openheartedness for any ethics of race, although it fails to generate ethical judgments (chapter 2). Ancient natural law theory, although never egalitarian, nonetheless opens the possibility for broad human equality (chapter 3). The coexistence of slavery with all of the classic moral systems turns out to depend theoretically on an overvaluation of the *form* of property ownership without regard for what may be owned (chapter 4). Christianity introduces a powerful notion of human equality, but not for mortal existence; and Christian emphasis on fictive entities is problematic for empirically grounded moral theory in general (chapter 5). Social contract theory, from Hobbes to Rousseau, vacillates between freedom for some and oppression for the sake of security, while at the same time allowing for crushing human inequalities in practical terms; Rawlsian justice-as-fairness does not correct this problem (chapter 6). Deontology and utilitarianism, both inspired by Rousseau, are promising for systems of universal human moral equality, despite the Eurocentrism of Kant and Mill (chapter 7). It does become possible to state a number of requirements for any ethics of race as a practice of global egalitarian humanism; this is an ethical and not a legal theory, but it goes beyond the ameliorations of egalitarian humanitarianism (conclusion).

This book has three implicit themes: the detachment of ethics from mores, the value of a cosmopolitan perspective, and the connection of philosophical ethics to ideas of government. Philosophical ethics has been limited by ideas of government, beginning with Plato's and Aristotle's invention of ethics from elite perspectives within the Greek city-state, extending to the limitations on ethics from ideas of the modern nation-state, and now coming to rest on the possibility of a global egalitarian humanism that depends on declarations and protections of international human rights. Nevertheless, in developing requirements for an ethics of race, I assume that the discourse of ethics is always able to assess government and that the practice of ethics can result in political change.

NOTES

1. Robert Coles, *The Moral Life of Children* (New York: Grove Atlantic, 1986), 142.
2. Until the early twentieth century in the United States, moral philosophy encompassed all of the humanistic subjects in philosophy and included political theory, aesthetics, philosophy of religion, philosophy of language, psychology, and philosophy of mind. But now the part of moral philosophy that addresses choices and values toward the general end of human well-being is known to philosophers as 'ethics,' 'moral theory,' and 'moral systems.'
3. The distinction drawn here between ethos and mores has been broadly accepted for some time. See, for instance, *The Concise Oxford Dictionary of Current English*, ed. H. W. Fowler and F. G. Fowler (London: Oxford University Press, 1954), 416 and 785.
4. After Plato, the main reference for philosophical discourse, spoken or written, became the written text. The transition from reading aloud together to reading si-

lently alone supported the individual as the primary audience for philosophers. For a historical account of how that transition was made possible by the addition of spaces between written words, see Paul Henry Saenger, *Space between Words: The Origins of Silent Reading* (Stanford, CA: Stanford University Press, 1997).

5. The poll was conducted during April 5–12, 2010, by *CBS News* and the *New York Times*. Results were released on April 14, 2010, at www.nytimes.com/2010/04/15/us/politics/15poll.html (consulted on April 16, 2010).

6. Consider this example: Soon after President Obama nominated Judge Sonya Sotomayor for the US Supreme Court, the media reported that she had said in the past that a wise Latina would make better rulings on the bench than a white male. During the Senate hearing for Sotomayor's nomination, Senator Lindsey Graham (R–South Carolina) said, in reference to that remark, "If I said anything remotely like that, my career would have been over." Peter Baker and Nela Lewis, "Sotomayor Vows 'Fidelity to the Law' as Hearings Start," *New York Times*, July 13, 2009, www.nytimes .com. Graham's indignation could have been enabled by his ignorance of what some observers of race in America see as white privilege. He was apparently unaware of the fact that statements of expertise based on race or ethnicity have different meanings when made by nonwhites than they do when made by whites, because of the history and ongoing reality of nonwhite disadvantage in US society. In denial of this history and reality, he purported not to know that nonwhites are permitted to say things about race that would sound racist if uttered by whites. While progressive commentators grasped all of this intuitively, as Graham's remark was circulated they did not explicitly refer to white privilege. Some of those same progressives went on to fault Sotomayor for telling the senators that good judges were and should be neutral vis-à-vis their own race, or any matter of race, in making decisions, thereby displaying their own apparent ignorance of her ongoing disadvantage as a Puerto Rican nominee for the US Supreme Court. There are several possibilities of interpretation here: progressives as well as Republicans in public life are unaware of the concept of white privilege; everyone is aware of the concept but deems it unacceptable for public mention; some of the officials and reporters are aware of the concept of white privilege but do not think that all or part of the public is, so they deliberately avoid the concept to avoid upsetting the unaware.

7. Jefferson thought that liberty was the gift of God and that it was only a matter of time, given that "his justice cannot sleep forever," before slavery would end, perhaps even by "an exchange of situation." See Thomas Jefferson, "Manners," pp. 95–107, in *Notes on the State of Virginia, Race and the Enlightenment: A Reader*, ed. Emmanuel Chukwudi Eze (Cambridge, MA: Blackwell, 1997): 96 and 97.

8. Ralph Waldo Emerson, "Compensation" (185), in *The Journals and Miscellaneous Notebooks of Ralph Waldo Emerson*, vol. 6, ed. Raph H. Orth (Cambridge, MA: Harvard University Press, 1966), 215.

9. See Jonathan Bennett, "The Conscience of Huckleberry Finn," *Philosophy* 49 (1974): 123–34. Bennett considers Huck to have a bad moral system as a standard. The claim here is that the practice of slavery was not a moral system but a matter of mores.

10. W. E. B. Du Bois, "The Conservation of Races," reprinted in *The Idea of Race*, ed. Robert Bernasconi and Tommy L. Lott (Indianapolis, IN: Hackett, 2000), 108–17.

11. I was tempted to frame this in terms of Audre Lorde's overused phrase about the master's tools being used to dismantle his house. However, Lorde's skepticism was more general than the problem I am intending to address here. She wrote: "What does it mean when the tools of a racist patriarchy are used to examine the fruits of that same patriarchy? It means that only the most narrow perimeters of change are possible and admissible." Audre Lorde, "The Master's Tools Will Never Dismantle the Master's House," pp. 94–101, in *This Bridge Called My Back: Writings by Radical Women of Color,* ed. Cherríe Moraga and Gloria Anzaldúa (New York: Kitchen Sink Press, 1983): 94. Lorde seems to be saying that any methodology developed in patriarchal regimes or disciplines is itself patriarchal or racist. My own view of cultural practices, assuming that philosophy is one, is that cultural practices are not monolithic. I think that if a philosopher holds racist views, both as a person and as expressed in his or her philosophy, this does not mean that the whole of the philosophy created by that philosopher is racist. The question of whether criticism of the part that is racist would be admissible, while a different issue, raises the further question, admissible by whom or what? I don't think a monolithic answer can be given to that question, either.

Plato's and Aristotle's Invention of Ethics

$\mathcal{S}$ome contemporary thinkers understand the importance placed on the state by Plato and Aristotle to be a lost appreciation of how human beings become human in community. One aspect of that reading of Plato and Aristotle is a critical view of the individualistic perspective of later political theorists in the Western tradition, particularly Hobbes and Locke. But contemporary communitarian values notwithstanding, the importance placed on political community by Plato and Aristotle is not egalitarian. Both philosophers were talking to rulers and future rulers. That audience is rhetorically indicated by the concern in their political writings with how members of the ruling class should behave, and it has historical support in Plato's active participation in statecraft and Aristotle's role as tutor to Alexander.[1]

Plato begins the main text of the *Republic* with the premise that an examination of justice in the state will illuminate justice as an individual virtue, not only because the state is the individual "writ large" but because the state, in the form of the city-state of his time, was the locus of individuals—man could realize his nature as human only within the city-state.[2] This locus was as much a physical place as it was a shared imaginary realm that was the source of moral ideals. According to Aristotle, man is a political animal by nature,[3] and the virtuous individual both requires a just state for education and development and is likely to participate in government.[4] While it is true that for Plato and Aristotle, ethics and morality are strongly tied to politics and human flourishing in the polis, it is more striking how each wrested ethics and morality away from mores (the customs of a people), and perhaps even ethos (the spirit of a people). Indeed, any distinction between ethics and mores that is viable today owes that debt to Plato and Aristotle. The focus of this chapter will be on Plato's and Aristotle's *invention* of ethics.

Plato and Aristotle wrested abstract ethics from concrete mores *in a way tied to the nature of rulers.* One result was that the stage was set for understanding the ruled as inherently inferior to their rulers. It was not just the condition of being ruled that made the many inferior to the few who ruled them. Running deeper than the *roles* of rulers and ruled was a division of humankind into groups fit and able to be either rulers or ruled. Both Plato and Aristotle wanted the best to rule because the best deserved to rule, the best would be made even better by ruling, and the whole of society would benefit from rule by the best. Plato and Aristotle viewed democracy as an undesirable form of government because it could allow the least qualified elements of society to rule. (Plato thought that democracy was an anarchic form of government that was a stage between oligarchy and tyranny; Aristotle held a similar transition theory and thought that democracy could degenerate into mob rule.)[5]

For Plato, the best were philosophers capable of contemplating the forms, and for Aristotle, they were virtuous aristocratic men. This ancient division of humankind into a ruling class and everyone else is not a self-evident political beginning. For instance, Plato and Aristotle could have denied that humankind is naturally divided into those who can and should rule and those who can and should be ruled. They could have held that all should rule, directly, by representation, or by taking turns. (Aristotle does entertain some of these arrangements within the ruling class,[6] but not for the whole of society.) However, Plato and Aristotle did not seem to think that any justification was needed for human social hierarchy or their own acceptance of it.

Still, in terms of the present inquiry for an ethics of race, it needs to be emphasized that a hierarchy of human groups is not in itself a racial taxonomy. Hierarchy can be based on gender, wealth, age, skill, or any one or more of myriad human attributes and circumstances. And while this is not to say that Plato's and Aristotle's ideas of hierarchy were free of what we would consider ideas of race, it is important to guard against anachronism. The science of modern biology enabled the classification of human groups into racial hierarchies (as was legitimated by varied pronouncements from Hume, Kant, and Hegel) in the eighteenth and early nineteenth centuries.[7] That is, race alone was held to be the principle for ranking human groups. Without these innovations of early biology, we would not have the ideas of human races that we have today. It is anachronistic to assume that thinkers had such ideas prior to the modern science of biology.

Some thinkers, who do locate ideas of modern race in time periods before modern biology, may be searching for a system of human division that is more general than race. Such a system would be capable of supporting, if not "generating," ideas of modern race.[8] For example, given a preexisting human hierarchy, differences in race could be lined up with it, so that the "best" race would be on top.

Without doubt, suggestions of a more general hierarchy, which also had elements of modern racial hierarchies, were present in Plato's and Aristotle's writings. Both assumed that part of the superiority of individuals worthy of ruling was their family genealogy. This is evident in Plato's breeding policy in the *Republic* and Aristotle's presumption in *Nicomachean Ethics* that in order to be virtuous, one must be well-bred.[9] Genealogy remains an important component of racial identity in common sense today, and until the acceptance of Mendelian heredity in the early twentieth century, genealogy was believed to be the mechanism for racial inheritance in biology.[10]

There is no anachronism in identifying the notion of a human division into hierarchical groups, together with the importance of genealogy, as the *historical foundation* of that modern system of biological race, which is now known not to have a scientific foundation. To put it more strongly, insofar as the architects of modern biological racial taxonomies took it for granted that humankind could be divided into a hierarchy of hereditary groups, the ancient assumptions formed a ready-made foundation for their project. Race could either be introduced as a new principle of hierarchy, or racial differences could be lined up with some other hierarchy. In either case, the overarching idea would be that there are natural rankings within humankind. Nevertheless, it is important to remember that hereditary hierarchies are not in themselves inevitably or exclusively linked to race, as they can also support divisions based on class or occupation (e.g., familial transmissions of farming, fishing, mining, sometimes ruling itself, and so forth). In a manner more detailed than a simple hierarchical structure, Plato's proposal in the *Republic* to tell the masses that humans were divided into gold, silver, and bronze types and that breeding should occur only within types appears to predate the social and legal segregation that constructed and supported modern racial divisions.[11] In a similar way, Aristotle's notion of born slaves,[12] which seems to have been a reference to differences in individual skill and aptitudes, was echoed in nineteenth-century justifications of specifically black slavery, although by then ideas of inherited aptitudes were used to categorize entire racial groups and not just individuals. Such social technologies of domination and segregation are of historical interest in studying the development of ideas of race and racial oppression.

However, the historical narrative of race, as a philosophical subject, is distinct from that of ethics. Plato and Aristotle invented philosophical ethics as patterns of thought distinct from mores. Their philosophical inventions were also cognitive directives for rulers that told them what to think about, and how. Plato wrote that, for the sake of society, rulers should think about the Forms of the Good and the True. Aristotle described how aristocrats could acquire the virtues that would make them good aristocrats. We can look back now and easily imagine that whole groups of those who would not have been approved by them to rule had identities similar to those who by the nineteenth century were designated not–white. Nevertheless, the invention of philosophical ethics as distinct from mores in the ancient world was not the invention of a racial taxonomy. Even if they assumed that only Greeks of specified lineages would rule Greece, this would not be a racial designation. Genealogy has been strongly associated with ideas of modern race, but modern racial taxonomy is a more general system of sorting than hereditary ties to specific peoples.

An ethical or political system based on human hierarchy is not the same thing as a taxonomy of either races or racial identities. That the content and methods of thought for rulers were later associated with the race of rulers is a separate issue. There is no evidence that Plato and Aristotle held that having what moderns would recognize as a certain racial identity was sufficient to rule. If it were necessary (i.e., all rulers as they described or could imagine them had it), then this would be part of the foundations of Western ethics that needs to be discarded in order to have what would count for us as an ethics of race. But neither is there any textual evidence that they considered anything like racial identity to be a requirement for ruling.

Apart from these considerations about how ancient ideas of political hierarchy and group differences compare with, and might have become historical foundations for, later ideas and practices of race, it is now possible to develop the main claim of this chapter: Plato and Aristotle invented ethics as patterns of thought distinct from existing mores—not only distinct from the mores of their time, but in principle distinct from all mores. We will see later how philosophical ethics developed over centuries with gaps and assumptions that left room for modern racial hierarchies and racism. But for now, the important issue is the distinct novelty of ethics. Ethics today has retained the same distinction from mores that it first had in the ancient world. After several centuries of race and racism, that distinction remains a powerful contribution to human equality and social justice.

PLATO'S INVENTION OF ETHICS FOR RULERS

Plato proceeds through three stages in his invention of philosophical ethics as distinct from mores: first, an application of metaphysical analysis to virtues; second, a development of value discourse for discussing ethics; third, the construction of an ethical system based on a description of an ideal state. The first stage starts with Socrates in the early dialogues, which record his questioning of received opinion. Socrates' questions not only revealed the fundamental ignorance of his contemporary experts in the arts, politics, religion, and even philosophy, but sometimes made his interlocutors appear silly, stupid, and unworthy of their status. Socrates revealed a lack in his interlocutors, as well as himself, that in retrospect can be viewed as ethical/moral in the sense of philosophical knowledge—they lacked a philosophical ethics. For example, when

Socrates brings young Hippocrates to a gathering at which the great sophist, Protagoras, is holding forth, the discussion begins with Protagoras' answer to what he can teach the youth: "The proper care of his personal affairs, so that he may best manage his own household, and also of the state's affairs so as to become a real power in the city, both as speaker and man of action."[13] Socrates objects that being a good citizen cannot be taught in the way specific skills and arts can. Protagoras counters that virtue is taught to young men, especially those from cultured and wealthy families, as a matter of course. Socrates then tries to shift the discussion to the nature of virtue, for example, asking if it is an integral whole, like a face that is made up of eyes and ears, or more like a piece of gold made up of like parts.[14] Protagoras has no satisfactory answer to Socrates' line of questioning because he is interested in success and goodness in a conventional sense while Socrates wants to pursue the metaphysics of virtue.

Socrates' encounter with Protagoras is superfluously technical, even in contemporary terms. In *Charmides*, *Laches*, and *Lysis*, Socrates applies similar philosophical methods to the virtues of sophrosyne (a quality combining self-knowledge and temperance), courage, and friendship. He forces his interlocutors to think and speak about virtues in a way different from their treatment in ordinary discourse, and they find that on the abstract ground that Socrates introduces they know very little about even well-received virtues. The abstract methodology is not new in itself, since it derives from analyses previously developed by the so-called pre-Socratic philosophers for considering the natural world. What is new is Socrates' sustained systematic application of such methods of thought to the virtues, or, more generally, to the human social and psychological worlds.[15] This application is the first stage in Plato's separation of ethics from mores.

The dialogues immediately preceding Socrates' death dramatically effect the philosophical separation between ethics and mores, showing in the process how philosophy illuminates values that transcend the concerns of normal existence. That is the second stage of Plato's shift from mores to ethics. The trial and death dialogues are rhetorically compelling because of their dramatic examples. While walking to his trial for practicing philosophy, Socrates dallies to converse with Euthyphro, a priest, who presents himself as exceptionally pious for having brought his own father to court on a charge of murder. On the pretext of seeking help for his own defense, Socrates mockingly draws Euthyphro out on his claim that piety is what the gods love. The result of their conversation can be expressed in the following problematic:

> Is an action pious (morally good/just) because the gods love it, or do the gods love it because it is already pious? If the first, then we have no solution to divine arbitrariness, because the gods often disagree (or there are conflicting religions). But if the gods love pious actions because they are already pious before they love them, then we still need to know what piety (goodness/justice) is.[16]

After Socrates leads Euthyphro in and out of this nested dilemma, which effectively severs a rational connection between morality and religion, he wants to begin again by returning to the original question of what piety is. Euthyphro rushes away—"Another time, then, Socrates, for I am in a hurry and must be off this minute"[17]—but the wider audience is left with the question that arises out of the incoherence of prevailing mores. What is piety (goodness/justice)? Socrates doesn't give an answer to this question or even give reason to believe that he himself has one. Socrates at that point is the historical Socrates as portrayed by Plato, to be distinguished from Socrates as Plato's philosophical alter ego in the *Republic*.[18] The historical Socrates presumably did not have a moral system. A moral system was among the things that the historical Socrates became famous for saying that he knew he did not know.

Socrates' apparent lightheartedness continues into his trial, where it becomes clear that although he does not take the trial itself seriously, he is deadly in earnest about what it is about, namely whether or not he has been impious and corrupted the youth of Athens.[19] He spars verbally with the young prosecutor, Meletus, propping him up so as to make a fool of him, as he did with Euthyphro. In their sham debate, Socrates recounts his past behavior in details that substantiate the charges against him, from exactly the perspective of those who do not follow his new way of addressing the virtues. He then asserts:

> You are mistaken, my friend, if you think that a man who is worth anything ought to spend his time weighing up the prospects of life and death. He has only one thing to consider in performing any action—that is, whether he is acting rightly or wrongly, like a good man or a bad one.[20]

The wording of this passage in itself suggests a transition from mores to ethics. One of the charges against Socrates is impiety. But Socrates, by here talking about being good and doing right, has raised with these terms a more important issue than piety in the sense of simply accepting the religion of his times. Moreover, compared to the value of being good and doing right, Socrates despises even concern about death. In saying that risk of life or death ought not to be taken into account by a good man, he removes fear of death, and perhaps even mortality itself, from his (moral) identity. And in making these assertions when he is on trial for his own life, he implies that being a good man and doing what is right is the primary principle of his own action.

Socrates underscores his implied moral identity by dismissing with apparent frivolity choices that would undermine it. (What he says appears frivolous to onlookers who do not understand him—it is not frivolous to those who do.) After he has been convicted and has the right to propose an alternative punishment, such as banishment, he suggests that he be given free meals in the Prytaneum (the public dining hall in Athens) in place of some Olympic athlete. His justification is that he gives people the reality of success, whereas the athletes provide only the semblance; also, they do not need maintenance, whereas he does.[21] When his death sentence is duly official, Socrates refuses assistance for an exile that would curtail his continuing to live in the ways in which he has so far conducted his life. As he dies, not just peacefully and serenely but blithely, he implies that his consumption of the poison, according to the instructions of the man who has prepared it, has been an ordinary medical procedure, requiring no more than the customary sacrifice: "Crito we owe a cock to Asclepius."[22] (That is, strictly speaking, Socrates was not executed but accepted his death sentence by carrying it out himself via what we would call "physician-assisted suicide.")[23]

We are given to assume by the facts brought out in his trial that the mores of Socrates' time and place accorded high value to conventional religious piety, the authority of the state, and the avoidance of death. But Socrates in each of these instances values something greater: being good and doing what is right. Still, in Plato's dramatization of his death, Socrates does not have a full-blown account or theory of the right and the good; Socrates dies without a moral system. That Socrates, in the absence of a stated moral system or theory, was able to convincingly present certain actions as unethical or immoral created a need for ethics as Plato later developed it. The fact that the need for a moral system precedes knowledge of the moral system suggests that some moral systems occur after the situations to which they can be applied. First occurs a sense of harm, confusion, indignation, or outrage, and then later in time the moral system that explains what has been done wrong is constructed.[24]

The moral system that we get in the *Republic* is a theory of the good state and how relations between rulers and those ruled should be organized. The right organization of higher and lower, exalted and base, is as important for the individual as it is for society. Socrates starts out seeking justice as an individual virtue but turns to the state because justice there is bigger and easier to discern:

> Is not the city larger than the man? . . . Then, perhaps, there would be more justice in the larger object, and more easy to apprehend. If it please you, then, let us first look for its quality in states, and then only examine it also in the individual, looking for the likeness of the greater in the form of the less.[25]

As a result of Socrates' methodology, we can say that for Plato the virtue of the individual is a matter of what we would call "applied ethics." In other words, the need to define individual virtue signals the need for a moral system, which Plato is able to provide by reading it off the ideal state as he imagines it. Only after the completion of that reading do we have a moral or ethical system for individuals. Hence, in book 9 of the *Republic*, Plato comes full circle to describe the nature of the just man as having the same internal psychic organization as the just state, where those with the most highly developed reason and the greatest knowledge rule:

> Then when the entire soul accepts the guidance of the wisdom loving part and is not filled with inner dissension, the result for each part is that it in all other aspects keeps to its own task and is just, and likewise that each enjoys its own proper pleasures and the best pleasures and, so far as such a thing is possible, the truest.[26]

The moral system that Plato reads off the ideal state in the *Republic* constitutes his philosophical invention of ethics as a pattern of thought and way of life radically different from existing mores. This is the third stage of Plato's separation of ethics from mores. The radical difference is located not only in a strict division of labor within society and in the psyches and behavior of rulers, but within the hearts and minds of all citizens. Education is therefore essential to support (we would say "continue to construct") the Republic. Children of all classes are to be educated so that they may be just, in the sense of having the proper internal organization:

> This is the purpose of the law, which is the ally of all classes in the state, and this is the aim of our control of children, our not leaving them free before we have established, so to speak, a constitutional government within them and, by fostering the best element in them with the aid of the like in ourselves, have set up in its place a similar guardian and ruler in the child, and then, and then only, we leave it free.[27]

The (superior) individual's goal for virtue is knowledge of the forms, particularly the forms of the good and true. Whether such knowledge is knowledge created by the mind through a process of philosophical reflection or is known by the mind about a source that exists outside of all minds—which is *the* fascinating question in interpreting Plato—does not matter in terms of how philosophers occupy themselves qua philosophers. Qua philosophers, philosophers think about the Forms. Clearly absent from their proper focus and also absent from the curriculum studied by their children is anything too closely related to existing culture, myth, and tradition. Teaching the child to develop reason requires the absence of art from the curriculum. As many have noted, one purpose of Plato's doctrine of censorship is to make sure that the minds of citizens are directly occupied with the truth as manifest in the forms themselves and not with copies (the artists' representations) of copies (existing objects represented by the artist) of the forms (reality). But overlooked in this attention paid to censorship is another, nonimaginative dimension of the arts in life whereby they express the myths, customs, and values of a people—its mores. In dismissing the arts as worthy of unrestricted learning, Plato focuses on the distorting practices of *individual* artists[28] and neglects the popularity of the arts as a social institution that expresses the core beliefs and concerns of a people. In overlooking the role of the arts as a unifying element in a culture, his introduction of censorship is as much destructive of existing culture as it is constructive of ideal culture.[29]

Plato has to dismiss the mores of his time, or any time, because one of the most striking features of his republic is its difference from known Greek, and even generally human, society. According to Plato, man becomes human in society, and, to change human nature, it is first necessary to change society. The *Republic* offers a description of how society should change toward an ideal, first through a change in how it is organized so that the most rational element rules, and second by a plan for reconstructing this most rational element in terms of its social relations and the activities of its individual members. Not all philosophers will be fit and able to rule, but only philosophers who have been trained in Plato's philosophy and are able to live according to its principles. The training of the first generation of philosopher-rulers is an intense version of the education that will later be appropriate for all citizens.

The early education of the whole guardian class (consisting of both the military/police/administrative and ruling parts) is to consist of 'music' (literature and art, as well as music) and gymnastic, which are supposed to counterbalance each other so that guardians are both sensitive and strong.[30] In music, portrayals of the gods and heroes in all of the old myths are to be purged of excessive passion, violence, deceit, insobriety, and anything else that suggests evil or vice, including sorcery. The young should believe that "God is not the cause of all things, but only of the good."[31] There is to be no comedy or tragedy. The auditory modes of music are to be limited to Dorian and Phyrgian, and harmony and rhythm are to correspond to the simple and uplifting qualities of approved poetry.

The gymnastic program, which will begin a lifelong practice with direct application to soldiering, is to consist of training that will support the virtue of temperance. Closely related to exercise for physical strength is a minimalist type of medical practice that will benefit only those who are basically healthy, leaving the constitutionally weak and self-indulgent to perish. This principle of limited medical treatment is said to correspond to a certain strictness in the law:

> And these arts will care for the bodies and souls of such of your citizens as are truly wellborn, but those who are not, such as are defective in body, they will suffer to die, and those who are evil-natured and incurable in soul they will themselves be put to death.[32]

The next phase of education for rulers, continuing until age thirty-five, consists of reckoning, arithmetic, geometry, and contemplation of the forms, finally arriving at direct contemplation of goodness and truth. The future ruler is then sent "back into the cave" to serve as a guardian and administrator of affairs of state for fifteen years. At age fifty, he or she would rather retreat to a purely philosophical life but instead "must be brought at last to the goal."

> We shall require them to turn upward the vision of their souls and fix their gaze on that which sheds light on all, and when they have thus beheld the good itself they shall use it as a pattern for the right ordering of the state and the citizens and themselves throughout the remainder of their lives, each in his turn, devoting the greater part of their time to the study of philosophy, but when the turn comes for each, toiling in the service of the state and holding office for the city's sake, regarding the task not as a fine thing but as a necessity.[33]

The lifestyle of the rulers differs from age-old ideas of the luxury enjoyed by patriarchs. The rulers are to live plainly and own no private property, which would distract them from their public duties by providing incentives for personal accumulation and enjoyment. Social as well as economic practices are to be radically revised so that the most important goal and preoccupation of rulers is preserved, that is, the good of the whole society: marriage and the family will not exist in traditional forms. There will be no couples in sexually exclusive relationships and children are to be raised communally, not knowing who their parents are. Moreover, girls who are deemed intellectually and physically qualified to rule will receive the same training as boys in that category and can achieve the highest office.[34]

To sum up, Plato invented philosophical ethics as a stated result of his description of the ideal political community. There are several general questions raised by this project in terms of its suitability for an ethics of race or an ethics that could be applied to contemporary issues of race. Is the dependence of ethics on political structure compatible with an egalitarian ethical system? Yes, if the political structure were itself egalitarian. If it were not egalitarian, it would have to be fair: where there were not equal opportunities for everyone to rule, the qualifications for being able to rule would be determined by the tasks that rulers were expected to perform and there would be equal—or fair—opportunities for acquiring those qualifications.

A deeper question is whether an ethical system so closely tied to a political system is a practical ideal or even true to the nature of ethics as we understand it today. It is very difficult to change entire political systems or create viable new ones. Also, in order to construct the ideal state or even imagine it, it may be necessary to begin with some nonnegotiable ethical intuitions. We are left with the question of what these intuitions might be, if they are not to come from existing mores. This is not to say that they might not come from elsewhere but to note that Plato's ultimate source of the Good in the Forms is not viable for (probably most of) us.

Plato's main problem with existing mores was that they did not allow for higher goods as he conceived of them philosophically. In the absence of strong intuitions or convincing argument about the existence and/or value of his higher goods, it is difficult to see how one can say anything conclusive about the content of his criticism of existing mores beyond the fact that he and Socrates both loved the activity of philosophical discourse. The high value he places on his conception of philosophy is also his ultimate justification for his ideal state, and thus derivatively for the ethical system that is read off it. For present purposes, while there is nothing antithetical to an ethics of race in Plato's moral system (that is, nothing inherently racist about it), neither is there anything strongly ethical about it. The value of philosophy as a foundation for ethics is not even universal among philosophers!

Nevertheless, it is very important to recognize that the practice of ethics begins with Socrates and Plato as a new form of discourse. In both private and public conversation, good and bad values and right and wrong action are described, examined, analyzed, and assessed. This highly critical process is very different from assent to preexisting values and compliance with established rules. The critical process about values and action distinguishes the discourse of ethics from the practice of mores—to this day. That new critical process is Plato's invention of ethics, in a sense more general and comprehensive than his own ethical system based on the high value of philosophy.

As I have already indicated, another enduring contribution made by Plato, which is of great relevance to the present project, is his demonstration that it is possible to have a system of values that might not yet be an ethical system but is independent of existing customs, beliefs, and group values and traditions. Moreover, this value system or 'proto-ethical' system might be inspired or motivated by specific situations or incidents that reveal a moral lack. (The main examples here have been Socrates' frustration with Euthyphro's inability to define piety, Protagoras' inability to analyze virtue, and Socrates' apprehension of a value higher than preserving one's own life while he was on trial for his manner of discourse.)

ARISTOTLE'S VIRTUES FOR RULERS

As we know, Aristotle said that man is a "political animal."[35] But Aristotle departs from Plato's belief that the structure of virtue in an individual is analogous to that of the state, and he does not use Plato's methodology of "reading" the ethics of an individual off the description of the virtuous state. Rather, according to Aristotle, there is the practical matter that a just state supports virtue in the citizen, who, as a matter of course, will participate in government.[36] Theoretically, the connection of ethics to politics is more architectonic for Aristotle than Plato. According to Aristotle, in order to study ethics we must study politics; the study of ethics is a subpart of the study of politics. He tells us in his introductory remarks in *Nicomachean Ethics*:

> [This is properly called political science;][37] for though admittedly the good is the same for a city as for an individual, still the good of the city is apparently a greater and more complete good to acquire and preserve. For while it is satisfactory to acquire and preserve the good even for an individual, it is finer and more divine to acquire and preserve it for a people and for cities. And so, since our investigation aims at these [goods for an individual and for a city], it is a sort of political science.[38]

It is interesting for moral theory that Aristotle's conception of ethics in this passage appears to be either communal or utilitarian, insofar as the good for a city is "finer and more divine" than the good for an individual. It would be communal if a city in being a community is more important than an individual, but utilitarian if a city is a collection of individuals. That is, the interpretation as communitarian or utilitarian turns on whether the city is in itself an integral whole for Aristotle. I don't think that this issue substantially detracts from the importance of the (city) state as the locus of ethics. (If it does detract, it would also detract from the importance of the state according to Plato, if we held him to a kind of "methodological individualistic" analysis, whereby his ideal state would be nothing but a collection of individuals.)

Unlike Plato, Aristotle does not reject the mores of his time, or known mores in general, as a foundation for the government of an ideal society, as the basis for the values of an ideal society, or in order to specify the nature of the rulers of an ideal society. He does not even pursue the project of describing an ideal society but instead confines himself to describing the virtues in his contemporary society. According to Aristotle, because man is by nature "political," which in our terms would include "social," human organization has developed from the family, consisting of men and women and masters and slaves, into villages and communities. Because man is social by nature and has speech, the state is the end or goal of human organization.[39] Aristotle is "naturalistic" in comparison to Plato because he neither posits the state as a source of abstract ideals nor posits an ideal state. Aristotle also takes Plato up on a number of his specific innovations by rejecting the feasibility of communal family life, the abolition of private property, and the political equality of women for the sake of having a communal ruling class. He rejects these innovations on the grounds that they require too much sameness among citizens, community property will create conflict and violence, and communal family life will destroy natural human bonds.[40]

Like Plato, Aristotle holds that behaving virtuously or having certain virtues makes us happy. He takes great care to emphasize that happiness is not a feeling but an activity of the excellent rational soul, expressed in virtuous activity; happiness supervenes on a whole human life.[41] For Aristotle, reason is the primary human trait that is relevant to ethics. Although unlike Plato, he does not hold reason to be the highest human faculty but rather a distinctively human and active part of the soul, in the sense of a capacity rather than a literal part.[42] So we could say that for Aristotle, the focus is on reasoning. And although all humans are reasoning animals, there are certain contingent qualifications for studying virtue and becoming virtuous. To study virtue, "we need to have been brought up in fine habits."[43] To become virtuous, it is necessary that we have resources in friends, wealth, and political power.[44] Moreover, if we are deprived of good birth, good children, and beauty, or if our children and friends have died, our "blessedness" will be marred and we will not "altogether have the character of happiness."[45] Thus, while it is necessary to be virtuous to achieve happiness, virtue is not "altogether" sufficient for happiness in the absence of external good fortune: "Some maintain, on the contrary, that we are happy when we are broken on the wheel, or fall into terrible misfortunes, provided that we're good. Willingly or unwillingly, these people are talking nonsense."[46]

Given the external requirements for becoming virtuous and happy, it is not surprising that the virtues of character treated by Aristotle appear to be those of the privileged class of free male Athenians: bravery, temperance, generosity, magnificence, magnanimity, the virtues concerned with small honors, mildness, friendliness in social intercourse, truthfulness in social life, and shame.[47] Is Aristotle's theory of virtue or virtue theory, as opposed to his virtue system, applicable in an egalitarian way? It is, because reason, especially practical reason, is common to all human beings. Once the distinction is made between Aristotle's more general virtue theory and his virtue system of specific aristocratic virtues, there is no problem in his restriction to a privileged few of the acquisition and practice of the specific virtues he discussed. Only the aristocratic few of his time and place would have had the abilities, external resources, and opportunities to acquire and practice all of his specific virtues. However, nothing bars the identification or creation of a new list of 'Aristotelian' virtues that are developed and practiced as he generally described. Aristotelian *virtue theory* is not only far more democratic than Aristotle might have envisioned, but more open-ended. If we still think that happiness is the primary good, we need to decide what our secondary goods are in different contexts before we can determine the appropriate virtues for achieving them.

The radical philosophical dimension of Aristotelian ethics, both as restricted to elites and democratically accessible, is their how-to/can-do quality, which is to say their *psychological technology*. That is, Aristotle invented moral psychology. Aristotle offers a plausible account of the balance between free choice and settled character, which amounts to instruction on how to become virtuous, independently of what the virtue in question is. It is this technology of virtue-construction that constitutes Aristotle's invention of ethics as distinct from mores. This is not a completely philosophical invention, however, because it depends on the accuracy of his description of what human beings are capable of doing with themselves.

Aristotle's description of internal human capabilities does seem to capture universal capacities. According to Aristotle, apart from the varied external requirements that he specified for achieving the virtues he discussed, we have the ability to become virtuous based on processes of deliberation and choice that are under our control. Aristotle's general virtue theory holds that virtues of character are not present in us naturally but result from habitual action that is not against our nature. The habit built up is the result of repeatedly activating the virtue in question. We are trained in certain virtuous habits in youth, but when we recognize those virtues as such in adulthood and deliberately act in accordance with them, we create our own character in ways that make us responsible for it. Our deliberate actions in accordance with a virtue are the result of a preexisting habit, a contribution to the continuance of the habit of the virtue, and an expression of the virtue. Moreover, our enjoyment of the state of having the virtue, in addition to doing the actions of the virtue, is evidence that we have that virtue, as well as an important part of having it.

> We must take as a sign of someone's state his pleasure or pain in consequence of his action. For if someone who abstains from bodily pleasures enjoys the abstinence itself, then he is temperate, but if he is grieved by it, he is intemperate. Again, if he stands firm against terrifying situations and enjoys it, or at least does not find it painful, then he is brave, and if he finds it painful, he is cowardly.[48]

The products of crafts are good if they are good products, regardless of the state of the craftsman who produced them. In contrast, virtuous actions require that their agent be in the right state when he does them: he must know that he can do a virtuous act, decide to do it, decide because the act is virtuous, and perform the action on the basis of an established character trait of the virtue in question.[49]

For Aristotle, virtues are states which are usually "means" or intermediates between some excess and deficiency. However, the mean will always be relative to the agent in a given situation and there is no mechanical way to prescribe or generalize what it will be over all of the virtues, or for any particular virtue:

> Hence, it is hard work to be excellent, since in each case it is hard work to find what is intermediate; e.g., not everyone, but only one who knows, finds the midpoint in a circle. So also getting angry, or giving and spending money, is easy and anyone can do it; but doing it to the right person, in the right amount, at the right time, for the right end, and in the right way is no longer easy, nor can everyone do it. Hence [doing these things] well is rare, praiseworthy and fine.[50]

We can see from this that practical wisdom for Aristotle consists not only in identifying the right virtue for the right situation but in having good reasons for an action that is a deliberate extension or application of a settled habit. One does not merely choose to do something but chooses exactly how to do it, down to precise details of who will be affected by our action and to what degree. The agent must examine the reasons for a particular action and calibrate the extent and intensity of the action with its goal. The action has to be correctly timed. Also, we must know ourselves well enough to correct for our weaknesses of character and deficiencies of temperament at any one of these stages.[51] And finally, all this must be done with the general knowledge that our ability to make predictions is inexact, so that we cannot know "what the cumulative effect of particular actions will be."[52]

In an egalitarian interpretation of Aristotle's virtue theory, it should be noted that before one can practice a new virtue, new educational exposure might be necessary. But insofar as moral excellence requires at least minimal cognitive independence, if not full maturity, the process of acquiring and developing new virtues would seem to be what is meant now when we say that people change. Changes based on new habits are already common in our society in a large number of self-help practices, therapies, conversions, identity constructions (including racial and gender identities), parenting, adult education, professional education, and even ordinary college education among those aged eighteen to twenty-two. Not only are such processes independent of racial privilege or disadvantage, but the ongoing maintenance of found or established racial identities requires them if racial identities are virtues. If racial identities are not virtues, but vices, the same holds for their deconstruction.[53]

SUMMING UP PLATO'S AND
ARISTOTLE'S INVENTION OF ETHICS

The invention of ethics as a critical activity, begun by Plato, is completed by Aristotle, who adds practical action to a discourse of thought, speech, and writing.[54] The critical and deliberative nature of this discourse distinguishes it from conformity to mores for the individual, and it distinguishes the ethical practice from the application of mores within the group, as a group practice. There is more room for disagreement about ethical principles and outcomes than there is within the transmission and practice of mores. The outcome of ethical assessment, given the complexity of ethical behavior and the possibility of disagreement is, like the outcome of actions, (very) unpredictable.

Aristotle further deepens the Platonic practice of ethics as a discourse by adding the inner conversation that constitutes phronêsis, or practical wisdom. (Although he did not identify that conversation as "inner" as we would think of subjective activities.) The importance Aristotle places on knowing what the right thing to do is, as well as identifying the virtue called for in a given situation, sets up an inner dialogue that could be viewed by us as the origination of later senses of obligation and conscience. The element of practical wisdom culminating in action, but based on inner deliberation and choice, thus originates a prototypically modern, if not also contemporary, model of ethics or morality, with certain components: an internal thoughtful process, memory of past behavior, knowledge of certain virtues, the deliberate activation of dispositions based on habit, and the correction of known temperamental biases.

Despite what we can infer as the inner process of phronêsis, and because humans become human together, Aristotelian ethical activity is public in several ways: good and bad actions are visible to all in a relevant reference group; the moral system is a system for the reference group; and an individual's reasoning and deliberation can be followed, retraced, criticized, and revised for the future. The individual mental components of moral knowledge and its application do not entail that the moral system and reasoning and deliberating about it are the exclusive property of one or more particular individuals. On the contrary, it is in the nature of a moral system that if one person has it, she wants to share it, publicize it even. Also, just as Plato's inquiries into the good required dialogue, Aristotle's virtue theory requires discussion to determine the right virtues and how to apply them in any given context.

Aristotelian phronêsis, practiced in a polis, brings action into ethics, so that it is not merely a discourse. In terms of an ethics of race, discourse and dialogue retain their critical importance, especially in contexts where members of nonwhite populations have not had "permission to speak" until recently. In addition, an ethics of race would require knowledge and practice of distinctive virtues, for example, fairness and benevolence in racially diverse contexts, while it would at the same time identify bias and malevolence as vices.

Taken together, Plato and Aristotle give us an idea of what ethics is, something necessary to understand before there can be an ethics of race. Lacking, from both Platonic discourse and Aristotelian virtue ethics, is something that would enable a good attitude and good actions in contexts where not everyone was of the same race. This is the second necessity, because an ethics of race would be about 'race relations.' From the ancient world until today, cosmopolitanism would appear to offer the right kind of support for an attitude and actions relevant to race relations. Ancient cosmopolitanism and its modern forms will occupy chapter 2.

NOTES

1. Cornford makes a convincing case that Plato believed his ideas of government could be put into practice but was checked by the dangers of principled behavior in public life, mainly by Socrates' trial and subsequent death. Plato could have chosen a dangerous political career, but he prudently chose philosophy. However, there is evidence that he tested the waters of direct political reform in his visit to the court of Dionysius I in Syracuse, when he became friends with Dionysius' brother-in-law, Dion. See Francis Macdonald Cornford's introduction to his translation of *The Republic* (London: Oxford University Press, 1945), xv–xxix, esp. xxv–vi. Aristotle served as tutor to Alexander for three years upon an invitation of Philip of Macedon, after Plato's death in 343/2 B.C.E. Richard McKeon, introduction to *The Basic Works of Aristotle*, ed. Richard McKeon, trans. W. D. Ross (New York: Random House, 1941), xiv.

2. These are two distinct arguments. If the state is simply the individual writ large, then they are the same kind of entity so there is no "humanity" of the individual that does not also exist in the entity of the state. The second argument is in book 2 of *The Republic* where Plato posits the state as necessary for the survival of the human individual, when he begins to describe the state in terms of a division of labor, in saying that the individual cannot exist without others: "The origin of the city, then, said I [Socrates], in my opinion, is to be found in the fact that we do not severally suffice for our own needs, but each of us lacks many things. Do you think any other principle establishes the state? No other, said he [Adimantus]." Plato, *Republic*, trans. Paul Shorey, in *Plato: The Collected Dialogues*, ed. Edith Hamilton and Huntington Cairns (New York: Random House, 1964), 615 (book 2, 369b–c).

3. Man's political nature for Aristotle, as for Plato, refers to man as living a life that is already social. This is not only man as he is found, but man as he is "normal." For both Plato and Aristotle, the starting point is normal man. "Hence it is evident that the state is a creation of nature, and that man is by nature a political animal. And he who by nature and not by mere accident is without a state, is either a bad man or above

humanity." Aristotle, *Politics*, in *Basic Works*, ed. Richard MacKeon, trans. W. D. Ross (New York: Random House, 1941), 1129 (book 1, ch. 2, 1253a1–5).

4. This is a complex interrelationship of several elements. First, lawmakers should be virtuous: "The true politician seems to have spent more effort on virtue than on anything else, since he wants to make the citizens good and law-abiding." Aristotle, *Nicomachean Ethics*, trans. Terrence Irwin (Indianapolis, IN: Hackett, 1985), 29 (book 1, ch. 13, 1102a5–10). Second, Aristotle claims that moral education requires correct laws and that legislators should encourage the virtuous and correct those who disobey the laws, expelling the incurable. Aristotle, *Nicomachean Ethics*, 293 (book 10, ch. 14.2, 1179b30–1180a10). Third, there is an assumption that virtuous men in Aristotle's exclusive sense will be free citizens and that their virtue as individuals will overlap with the virtue of the government, depending on how virtuous the government is. Aristotle, *Politics*, 1180–81 (1276b15–1277b5). But fourth, none of this amounts to a claim that the political life is the best choice for happiness. Aristotle, *Nicomachean Ethics*, 7–8 (book 1, 1095b20–1096a). Still, a citizen by definition "shares in the administration of justice, and of offices." Aristotle, *Politics*, trans. Benjamin Jowett, 1176–77 (1275a20–25).

5. Plato, *Republic*, 785–92 (book 8, 557a–564a); Aristotle, *Politics*, 1212–13 (book 4, ch. 4, 1292a).

6. Aristotle, *Politics*, 1200–4 (McKeon, book 3, ch. 15, 1286b–1288a30, pp. 1200–1204).

7. Hume assumed that there were races and Kant made the same assumption, beginning with an observation of the existence of mixed race and ending with a reliance on Hume's assumption. Both Hume and Kant assumed that whites were superior to all other races. Hegel asserted that Africans are childish as a result of the geographical nature of Africa. Put in these terms, their views now appear idiotic, but these learned positions had great authority in the biological sciences and humanities for a very long time. For textual references see Naomi Zack, *Philosophy of Science and Race* (New York: Routledge, 2002), 9–24 and 27–31.

8. Berel Lang makes a different case that racism has metaphysical foundations in the history of ideas, particularly with regard to anti-Semitism. Lang thinks that while race may or may not have biological foundations as an idea, racism predates modern biology. See Lang, "Metaphysical Racism (Or: Biological Warfare by Other Means)," in *RACE/SEX: Their Sameness, Difference and Interplay*, ed. Naomi Zack (New York: Routledge, 1997), 17–28.

9. Plato, *Republic*, 698–700 (book 5, 459d–461c); Aristotle, *Nichomachean Ethics*, 6 (book 2, 1095b4–5).

10. The difference is that genealogical inheritance picks out whole organisms as predecessors, whereas according to Mendelian heredity only half of all inherited material comes from each parent, and it is impossible to predict which half, which genes, will get passed on at conception. For more comprehensive discussion and sources, see Zack, *Philosophy of Science and Race*, 59–86.

11. Plato, *Republic*, 658–60 (book 3, 414–415c). So-called antimiscegenation laws in the United States, which regulated racial intermarriage (and were struck down by

the US Supreme Court only in 1967), were a legal mechanism for ensuring racial purity, especially among whites.

12. Aristotle, *Politics*, ed. McKeon, trans. Jowett, 1132–33 (book 1, ch. 5, 1254a15–1255, pp. 1132–33).

13. Plato, *Protagoras*, trans. W. K. C. Guthrie, in *Plato: The Collected Dialogues*, ed. Edith Hamilton and Huntington Cairns (New York: Random House, 1964), 317 (318e).

14. Plato, *Protagoras*, 341–42 (349).

15. According to Cornford, Socrates brought into philosophy teleological questions about the purpose of the universe and normative questions of right and wrong. See Francis Macdonald Cornford, *Before and After Socrates* (New York: Cambridge University Press, 2007 [1932]), 1–4.

16. Plato, *Euthyphro*, trans. Lane Cooper, in *Plato: The Collected Dialogues*, ed. Edith Hamilton and Huntington Cairns (New York: Random House, 1964), 169–85. The "problematic" described above is an overall result of the dialogue, although Cooper's interpretation is that Socrates establishes that "the good is not good because the gods approve it, but the gods approve it because it is good" (169).

17. Plato, *Euthyphro*, trans. Lane Cooper, in Edith Hamilton and Huntington Cairns, eds. *Plato: Collected Dialogues*, 185 (15e4–4), p. 185.

18. Cornford, in comparing the accounts of death given by Socrates in the *Apology* and *Phaedo*, notes that even though Plato wrote the *Apology* years after Socrates died, he had no motive for misrepresenting Socrates' claim in that dialogue that he did not know what death was (Cornford, *Before and After Socrates*, 33). Also, Xenophon's *Memorabila* presents the historical Socrates without Plato's full philosophy.

19. Plato, *Apology*, trans. Hugh Tredennick, 5–10 (19b–20c).

20. Plato, *Apology*, 14 (28b).

21. Plato, *Apology*, 22 (36e).

22. Plato, *Crito*, trans. Hugh Tredennick, in *Plato: The Collected Dialogues,* ed. Edith Hamilton and Huntington Cairns (New York: Random House, 1964), 98–99 (118e–118).

23. I am interpreting this passage narrowly and literally as meaning that the sacrifice customarily given by the sick for a cure is intended by Socrates to be an offering in thanks for the effectiveness of the poison and not to symbolize a belief that "death is a cure for life," as some commentators suggest. See, for example, the translator's footnote in *Phaedo*, trans. G. M. A. Grube, in *The Trial and Death of Socrates*, by Plato (Indianapolis, IN: Hackett, 1975), 58. Grube's reading may be in keeping with Plato's idea of death as involving an afterlife, but it also fits the position that we know nothing about death, a position that is attributed to the historical Socrates. The choice of interpretation turns on how sharp a line is drawn between Plato's depiction of the historical Socrates in the dialogues wholly about Socrates and his depiction of Socrates to exposit Plato's mature thought. (See note 18, above.) It's not inconceivable the *Phaedo* has elements of both.

24. Although, of course, for Plato, but not the historical Socrates, the knowledge of the moral system he was to construct would not have been new knowledge but

knowledge already residing in the soul, as he presented geometry to be innately known by Meno's slave.

25. Plato, *Republic*, 615 (book 2, 368e–369a).

26. Plato, *Republic*, 814 (book 9, 586e).

27. Plato, *Republic*, 818 (book 10, 590e–591a).

28. The references to the arts that Plato wants to censor in the *Republic* seem fairly consistently to refer to the fallibility of individual artists, and not to the arts as a part of culture. Thus, Socrates considers the kind of literature and music appropriate for the Republic, in terms of the productions of specific artists. See, for instance: "Is it, then, only the poets that we must supervise and compel to embody in their poems the semblance of the good character or else not write poetry among us . . . or must we keep watch over the other craftsmen and forbid them. . . ." (Plato, *Republic*, 646 [Ibid., 401b], p. 646); "Hesiod and Homer . . . composed false stories" (624 [Ibid., 377d], p. 624); "If a man, then, it seems, who is capable by his cunning of assuming every kind of shape and imitating all things should arrive in our city, bringing with himself the poems which he wished to exhibit . . . we . . . should say to him that there is no man of that kind among us in our city, nor is it lawful for such a man to arise among us." (642–43 [Ibid., 398a], p. 642–43). Whether or not this was a deliberate rhetorical distraction on Plato's part, the focus on individual artists deflects concern about the role of the arts for a people or community, as a totality.

29. For us, as heirs to romanticism, as well as the Enlightenment, art can function as a revolutionary force, besides expressing something about the individual artist. But in the context of Plato's *Republic*, the notion of the ideal state is the revolutionary force, and the artist represents conservative ideas and values. Furthermore, we are apt to view censorship as a limitation on individual choice and individual self-expression, as an obstacle to cultural innovation. But when censorship is a mechanism for cultural innovation, as it was for Plato, group choices and expressions are being blocked or erased. I think that this radical and "progressive" nature of Plato's ideas for censorship has led to a certain reluctance of scholars to criticize him as harshly as they would a conservative apologist for censorship.

30. Plato, *Republic*, 655–56 (book 3, 411b–412c).

31. Plato, *Republic*, 627 (book 2, 380c).

32. Plato, *Republic*, 654 (book 3, 410a).

33. Plato, *Republic*, 771–72 (book 7, 540b–c).

34. Plato, *Republic*, 689–704 (book 5, 449–465). This liberation of women is to occur only within the ruling class and is proposed to destroy the traditional family structure, rather than for the sake of the women. See Susan Moller Okin, "Philosopher Queens and Private Wives: Plato on Women and the Family," in *Feminist Interpretations and Political Philosophy*, ed. Carole Pateman and Mary Lyndon Shanley (University Park: Pennsylvania State University Press, 1991), 11–31.

35. See note 3, above.

36. See note 4, above.

37. Aristotle, *Nichomachean Ethics*, Irwin, trans. [Translator's insertions] 3 (1094b), translator's insertions p. 3.

38. Aristotle, *Nicomachean Ethics*, 3 (1094b, 10–15), translator's insertions.

39. Aristotle, *Politics*, trans. Jowett, books 1–2, 1127–29, 1252a25–1253. Aristotle specifically may have had the city state of Athens in mind when he spoke of the state in this way, but he was not fully true to his own time in this regard, because Macedonia was becoming a political empire, which was far more than a city-state at the time he wrote the *Nicomachean Ethics*. Terrence Irwin, introduction to *Nicomachean Ethics*, trans. Terrence Irwin (Indianapolis, IN: Hackett, 1985), xiv–xv.

40. Aristotle, *Politics*, trans. Jowett, 1146–49 (book 2, 1–3, 1160b30–121262m).

41. Aristotle, *Nicomachean Ethics*, 18–23 (book 1, 1098b–1099).

42. Reason and virtue are intertwined. In his definition of virtue, Aristotle writes: "Virtue, then, is (a) a state that decides, (b) [consisting] in a mean, (c) the mean relative to us, (d) which is defined by reference to reason, (e) i.e., to the reason by reference to which the intelligent person would define it." Aristotle, *Nicomachean Ethics*, 44 (book 2, 1107a). (This is a very different approach from the line of reasoning Socrates posed to Protagoras when he tried to embark on an analysis of virtue as though it were a physical property, like the face. See note 14, above.) Aristotle has brought the things that we know about action and deliberation into philosophy, not metaphysically, but as an extension of common sense.

43. Aristotle, *Nicomachean Ethics*, 6 (1095b4–5).

44. Aristotle, *Nicomachean Ethics*, 21 (1099b1–5).

45. Aristotle, *Nicomachean Ethics*, 21 (1099b1–5).

46. Aristotle, *Nicomachean Ethics*, 203 (1153b, 16–20).

47. Aristotle, *Nicomachean Ethics*, 53–115 (books 3 and 4).

48. Aristotle, *Nicomachean Ethics*, 37 (1104b3–9).

49. Aristotle, *Nicomachean Ethics*, 40 (1105a30–35).

50. Aristotle, *Nicomachean Ethics*, 51 (1109a25–30).

51. Aristotle, *Nicomachean Ethics*, 54 (1109b1–6).

52. Aristotle, *Nicomachean Ethics*, 70 (1114b30–1115a5).

53. Aristotle does not address the deconstruction of vices, but the psychological technology for getting rid of them would seem to be the reverse of the process for acquiring a virtue: identify the vice, recognize an immediate situation in which one is disposed to practice the vice, and decide not to practice the vice, for the right reasons. This process has been made well-known in contemporary life by those who follow various therapies and self-help programs for correcting addictions.

54. Aristotle cautioned against philosophical study alone as sufficient for ethical practice: "Virtue requires habituation, and therefore requires practice, not just theory. . . . The many, however, do not do these actions but take refuge in arguments, thinking that they are doing philosophy, and this is the way to become excellent people. In this they are like a sick person who listens attentively to the doctor, but acts on none of his instructions. Such a course of treatment will not improve the state of his body; any more than will the many's way of doing philosophy improve the state of their souls" (*Nicomachean Ethics*, 40 [1105b12–17]). But millennia later, Aristotle's virtue theory is still not broadly understood among the many who are intellectually concerned with moral matters. He may have overestimated the degree of understanding of those who argue, as well as those who only listen to their doctors. The nature of ethics as a subject of philosophy, both lay and academic, is still under debate, as is the question of whether we should have ethics

in some contexts governed by mores. Therefore, what I am calling the "discourse" of ethics and what Aristotle may have been referring to as "arguments" is itself a practice that has not caught on among the many. If, however, Aristotle meant that philosophy itself is more than a discourse and that we are to follow him in including practical action as a part of philosophy, then my concluding remarks to this chapter are inadequate to the task of Aristotelian virtue ethics.

• *2* •

Cosmopolitan Contributions
to an Ethics of Race

$\mathscr{I}$n 1740, David Hume cautioned philosophers that normative language requires some justification and explanation because "ought" cannot be logically deduced from "is."

> In every system of morality, which I have hitherto met with, I have always remark'd, that the author proceeds for some time in the ordinary way of reasoning, and establishes the being of a God, or makes observations concerning human affairs; when of a sudden I am surpriz'd to find, that instead of the usual copulations of propositions, *is*, and *is not*, I meet with no proposition that is not connected with an *ought*. Or an *ought not*. This change is imperceptible; but is, however, of the last consequence. For as this *ought*, or *ought not*, expresses some new relation or affirmation, 'tis necessary that it shou'd be observ'd and explain'd; and at the same time that a reason should be given; for what seems altogether inconceivable, how this new relation can be a deduction from others, which are entirely different from it.[1]

Despite his casual tone, Hume here sweeps the entire history of moral philosophy. More than two thousand years before him, Plato and Aristotle had already made what ought to be the case a distinctively philosophical subject. Now, almost three hundred years after Hume's challenge, there is still no philosophical consensus on how to answer him. That philosophers engaged in normative discourse still find Hume's problem a live issue, while it seems not to perplex thinkers in other fields when they are engaged in normative inquiry, says something about the nature of philosophy (besides the fact that it moves very slowly), but more about this later.

One quasi philosophical answer to Hume's problem, which avoids the derivation of an *ought* from an *is*, is cosmopolitanism. In a historical assessment of Western philosophical ethics for an ethics of race, it therefore now makes

23

sense to consider ancient cosmopolitanism along with several contemporary innovations. The moral perspective of cosmopolitanism emerged during the time of Plato and Aristotle in the fourth century B.C.E. Cosmopolitanism, as a normative tradition, has at least four distinct strands: the social subject of how individuals should regard and interact with people who, to borrow Franz Boas's terminology, belong to "types distinct from our own";[2] personal identity development; political cosmopolitanism and ideal global structures; and religious and spiritual cosmopolitanism. Although these strands are not altogether distinct in cosmopolitan writings, they are each in different ways problematic for philosophers because neither taken separately nor combined do the strands share what is distinct about philosophy as a discipline. It is more unwieldy to furnish a philosophical exposition of cosmopolitanism than it is to criticize it. The main subjects of this chapter are social cosmopolitanism with its international aspect and cosmopolitan personal identity development, including religion. Further discussion of cosmopolitanism will be incorporated into discussion of natural law and Christianity in chapters 3 and 5. Political cosmopolitanism and ideal global structures will be taken up in chapter 7 and further developed in the conclusion, although the subjects will by then be revised into universalism and internationalism. But the ethical principle at issue with cosmopolitanism is the same in universalism and natural law: how to treat 'others' who are distant in various ways.

ETHICS AND COSMOPOLITANISM COMPARED

Philosophical ethics is a self-sufficient normative discourse, whereas cosmopolitanism begins by accepting the world. Philosophical ethics doesn't need real-time examples to make its points, whereas it's expected that cosmopolitan ethics will be grounded in an interest in the existing world. Cosmopolitan ethics really just has the one subject, the real existing world, taken more or less as it is. Philosophical ethics can be about anything in the world, or any aspect of it, but taken abstractly rather than in terms of what exists. There is an openness to cosmopolitanism that contrasts with the 'hermetics' of philosophy.

The undergraduate philosophy major is required to read preliminary texts, take lecture notes, and learn how to write in a distinctive way, for instance by filling in all gaps in reasoning and avoiding rhetoric and unsubstantiated opinion. By graduate school, all of one's professional peers and academic instructors and evaluators will have undergone the same training. In smaller and smaller circles of participants, the student acquires a profession that in the best sense is a vocation (calling). College teaching aside, the professional aspects of philosophy are scholarly and other professional philosophers are the audience. Occasionally, attempts are made to interact intellectually with those in other disciplines. Sometimes, there are texts written and lectures given with the intention of addressing "general" audiences. In the United States, it is not easy for philosophers to become public intellectuals and remain philosophers.

All extradisciplinary efforts made by philosophers in the United States tend to be treated with condescension by the obscure majority of the profession. American philosophers read, teach, talk, and write ethics among themselves. Despite a few exceptions in philosophical cosmopolitanism, applied philosophy, and philosophy of science, we are not cosmopolitans in our intellectual work life. Unsurprisingly, canonical encyclopedias of philosophy have not always had entries for "cosmopolitanism."[3]

No matter their personal experience, cosmopolitanism is not easy for philosophers to accept intellectually because its starting premise appears to be an assertion about the political world that is not credible. The core idea of cosmopolitanism is the view attributed to Diogenes of Sinope, by Diogenes Laëtius, that all human beings are by nature citizens in a world community.[4] All divisions into nationalities and other political groups are the result of convention only. To a philosopher, this idea of world citizenship is at best an ideal or an agreeable fantasy insofar as citizenship in reality is official membership in specific sovereign states. There is no world organization as yet in which every human being can claim "citizenship" in the same way as the word is used for citizens of France, Germany, India, the United States, New Zealand, Argentina, and so forth. Since history has resulted in a concept of citizenship that is tied to certain geographical locations smaller than the whole world, it could be claimed that it is citizenship in this historical sense that is natural, as opposed to citizenship in the ideal cosmopolitan sense. That would be the obvious philosophical objection to the core idea of cosmopolitanism, and philosophy is cold and abstract in ignoring the moral motivations for claiming world citizenship.

Cosmopolitans begin with an abstract framework that in principle includes everyone, whereas philosophical ethical systems, starting as we have seen with Plato and Aristotle, begin by addressing an intellectual and social elite. Such exclusive philosophical moral systems can be opened up to include everyone—everyone can develop virtues for instance—but that requires revision. Before the twentieth century, universal inclusion and its unequivocal expression was not a fundamental, beginning assumption in philosophical ethical systems. After World War II and especially after the 1960s, philosophical ethicists have accepted a moral obligation of inclusiveness. No one now advocates or develops a moral system that on its face excludes the same treatment as is afforded middle- or upper-class, able-bodied, heterosexual, white men for those who are female, poor, disabled, nonheterosexual, or nonwhite. Still, inclusiveness may not be a deep assumption in some moral thinking, but tacked on as an afterthought.

Overall, cosmopolitanism and philosophical ethics feel like different sorts of projects with different subjects—the rational, ethical human being versus anyone and everyone. The ethical human for philosophers remains a privileged person, currently in fortunate circumstances that do not have to be disturbed for the sake of moral development, a fact that can still be discreetly disclosed for rhetorical purposes that have nothing to do with the claims or arguments put forth.[5] Philosophical ethics is still addressed to those taken to be superior to some mass, and it is all about that audience and not so much about the mass. Philosophical ethics in the Western tradition therefore has to be approached carefully in terms of race because it shares with the problematic aspects of racial whiteness an atmosphere of exclusivity. Philosophical ethical questions have continued to proceed from the perspective of the few (privileged) "we's" in stable, comfortable circumstances, even if they do not have great power or wealth. How should we (enlightened ones) relate our lives to ideals? How should we (superior ones) develop ourselves so that our lives are fulfilled and we flourish? How should we (who have been properly brought up) treat our peers? What do we (who can take care of ourselves) have a right to expect from government? What do we (who possess many of the goods of life) owe those less advantaged? How and why should those who are more powerful than we (who have sufficient power among ourselves) leave us alone? How should we (who have the capabilities and opportunities to live pleasant lives) define happiness? Overall, the ethical questions that arise from the tradition of philosophy concern how we few (who know that we have choices) *should* live. The many of the world are not fortunate enough to devote serious attention to such normative questions because they are preoccupied with matters that more directly concern whether or not they *can* live or will remain alive. To those many, the normative questions that preoccupy most moral philosophers would be exquisite. And while that could be said of all philosophical subjects, it glares in ethical discourse that now purports to be universal and inclusive.

COSMOPOLITANISM AND AN ETHICS OF RACE

Cosmopolitanism seems more likely than Western philosophical ethics to include as its human subjects those for whom life itself is tenuous. Diogenes, the first explicit cosmopolitan, has been interpreted as refusing to be defined by his local origins.[6] This entails that his concerns as a citizen of the world went beyond his concerns as a resident of Sinope or Athens. Diogenes' kind of cosmopolitanism has the potential to unite the concerns of those who can be preoccupied with questions about how they should live with those who are preoccupied with questions about whether they can, or will, remain alive. Today, a global majority of those for whom life is tenuous are nonwhite. In terms of race, the cosmopolitan union goes beyond an ethics of race that is motivated by concerns about race in the United States. Race within the United States is not now generally an issue of genocide, war, ethnic cleansing, disaster, or, in stark terms, who can and will live (although in the past it has been and sometimes still is). But an ethics of race that ran deeper than the preoccupations of privilege would have to address such concerns.

Cosmopolitanism, in contrast to philosophical ethics, is first and foremost an attitude toward others who exhibit differences that we might otherwise be adverse to, have distain for, or simply be content to live in ignorance of. Cosmopolitanism addresses the moral, as well as geographical, distances between its subjects and those who are 'other' to them. That is, in both the ancient and modern cases there are moral and physical distances, and differences in culture and history, between privileged cosmopolitans and those others toward whom it would be morally good to have a cosmopolitan attitude. Cosmopolitanism, in contrast to philosophical ethics, begins with an intuition that those who are different from us merit our serious moral consideration. This is symmetrical, because cosmopolitans would also want cosmopolitan treatment for themselves. (Accounts of the outrageous behavior of Diogenes of Sinope, which included "raising his leg" on those at a banquet who threw him bones as though he were a dog,[7] suggest that the cosmopolitanism he introduced was partly a matter of his fellow Athenians tolerating him.)

Even though philosophical ethics and cosmopolitanism seem to be different kinds of projects, any ethics of race would share cosmopolitanism's acceptance of difference. And it's not only that motivations for an ethics of race and for cosmopolitanism are similar. Race itself is an idea of a typology or taxonomy or system of classification that applies to the whole of humanity and not just the residents of one nation. The idea of race is inherently cosmopolitan, although historically not in the sense of benevolent inclusion and approbation that is associated with cosmopolitanism.

However, and this is the first criticism of cosmopolitanism concerning an ethics of race, in ancient Greece and Rome as well as contemporary Northern Europe and America, cosmopolitan benevolence and approbation often proceed from those on the top of human hierarchies of race (and class). It is easy for cosmopolitans to unintentionally condescend at the same time that they reach out. Martha Nussbaum, for example, applies the cognitive theory of emotions held by the Stoics to the idea of a racially egalitarian cosmopolitan education. But her example seems to be about education for relatively privileged white children (because they have cosmopolitan parents and teachers). Nussbaum writes:

> Certain especially pernicious forms of anger and hatred can indeed be eradicated by patient reform following Stoic conceptions. The hatred of members of other races and religions can be effectively addressed by forms of early education that address the cognitive roots of those passions by getting children to view these people in the Stoic cosmopolitan ways, as similarly human, as bearers of an equal moral dignity, as members of a single body and a single set of purposes, and as no longer impossibly alien or threatening.[8]

If cosmopolitanism were thoroughly egalitarian, it would not depend on generosity and charity from cosmopolitans but would be a moral standard for interactions among equals.

There is an egalitarian unconventionality of ancient cosmopolitanism, resembling Plato's elimination of the traditional family, although it is less for the sake of an ideal and more an expression of individual freedom and open-mindedness. Diogenes Laëtius relates of Diogenes of Sinope:

> He played . . . with the topics of noble birth, and reputation, and all things of that kind, saying that they were all veils, as it were, for wickedness. . . . Another of his doctrines was that all women ought to be possessed in common; and he said that marriage was a nullity, and that the proper way would be for every man to live with her whom he could persuade to agree with him. And on the same principle he said, that all people's sons ought to belong to everyone in common; and there was nothing intolerable in the idea of taking anything out of a temple, or eating any animal whatever, and that there was no impiety in tasting even human flesh; as is plain from the habits of foreign nations; and he said that this principle might be correctly extended to every case and every people.[9]

Racial minorities within nations and entire nations and continents peopled by nonwhites, who make up our global human majority, have cultural practices (mores) that diverge from dominant white Euro-American culture (mores). In the context of white Euro-American mores, the mores of these non-whites—and their recognition and affirmation without condescension—are unconventional. As Kwame Anthony Appiah puts it in his introduction to *Cosmopolitanism: Ethics in a World of Strangers*, "The foreignness of foreigners, the strangeness of strangers, these things are real enough. It's just that we've been encouraged, not least by well-meaning intellectuals, to exaggerate their significance by an order of magnitude."[10] The basic principle here is the Roman playwright Terence's famous maxim, "I am a man, I consider nothing that is human to be alien to me."[11]

However, the awareness of different ways of life and overall willingness to accept and be comfortable with those who are different, together with affirmation of cultural difference associated with race, are not sufficient to suggest that an ethics of race should or could simply be racial cosmopolitanism. Racial cosmopolitanism would be an attempt to accept not only differences in race but also differences in mores associated with different races. Racial cosmopolitanism would critique and change insular perspectives of individuals, their identities, and ideas of ideal political structures. An ethics of race, by contrast, would attempt to evaluate perceptions of differences in race and also different mores associated with racial difference. One could argue that certain practices, associated with the cultures of different races, are morally wrong, in departure from the cosmopolitan project of understanding and toleration. The goal of an ethics of race would be the defense of certain values and the construction of certain principles that would be standards for individual identity and race-based interactions between individuals and groups. A philosophical ethics of race could, and probably would, be much more critically aggressive than racial cosmopolitanism.

An ethics of race would allow for criticism of the idea of race itself, whereas racial cosmopolitanism would tend to accept racial divisions and distinctions as they have been socially constructed and persist in living history. An ethics of race would allow for racial eliminativism, or a prescription that the concept of race be replaced with something else on account of its false biological foundations. Racial cosmopolitanism could not easily advocate such a change in discourse so long as members of some groups thought and spoke about race in the old way. Moreover, there is a paradoxical difference in abstraction between an ethics of race and racial cosmopolitanism. An ethics of race would be universal, whereas racial cosmopolitanism would be pluralistic, if not relativistic. In other words, an ethics of race would determine what ought to be the case in a diverse world, for everyone. By contrast, racial cosmopolitanism would seek to accommodate conflicting differences, without universal normative judgment.

DIFFERENCES BETWEEN COSMOPOLITAN AND PHILOSOPHICAL ETHICAL OBLIGATIONS

Awareness of the difference between a cosmopolitan obligation that is something like "we ought to get along" and a philosophical ethical obligation that is something like "we ought to do the right thing" can help one understand contemporary crises about race. Consider, for example, the broad public indignation when the president of the United States said, in July 2009, that a white policeman had "acted stupidly" in arresting a black Harvard University professor in his own home when he had not committed a crime nor appeared likely to immediately do so.[12] From the outset, this incident was beset with different normative perspectives based on race: many blacks saw the incident as racial profiling or bias on the part of the police officer, whereas many whites saw it as a simple case of a policeman doing his job by maintaining order, because the professor yelled at him. The black view, which the president seemed at first to express, is that racial profiling is a widespread moral wrong and that the white policeman behaved unethically insofar as his arrest of the professor was an instance of racial profiling. But the president almost immediately backed away from his initial comment that the policeman had acted stupidly.

Why did the president rescind his use of the word "stupid"? Because it sounded like the result of an ethical judgment that an act of racial bias had been committed, and the majority of the white public, particularly members of police departments throughout the country, wanted the president to remain neutral about conflicting mores associated with black and white racial groups. That is, the white majority wanted the president of the United States to be a cosmopolitan about different race-based moral views. The president obliged by inviting the professor and the policeman to drink beer with him at the White House so that he could neutrally moderate their disagreement. Did he appear to become a cosmopolitan so quickly because it was his underlying perspective all along, or did he merely conceal an ethical perspective so as not to alienate many white voters? Or, did he realize that US police departments answer to local rather than federal authorities and thus choose not to overextend his administrative powers? Whatever the reasons or causes contributing to how it was resolved, the entire incident highlights conflicts between black and white race-based mores. Black mores, as associated with black race, are more likely to result in perceptions of racism than those of whites, and with the perceptions of racism come moral judgments. The mores associated with white race hold that the police are right in the absence of strong evidence to the contrary, particularly in parts of the United States where police and fire departments have historically been made up of "ethnic whites," such as Irish Americans in Boston. (The incident also suggests that in the summer of 2009 purely ethical discussions of race-related matters were not popular in the United States.)[13]

During the 2008 presidential campaign, Barack Obama, as the first African American presidential candidate, expressed an intention to "move on" concerning matters of race. The professor and the police officer were also reported as wanting to "move on." But moving on means different things to blacks and whites in the United States. To blacks and other minorities it means making progress toward more racial equality, while to whites it often means avoiding the subject of race completely. There is yet another comparative paradox here: cosmopolitanism, which purports to be progressive in accepting differences, can in reality play out as conservative regarding racism, whereas philosophical ethics, although more insular and abstract, has the potential to further social justice by confronting racism directly.

Nevertheless, cosmopolitanism remains necessary for an ethics of race, mainly because one big danger for an ethics of race is self-righteousness. Because construction of an ethics of race would be motivated by the need to correct race-based injustice and oppression, there need to be limits on the corrections proposed and the rhetoric deemed appropriate. Otherwise, an ethics of race runs the risk of going too far into anger, blame, and vengeance and thereby becoming unethical. Thus, the values generally understood to be placed by cosmopolitans on peace, toleration, and self-restraint (whether via a cognitive programming or reprogramming of the emotions as Nussbaum describes or via direct self-control) would be worthy constraints to an ethics of race.

Still, we need to be prepared that the cosmopolitan contribution to an ethics of race will not facilitate judgment about those conflicting mores related to race that are bound up with practices of oppression. We should not expect cosmopolitanism to generate such judgment in fine-grained ways because cosmopolitanism is committed to toleration, and judgment may not be tolerant. Even in its most aware and sophisticated applications, cosmopolitanism seems to be incapable of generating condemnation of racism within other cultures that are otherwise embraced, understood, accepted, or tolerated.

Cosmopolitanism does its work without being offensive or causing offense. But any philosophical ethics, and especially an ethics of race, may be as offensive as the arguments it tracks require. Cosmopolitan analysis does not just stop short of racism, it also leaves other practices, such as incomplete civil rights for women and animal cruelty, uncriticized. The overall goal of cosmopolitanism seems to be that people should get along, reserving condemnation only for practices and beliefs, for example terrorism motivated by Islamic fundamentalism, that violate the most general and essential human goods.[14] However, as Appiah analyzes "getting along," it does not require shared values (which may lead to intense conflict), the same view of the world, or indeed very much at all that could be the result of changing one's mind based on rational argument. He writes, "We can live together without agreeing on what the values are that make it good to live together; we can agree about what to do in most cases, without agreeing on why it is right."[15]

Appiah holds that the primary requirement for getting along is getting used to people who are different by peacefully living among them and interacting with them. As a broad description of how humans behave socially, I think

Appiah is right. In major metropolitan areas with multinational, multiracial, and multicultural populations, people get along by functioning together in schools, businesses, services, and entertainment venues, often without knowing very much about the different identities of others. Appiah's description is also useful for a philosophical perspective allowing for pragmatic principles of action in ways that go beyond cosmopolitanism. We can use its prescriptive form in family relationships, as well as relations between nations. But even turned into a prescription—Get along!—this prescription is not helpful for the development of philosophical ethical discourse. It is easy to agree that violations of the broadest principles of human justice are bad, but what the philosopher of racial ethics would need are specific tools or rules of discourse to allow for criticism of violations of more narrow principles of human justice, such as racial profiling.

CICERO'S CIRCLE

The foregoing is not to say a cosmopolitan perspective is morally lax, as it can very rigorously be used to tell us that we have obligations to all other human beings on the planet and can translate such obligations into proposals to end third-world poverty (as Appiah does in the last chapter of *Cosmopolitanism*).[16] There are many impassioned scholarly books about moral issues in race relations in the United States that have little engagement with topics or practices of race outside of the United States, except for identifying and situating references to continents of ancestral origin. There is little in African American philosophy about obligations to present-day Africans who suffer great disadvantages from terrorist wars against civilian populations, inadequate food and water, and disease, and even less concern expressed for the rural poor in India or indigenous groups in Scandinavia.[17]

Cicero provided a model of our relations with and obligations to others, based on the metaphor of concentric circles. Our first duties are to close relatives in the central area of the circle. Next come bands representing extended families, neighbors, fellow city dwellers, compatriots, and finally all of humanity. Cicero's ideal was that we should draw those in the band closest to the circumference of the circle into the central sphere of those to whom we are immediately connected, although Nussbaum notes that there is a tension in interpretation over whether Cicero intended to claim that our primary service is owed to those with whom we are immediately connected or to humanity as a whole.[18] But whatever the ranking, the inclusion of obligations to humanity constitutes another contribution from cosmopolitanism to an ethics of race, to guard against ethnocentrism.

However, in addition to the expanding inclusive quality of Cicero's cosmopolitanism, we need to remember that the loving egalitarianism in the center of his circle cannot be taken for granted. In contemporary familial centers of human life (at least in the United States and Europe, perhaps not all over the world) there are child abuse, violence against women, disregard for the elderly, emotional neglect, adultery, mental illness, alcoholism, and drug addiction. The distribution of work in the family is also notoriously unfair to women. When people see psychologists and psychiatrists who offer talking therapies, except for post-traumatic stress disorders incurred in adulthood, the psychic pain and damage that necessitates treatment is usually rooted in childhood experiences within the patient's family. So before conduct in intimate relationships is accepted as an ideal for how to behave toward foreigners and strangers, we need to be clear about what our ethical standards are for intimate relationships. Merely that the relationships have existed, are highly valued, and are given high priority by most people is not sufficient for them to qualify as ideals for human interaction.

However, philosophical ethics has unfortunately not created a robust tradition of examining intimate relations. And it may be that philosophical ethics is inherently inadequate to the task. Michael Stocker has argued that traditional ethical systems—egoism, utilitarianism, and deontology—are primarily concerned with our reasons for actions. We are supposed to have good reasons that can justify our actions, on the grounds that we are doing our duty, maximizing pleasure or happiness, or acting in our own best interests. Stocker thinks that this emphasis on reasons cuts agents off from their motives. Stocker concentrates on love and concern for particular persons as a primary motive. We love our spouses, parents, children, and friends as concrete particular beings who are irreplaceable. As a result, the reliance on ethical reasons is external to an intimate relationship and external to the individuality of agents involved.[19] Stocker does a good job of explaining the gap between philosophical ethics and personal life, but he does not ask whether we can expect family life to conform to external moral principles and values. Doing something in an intimate relationship for the reason that it is one's duty is not sufficient to fulfill affective expectations. But might it not be necessary? For example, a parent has a duty to feed her children and she does that. Stocker and the rest of us want her to feed them out of her love for them as her children. But if her love for them misguidedly leads her to starve them, something would be seriously amiss precisely because she has not fulfilled her duty.

Suppose we do bring the stranger/foreigner into the center of Cicero's circle. On Stocker's view, we would be expected to love that person. If there are already failures of love and derelictions of duty in the inner circle, to bring the foreigner/stranger into it may be neither kind nor benevolent. But if the center of the circle is loving and healthy, based on a history of love, respect, care, and friendship, bringing the foreigner/stranger in may be too kind and benevolent, that is, it may be inappropriate. When all is well in the family and among close friends, the privacy surrounding these relationships refers to the possession of shared histories and bonds to concrete individuals that are not only based on positive and nurturing behavior but on the fact that people are related to each other in the ways that they are, for instance, brother, mother, father, sister, lifelong friend.

Perhaps the cosmopolitan should get out—leave home—and encounter the foreigner/stranger in his or her different setting or in some neutral place. There is a well-known proclivity of people we call "cosmopolitans" to do exactly that. More than literal world travel, suggested here is the need for a movement from the mores of the cosmopolitan's origins, including the family center, into exactly the kind of public and semipublic physical and psychic spaces that require actions have reasons based on external values and rules. The impersonal nature of the rules and values outside of the center of Cicero's circle may be exactly what is required for the individual cosmopolitan to come into her own, not only as a cosmopolitan but as an autonomous individual who rebels against her nearest and dearest.[20]

COSMOPOLITAN PERSONAL IDENTITY DEVELOPMENT

Cosmopolitanism is about people in motion, both physically and psychically. Even when it is a matter of attitudes, as in how we should regard strangers, there is movement and change in the fact that we are preparing ourselves for dealing with what and whom we do not yet know. The idea of a technology of the self, which began with Aristotle's theory of the acquisition of virtues, is extended in cosmopolitan ideas about personal identity development. To borrow from Sartre, one makes an appointment with oneself in the future as a person changed from who and what one is now. In the case of cosmopolitan personal identity development, one aims to change who one is as one has been initially defined or posited by a community of origin. One might morph into a member of a different community or one might become permanently mobile and at ease with anonymity.

Cosmopolitan anonymity is facilitated by life in modern and postmodern cities, regardless of how divided by ethnic neighborhood such cities may be.[21] Iris Young has presented an ideal version of a flourishing and nonoppressive city to model a radical politics of difference that requires neither face-to-face community interaction nor assimilation. She writes:

In such public spaces the diversity of the city's residents come together and dwell side by side, sometimes appreciating one another, entertaining one another, or just chatting, always to go off again as strangers. . . . City life implies a social exhaustibility quite different from the ideal of the face-to-face community in which there is mutual understanding and group identification and loyalty. The city consists in a great diversity of people and groups, with a multitude of subcultures and differentiated activities and functions, whose lives and movements mingle and overlap in public spaces. People belong to distinct groups or cultures and interact in neighborhoods and work places. They venture out from these locales, however, to public places of entertainment, consumption, and politics. They witness one another's cultures and functions in such public interaction, without adopting them as their own. The appreciation of ethnic foods or professional musicians, for example, consists in the recognition that they transcend the familiar everyday world of my life.[22]

Young's passage leaves unanswered the question of how in their hearts and minds, in the privacy of the self, people are changed by contemporary urban encounters. The phrase "always to go off again as strangers" is not relieved of its anomie by the description following it of public consumption and entertainment that flows from a diverse urban marketplace. One is left to wonder whether the public places of politics are similarly packaged for mass consumption.

The cosmopolitan project of finding oneself by leaving home needs to be illuminated by accounts of the internal identities of those who leave the mores of home. In terms of ethnicity and race, we first need an account of what it is like to be constricted in staying home, and, second, we need a general description of personal cosmopolitan growth through leaving home. Insofar as cosmopolitanism is about the actual human world, specific examples are in order. Interesting in this regard is Jean-Paul Sartre's analysis of the French anti-Semite and Jason Hill's analysis of the noncosmopolitan nature of what he calls "Jewish tribal identity." Hill has also provided both religious and secular accounts of cosmopolitan personal identity development that are highly relevant to this discussion.

In his 1948 *Anti-Semite and Jew*, Sartre does not present an explicit statement of his commitment to cosmopolitanism, and neither does he set out a general ethical system or an ethics of race or ethnicity. Sartre was not a Jew so his cosmopolitanism is implied by his condemnation of anti-Semitism. Sartre begins with a claim that anti-Semitism cannot be accepted as a mere opinion. He writes: "I refuse to characterize as opinion a doctrine that is aimed directly at particular persons and that seeks to suppress their rights or to exterminate them. . . . Anti-Semitism does not fall within the category of ideas protected by the right of free opinion."[23] Sartre's grounding moral values are evident in how he contrasts them with the traits of the anti-Semite: "A man who finds it entirely natural to denounce other men cannot have our conception of humanity; he does not see even those whom he aids in the same light we do. His generosity, his kindness are not like our kindness, our generosity."[24]

Sartre's analysis of the psychology of the anti-Semite presupposes the moral freedom to choose virtues or vices. The anti-Semite has chosen passion as opposed to reason, as his hatred of Jews is not based on experience. For Sartre, the anti-Semite has what we would call an essentialist idea of Jewish identity, whereby everything a Jew does is conditioned by the fact that he is a Jew—the anti-Semite cannot conceive of Jewish "redemption." The anti-Semite is neither an aristocrat nor a worker and decidedly not an intellectual. He takes refuge in his own mediocrity and in the crowd of other anti-Semites. The anti-Semite does not want to recognize or make use of his own freedom but would rather be a thing, so that everything he values about himself may be given to him without any effort on his part. As the ultimate anticosmopolitan, the anti-Semite sustains the fantasy of a mystical connection to a particular place based on his genealogy:

> The true Frenchman, rooted in his province, in his country, borne along by a tradition twenty centuries old, benefiting from ancestral wisdom, guided by tried customs, does not *need* intelligence. His virtue depends upon the assimilation of the qualities which the work of a hundred generations has lent to the objects which surround him; it depends on property. It goes without saying that this is a matter of inherited property, not property one buys.[25]

Sartre's description of the French anti-Semite is meant to be an analysis of a pernicious form of *bad faith*, in the sense of individuals not assuming responsibility for their ability to choose and shape their own lives. It does not follow from this that members of a group hated in such bad faith are themselves all, or always, in good faith. Jason Hill in *Beyond Blood Identities: Posthumanity in the Twenty-First Century* critiques Jewish identity from an explicitly egalitarian cosmopolitan perspective.[26] Hill claims that according to Jewish religion, the "Jewish soul" was chosen by God before God created the rest of humanity. He argues that this heritage of having been chosen by God constitutes a readymade identity that sets Jews apart from the rest of humanity. Hill writes:

> If a group is singled out and chosen by God, stamped with the imprimatur of his meta-ontological insignia, then that group and its members are both structurally and ontologically outside the domain of the ordinary. If one is exceptionalized in this robust ontological manner, then one is both de-humanized and un-humanized because one is taken outside the world.

De-humanization is articulated non-pejoratively. It suggests that one is evacuated of one's own personal and ordinary humanity and singled out as the paradigmatic example of moral excellence. . . . This metaphysical sleight of hand places a reciprocal burden on Jewish agency which deprives it of its freedom to make its way towards its own humanity.[27]

Apparently, Hill is not talking about Jews as an actual historical people, but Jews as they might view themselves according to one interpretation of their religious tradition. (Like Sartre, he is criticizing what he imagines to be "the imaginary" of others.) The problem for cosmopolitan identity that Hill raises here is the result of shirking the same kind of commitment to the work of making oneself that motivates Sartre's castigation of the French anti-Semite. The deprivation of "freedom to make its own way towards its own humanity" posited by Hill is similar to Sartre's description of the anti-Semite's embrace of passion over reason. Hill's description of receiving the heritage of having been divinely chosen parallels Sartre's description of passive Frenchness. Unlike Sartre, who deploys a framework capable of critiquing all religious choices,[28] Hill seems to be focused on the particular religious choice of being a religious Jew. Thus, his proposed alternative to acceptance of having been chosen is not a rejection of religion per se but an endorsement of St. Paul's cosmopolitan religious teachings. According to Hill, Paul, who was an elite member of a tiny Hebrew sect, universalized Judaism as a form of cosmopolitanism after his revelation "on the road to Damascus." That the result of this universalization just happened to be the religion of Christianity seems not to be central to Hill's analysis, although it is impossible to overlook. Hill quotes Paul's views:

For you are all children of God through faith in Christ Jesus. For as many of you were baptized into Christ have put on Christ. There is neither Jew nor Greek; there is neither slave nor freeman, there is no male and female: for you are all one in Christ Jesus. And if you belong to Christ, then you are Abraham's offspring, heirs according to the promise. (Galatians 3:26–29) [italics from Hill's text][29]

If we step outside of religious beliefs, a Sartrean framework would allow for choosing this or that religion, choosing no religion, or choosing the religion of one's family that had been drummed in since infancy. What is important existentially for constructing the self is that the individual choose who he or she wants to be and be aware of choosing.[30] Existentialist identity construction would thus resemble Aristotelian virtue construction. For a cosmopolitan, the structure of choice would entail freedom to choose the group of people to whom one belongs. The self-aware freedom to choose mores and racial/ethnic identities distinct from those of one's origin means that a cosmopolitan can choose to leave home.

In *Becoming a Cosmopolitan: What It Means to Be a Human Being in the New Millennium*, Hill offers a secular view of the construction of cosmopolitan personal racial/ethnic identity that is based on the idea that one could and often should leave one's family culture when it obstructs growth and flourishing.[31] Hill proceeds from a cosmopolitan ideal of an egalitarian world in which individual human dignity is a primary value. Insofar as identities of race, ethnicity, nationality, and gender are imposed as expectations on individual perspectives and development, they should be sites of rebellion. Such rebellion is part of becoming an adult, part of maturing, and it is morally creative. Hill writes: "One who clings to a racial and ethnic identity attempts quite often to wring a great deal of virtue out of it without adding anything, such as, say, moral behavior of a certain type, to make the concept content specific." The individual not only has a right to forget her origins but at times a positive duty to do so. Hill calls for nascent cosmopolitans to "come out of the closet." He recognizes Nussbaum's distinction between radical cosmopolitanism that would exhort one to be a citizen of the world, with obligations to all of mankind, and moderate cosmopolitanism that allows for putting kith and kin first. His own ideal, partly realized through writing, is the radical version:

> At the moment I am situated somewhere between the two types of cosmopolitanism. Existentially, I have not yet grown into a full-fledged radical cosmopolitan, although I remain one in principle. I write, however, in order to become the person I would like to be. The radical cosmopolitan represents an Ideal. Its ethos is the one I would most like to see saturate the culture in which I live because it is predicated on and attempts to capture crucially salient (but infrequently exercised) features of the human condition: becoming and moral maturity.[32]

Given the possibilities for an individual's identity of religion or no religion, this religion or that religion, this race and culture or some other race and culture, or perhaps no race or culture, the cosmopolitan contribution to an ethics of race would be to respect and protect an individual's right to make choices in such matters, including the choice to leave home. This means that on the grounds of ethics, mores can be chosen. Radical cosmopolitanism not only allows for personal choice toward leaving home, but generally encourages or advocates it. It is difficult to imagine that any such choice, including the choice not to change one's mores of origin, could be advocated or prohibited on philosophical ethical grounds, provided that the choice itself does not involve harming others. A philosophical ethics of race would probably stop short of such outright encouragement or advocacy. Philosophers generally avoid telling people what they should do, although this does not mean that they hesitate to point out what should not be done. (In this sense, philosophers are analogous to political liberals who locate freedom in what is not explicitly prohibited by law.)

SUMMING UP AND RETURNING TO HUME'S *IS-OUGHT* PROBLEM

To sum up, the unexceptionable cosmopolitan contribution to an ethics of race would be openhearted and open-minded approaches to people who belong to "types distinct from our own," both racially and culturally. Cosmopolitanism would thus have the first word in an ethics of race. The cosmopolitan commitment to get along, accept, and tolerate would be energized by philosophical ethical judgments based on values such as justice and equality. Sometimes, in small matters, the value of getting along would outweigh serving justice, but justice will have to be served in matters of significant human well-being. For example, on the ground of a philosophical ethics of race, a person of color might overlook a mild racist remark or choose not to directly confront an atmosphere of white supremacy in the workplace. But an overt racist remark made by an otherwise responsible person should not be ignored and neither should outright racially discriminatory action.

Cosmopolitanism could also make an important contribution to an ethics of race by introducing a sense of obligation to further the well-being of members of types distinct from our own, although such obligation need not be part of cosmopolitanism itself. As Appiah has recently reinterpreted it, cosmopolitanism is a worldwide practice of conversation and not an exchange of moral exhortations.[33] And, finally, the cosmopolitan individual may be more likely to imagine and create racial and ethnic identities for the self that differ from expectations first encountered at home. Such innovations would not only benefit the individual as what John Stuart Mill called "experiments in living" but might serve as illuminating examples to others.

Methodologically, cosmopolitanism could contribute to a philosophical avoidance of Hume's *is-ought* pincer. The cosmopolitan usually proceeds from a foundational normative premise that we should accept and tolerate those who are different and then seeks ways to make this possible. In contrast, cowed by Hume, a moral philosopher often begins an ethical inquiry by trying to derive an *ought* from some *is*. For example, the philosopher, who is herself empathetic, might have an intuition that because empathy is a nearly universal human trait, we all ought to be empathetic. This puts us back in Hume's pincer. From the fact that empathy is a nearly universal human trait, it does not logically follow that we ought to be empathetic. If the philosopher wants to assert that we ought to be empathetic, with philosophical justification, then any of a number of complicated and futile projects may be launched: show the benefits of empathy, show how empathy can generate other human virtues, deny that there is a problem connecting *is* and *ought* by positing values as already in the world. These projects are futile because regardless of whether or not what is morally good is a natural something, the moral nature of the *ought* in what I or others ought to do concerns choice and the freedom to make choices. This moral *ought* has to do with exercising liberty and/or suppressing or expressing an unbounded freedom. It is on those grounds alone, far and away from anything that *is*. Its regard for the future makes it undetermined.

So why shouldn't a philosopher just avoid Hume's pincer in the cosmopolitan way? We could say that there is no logical connection between what is the case and what ought to be, but that what ought to be can be logically deduced from more general statements of what ought to be. Thus, we don't have to derive an *ought* from an *is*, but only from another *ought!* That derivation would ultimately rest on a foundational normative statement so intuitively compelling that it can be posited as a universal foundational normative statement. Ultimately, we should proceed from an *ought* so powerful that it knocks on the head everyone who is tied to some *is*. We need an irresistible *ought*—or two, or more—not just for philosophical ethics in general, but for an ethics of race in particular. This is because differences in mores tied to race, as well as race itself, are already very compelling, emotionally, politically, practically, and normatively.

NOTES

1. David Hume, *A Treatise of Human Nature*, ed. L. A. Selby-Bigge (London: Oxford University Press, 1964), 469 (book 3, part 1, section 1)
2. Boas is an interesting source for this phrase because he was a German Jewish immigrant who tirelessly combated scientific racism in his studies of African and Native Americans. He used the phrase at the 1908 Annual Meeting of the American Association for the Advancement of Science in reference to recent immigrants from southern and eastern Europe, whom he lists as: "Italians, the various Slavic people of Austria, Russia, and the Balkan Peninsula, Hungarians, Roumanians, east European Hebrews, not to mention the numerous other nationalities." Boas continues: "There is no doubt that these people of eastern and southern Europe represent a physical type distinct from the physical type of northwestern Europe; and it is clear, even to the most casual observer, that their present social standards differ fundamentally from our own. Since the number of new arrivals may be counted in normal years by hundreds of thousands, the question may well be asked, What will be the result of this influx of types distinct from our own, if it is to continue for a considerable length of time?" Franz Boas, "Race Problems in America," pp. 839–49, *Science* 29 (May 1909): 840,

cited by Leonard B. Glick, "Types Distinct from Our Own: Franz Boas on Jewish Identity and Assimilation," pp. 545–65, *American Anthropologist*, vol. 82 (1982): 545.

3. For example, while the contemporary online Stanford Encyclopedia of Philosophy does have an entry for cosmopolitanism (plato.standford.edu/entries/cosmopolitanism/), the following sources do not: Paul Edwards, ed., *The Encyclopedia of Philosophy*, 8 vols. (New York: Macmillan, 1967); Simon Blackburn, ed., *Oxford Dictionary of Philosophy* (Oxford: Oxford University Press, 2005); Robert Audi, ed., *The Cambridge Dictionary of Philosophy* (Cambridge: Cambridge University Press, 2006).

4. The emphasis on Diogenes' world citizenship, as though it had been chosen by him, seems to have come after his lifetime. In the (online) Stanford Encyclopedia of Philosophy 2006 entry for "cosmopolitanism," after a discussion of Socrates' implicit cosmopolitanism, the authors write about Diogenes of Sinope: "It is said that 'when he was asked where he came from, he replied, "I am a citizen of the world [*kosmopolitês*]"'" (Diogenes Laëtius VI 63). "Cosmopolitanism," *Stanford Encyclopedia of Philosophy*, at plato.stanford.edu/entries/cosmopolitanism/ (consulted July 2009). The source of this account, *The Lives and Opinions of Eminent Philosophers*, written by Diogenes Laëtius, in the third century B.C.E., contains many anecdotes about Diogenes' witticisms, as well as biographical data. Diogenes Laëtius, "Diogenes," in *Lives and Opinions of Eminent Philosophers*, trans. C. D. Yong (London: Henry G. Bohn, 1853), 224–48 (book 6). Diogenes and his father were involved in coin adulteration in Sinope, which was part of the reason why Diogenes left Sinope for Athens. Diogenes was at times very poor and spent his last years as a slave in Xeniades' household, where he mainly worked as a tutor to Xeniades' children. When Diogenes was sold, Hermippus relates in his "Sale of Diogenes" that when asked what he could do, his answer was, "Govern men." The idea was the paradoxical one that he would be sold as a master. To justify this Diogenes referred to the obedience due to physicians and pilots who were slaves. ("Diogenes," 227 [book 4], and 245 [book 9]). It is evident that Diogenes was a highly skilled man with an outrageous sense of humor who did not set out to be a cosmopolitan as someone might today but developed the role, or vocation, in response to his circumstances. According to Diogenes Laëtius, he also referred to himself as homeless, if the following lines were correctly attributed to him:

> Houseless and citiless, a piteous exile / From his dear native land; a wandering beggar, / Scraping a pittance poor from day to day ("Diogenes," 230 [book 6]).

5. For example, a contemporary virtue theorist writes: "For certain kinds of pleasure are of course external goods along with prestige, status, power and money. Not all pleasure is the enjoyment supervening upon achieved activity; some is the pleasure of psychological or physical states independent of all activity. Such states—for example that produced on a normal palate by the closely successive and thereby blended sensations of Colchester oyster, cayenne pepper and Veuve Cliquot—may be sought as external goods, as external rewards which may be purchased by money or received in virtue of prestige. Hence the pleasures are categorized neatly and appropriately by the classification into internal and external goods." Alasdair MacIntyre, *After Virtue* (Notre Dame, IN: University of Notre Dame Press, 1984), 198.

The philosophical point about the cheese, oysters, and the old French champagne ("cleek-oh") is, of course, not that the author has the knowledge, discrimination, money, and disease-free palate to appreciate them. But the reader cannot help but notice the personally privileged nature of the example and its faint whiff of superiority.

6. Martha Nussbaum, "Patriotism and Cosmopolitanism," *Boston Review* 19, no. 4 (1994), at bostonreview.net/BR19.5/nussbaum.html.

7. Diogenes Laëtius, *The Lives and Opinions of Eminent Philosophers*, 234 (book 6V) l, p. 234. Also: "Once Alexander the great came and stood by him, and he said, '"I am Alexander, the great king.'; And I, said he, '"am Diogenes the dog.'" And when he was asked to what actions of his it was owning that he was called a dog, he said, "'Because I fawn upon those who give me anything, and bark at those who give me nothing, and bite the rogues.'" (Ibid., 239.)

8. Martha Nussbaum, "Kant and Cosmopolitanism," pp. 25–58, in *Perpetual Peace*, ed. James Bohman and Matthias Lutz-Bachmann (Cambridge, MA: MIT Press, 1997): 48.

9. Diogenes Laëtius, *The Lives and Opinions of Eminent Philosophers*, 244–45 (book 6).

10. Kwame Anthony Appiah, *Cosmopolitanism: Ethics in a World of Strangers* (New York: W. W. Norton, 2006), xxi.

11. Ronald Strickland notes that this maxim, so often attributed to Montaigne because it was inscribed on a roof beam in his study, comes from Terence's comedy, *Heautontimorumenos*, where, Strickland reports, it was said by a "busybody" to a neighbor who had suggested he mind his own business. Strickland, "Nothing that Is Human Is Alien to Me: Neoliberalism and the End of *Bildung*," *RiLUnE (Review of Literatures of the European Union)*, no. 1 (2005): 29–40. In fact, Chremes is more of a good neighbor than a busybody because he elicits from Menedmus a confession of problems with his son, which are the subject of the ensuing play and involve Chremes and his son, before everything is resolved. See Terence, "The Self-Tormentor (Heautontimorumenos)," trans. Palmer Bovie, in *Terence: The Comedies: Complete Roman Drama in Translation*, ed. Palmer Bovie, trans. Constance Carrier and Douglas Parker (Baltimore, MD: Johns Hopkins University Press, 1992), 71–145. Be this as it may, the "busybody" description raises interesting problems about this famous cosmopolitan maxim. For one thing, unsolicited concern about others is less lofty than what, through Cicero's appropriation of the maxim, has been taken to mean a cosmopolitan sense of solidarity with all humanity, based on respect for individual persons. (On Cicero's derivation, which was accepted and further developed by Kant, with no hint of a "busybody" origin, see Nussbaum, "Kant and Cosmopolitanism, 33 and 54n30.) And for another, such concern may be difficult to distinguish from idle or malicious curiosity. Idle curiosity accompanies life in small communities everywhere and is sometimes the source of malicious gossip. Both can take the form of a cynical interest in the lives of others, magnificently exemplified by Miss Marple, Agatha Christie's elderly sleuth. Nothing human is alien to Miss Marple, who very successfully catches murderers throughout England, on the premise that the terrible truths she has learned about human nature from observing misbehavior in her own tiny village can be applied to people anywhere. Miss Marple is thereby some kind of a reverse cosmopolitan, because instead of flowing from the world to her home, her knowledge and wisdom flow from her

home to the world. There is no formal term for this, although were her intuitions and projections false instead of true, she would be merely vulgar. Colloquially speaking, Miss Marple is the ultimate "yenta."

12. See, "After Beers, Professor, Officer Plan to Meet Again," *CNNPolitics.com*, July 31, 2009, at edition.cnn.com/2009/POLITICS/07/30/harvard.arrest.beers/?imw=Y (consulted July 2009).

There is also the possibility that President Obama was making a somewhat cynical and pragmatic judgment that went over the heads of the American media's public, when he said that Sgt. James Crowley had "acted stupidly" in arresting Professor Louis Gates. He may have meant that Crowley had miscalculated the effect of arresting a famous black Harvard University professor, implying that the arrest would not have been stupid if an obscure black person had been handcuffed in similar circumstances. If the President meant that there were no legal grounds for the arrest, then why didn't he simply say that Crowley had acted unjustly?

13. See Bob Herbert, "Anger Has Its Place," *New York Times*, August 1, 2009, A9. Herbert here rejects the presidential cosmopolitan view and expresses and calls for moral outrage in the form of public demonstration.

14. Appiah, *Cosmopolitanism*, 154–57.

15. Appiah, *Cosmopolitanism*, 71.

16. Appiah, *Cosmopolitanism*, 155–74.

17. This is not to say that individual African American philosophers do not go to Africa and express concern for the well-being of Africans. Also, in American society African Americans are expected to recognize special obligations to Africa, based on ancestry alone, regardless of their scholarly interests or whether they have any. Such expectations might be resisted by those who are sensitive to racial stereotyping. For example, in August 2009 the following "invitation" was circulated by e-mail on the Internet: "I am inviting you to participate in a new section we are launching on our website www .pfa-partnersforafrica.org, where prominent people in the African American community will be sharing their views on African Americans reconnecting to Africa. We are asking for a 2–3 paragraph note reflecting on your thoughts on this area that will be placed on our home page. You can use this opportunity to discuss not only your views on this subject, but also any of your own personal achievements and projects related to Africa."

18. Marcus Tullius Cicero, *De Officiis* (*On Duties* or *On Obligations*), I, 50ff. In "Kant and Cosmopolitanism," ed. and trans. P. G. Walsh (Oxford: Oxford University Press, 2000). Nussbaum notes that Cicero got the circle metaphor from Hierocles (32–33), citing Julia Annas, *The Morality of Happiness* (New York: Oxford University Press, 1993), 267.

19. Michael Stocker, "The Schizophrenia of Modern Ethical Theories," *Journal of Philosophy* 73, no. 14 (August 12, 1978): 453–66.

20. Rebelling has a bad name because adolescents do it and because (as Sartre claims in his analysis of Charles Baudelaire) the rebel may preserve that against which he rebels, so as not to revolt genuinely. See Jean-Paul Sartre, *Baudelaire*, trans. Martin Turnell (New York: James Laughlin, 1967), 59–75 passim. But "revolution" seems too strong a word to describe the actions of a young person who finds her family center constricting and strikes out on her own.

21. On the new multiplicity of immigrant neighborhoods on New York City since the Hart–Celler Act ended preferences for immigration from Northern Europe in 1965, see Joseph Berger, *The World in a City: Traveling the Globe through the Neighborhoods of the New New York* (New York: Random House, 2007).

22. Iris M. Young, "The Ideal of Community and the Politics of Difference," in *Feminism/Postmodernism*, ed. Linda J. Nicholson (New York: Routledge, 1990), 300–24.

23. Jean-Paul Sartre, *Anti-Semite and Jew*, trans. George J. Becker (New York: Schocken Books, 1995), 9.

24. Sartre, *Anti-Semite and Jew*, 21–22.

25. Sartre, *Anti-Semite and Jew*, 23.

26. Jason D. Hill, *Beyond Blood Identities: Posthumanity in the Twenty-First Century* (Lanham, MD: Rowman and Littlefield, 2009). Disclosure: Jason Hill is a friend and colleague of mine, who I believe has Jewish ancestry. My mother was Jewish and raised me by herself. At times I have felt a Jewish identity and, on those grounds, I had mixed feelings about Hill's critique of Jewish self-perception as "chosen" because not everyone who could be categorized as a Jew sees herself as chosen by God or believes that there is a God. (I have neither that perception nor that belief.) I also have reservations about the feasibility of claiming that a people is dehumanized in a "nonpejorative sense." My intuition is that to say a group of human beings is not human or is outside of humanity, without also claiming that they are super-human or god-like (e.g., contemporary fictional vampires) is always and inevitably pejorative.

27. Hill, *Beyond Blood Identities*, 289, prepublication manuscript.

28. Sartre's existentialism is without qualification atheistic. In his famous "Existentialism is a Humanism" essay, first published in 1945, he wrote, "Atheistic existentialism, which I represent. . . ." Trans. Bernard Frechtman, trans., reprinted in *Existentialism and Human Emotions* (New York: Philosophical Library and Carol Publishing Co., 1985). The essay is also available online at www.marxists.org/reference/archive/sartre/works/exist/sartre.htm. (Reproduced under "fair use" provisions.)

29. Hill, *Beyond Blood Identities*, 314, prepublication manuscript.

30. Sartre, "Existentialism Is a Humanism."

31. Jason D. Hill, *Becoming a Cosmopolitan: What It Means to Be a Human Being in the New Millennium* (Lanham, MD: Rowman and Littlefield, 2000).

32. Hill, *Becoming a Cosmopolitan*, 141.

33. This reinterpretation of cosmopolitanism was evident in Kwame Anthony Appiah's discussion at a seminar devoted to his ideas, sponsored by the Oregon Humanities Center at the University of Oregon, in Eugene, on May 26, 2010. See also Appiah's interview at www.philosophybites.com (consulted May 2010).

• 3 •

Natural Law and Inequality

*W*e saw in chapter 1 that although both Plato and Aristotle invented ethics against a political backdrop, ethics, as something separate from politics, was not their goal in constructing political theory; neither did they derive politics from ethics. Plato's goal was to describe justice (already a quasi-political ideal), and for Aristotle it was the prescription for the happiness (as supervening on lived excellence) of the best men in the best society. For both Plato and Aristotle, the condition of the state was a foundation for the ethical condition of the individual. Nevertheless, neither one regarded the individual as a significant political unit: in *Laws*, Plato wrote, "Neither your own persons nor the estate are your own; both belong to your whole line, past and future, and still more absolutely do both lineage and estate belong to the community." And in *Politics*, Aristotle concurred: "We must not regard a citizen as belonging just to himself: we must rather regard every citizen as belonging to the state."[1]

The present subject is not individualism versus communitarianism in our current sense, but the comparative foundations of philosophical ethics and philosophical ideas of the state or government. For ethics to motivate or ground political philosophy, a philosopher would need to begin with moral intuitions or a moral system that could be validated independently of the political realm. A description of the right kind of government could then be derived from that. Still, for present purposes, such a derivation is of hypothetical interest only, and only because ethics and politics are so closely connected for Plato and Aristotle in their inventions of philosophical ethics. That is, the present project is to figure out what would work as an ethics of race, and in the course of this inquiry, or perhaps antecedent to it, we have to know something about ethics and the architectonic of which it is a part.

Plato used his description of the right kind of government to support his moral intuitions, and Aristotle constructed a theory of virtues and their development on the assumption that ethics was a subfield of politics, so that good government would result in virtuous citizens, who would participate in that government. Plato and Aristotle shared a standpoint from the inside of the ruling class looking out, and down. It was from that standpoint that they invented philosophical ethics. But even if Plato's heuristic use of government for ethics and Aristotle's elitism are put to rest, the ancient connection between philosophical ethics and political philosophy permeates the history of social and political philosophy so that we can now reasonably *expect* positive or actual law to be ethical. And on that point, an ethics of race would part company with both Plato and Aristotle. We do not rely on government as a source of ethics. From the perspective of nonwhite racial liberation, there is a long and distressing history of the unethical nature of government with regard to race. Slavery, segregation, and apartheid were all legal practices, enforced by governments. Racism, in both private and institutional forms, has been repeatedly left undisturbed by government, as well as practiced by it.

NATURAL LAW AND INEQUALITY

If government can and has been racially biased, what about the laws themselves? Is there a system of law that is infallibly egalitarian? Aristotle, who believed that virtuous aristocratic men should always rule and be ruled by one another, distinguished between actual individuals and the law or their law, which was "reason without passion and . . . therefore preferable to any individual."[2] This value placed on laws rather than rulers as such (e.g., the president of the United States) or rulers as the specific persons they are (e.g., Barack Obama) has been reiterated countless times, especially in the modern period, to valorize "a government of laws not men." Emphasis on the importance of laws in government has sometimes fetishized the laws themselves in the service of particular interpretations of this or that law for the interests of some. But there is a disinterested democratic approach to legal procedures that relies on the application of laws to ensure fairness and justice, either toward fulfilling "equal treatment under the law" or to ensure that laws do not contradict what are taken to be egalitarian founding documents, such as the US Constitution.[3] Both of these valorizations of law(s) over individuals can refer either to positive law (e.g., in judicial review based on interpretations of a founding constitution) or to some other law that legitimates that, namely *higher law*.

After millennia of the dominance of Christianity in the West, we are apt to associate the idea of higher law with the imagined dictates of the Christian God. But historically, that is only one specific interpretation. Higher law is generally an ultimate normative guide for human interactions that derives from what has been known as "natural law." The idea of natural law was a strain of ancient Greek cosmopolitanism: everything that occurs in the universe follows divine orderly principles that enable each kind of thing to reach its full potential. In the ancient, medieval, and modern periods, for humans to live in accordance with natural law entailed the development of virtues that were in accord with their distinctive natures, particularly the cognitive virtues of rationality and the pursuit of knowledge and wisdom. Natural law was supposed to extend to all human beings, having the capacity to unite them in harmonious interactions if they lived according to its dictates.

However, as H. L. A. Hart pointed out, for modern thinkers the ancient idea of natural law, with its associated normative teleology that we *should* develop according to our capabilities for distinctively human excellence, has been confusing for two reasons. First, the description of order or regularities in nonhuman things is not the same as human order voluntarily undertaken by conscious beings in obedience to perceived higher powers. And second, the presumption of universal equality has not resulted in the equality of all those living under government. That is, both governments and individuals have developed and lived in violation of what are taken to be teleological principles of natural law.[4] This is not Hume's identified gap in reasoning from what is to what ought to be, but rather a gap in reality between what ought to be and what in fact is. (The gap is in reality and not just in thought if natural law is taken to be real.) Natural law theorists have, mistakenly, for thinkers in a post-teleological age, described what ought to be as though they were describing what is.

We saw in chapter 2 how cosmopolitanism in both ancient and modern forms can bypass questions about the formation of government toward an acceptance of the world as it is, complete with all of its different peoples, nations, and their customs and beliefs. Cosmopolitanism also bypasses or seeks to transcend certain kinds of local attachment, including patriotism. Apart from its apparent political neutrality, cosmopolitanism in this sense lacks a political theory that would apply to the formation of government within a society. Also absent is a normative framework for assessing different forms of government and their concrete expressions. In the normative mode of acceptance for the cosmopolitan, different governments would go along with different cultures and peoples, and, provided that they did not propound and practice extreme forms of hatred or genocide—or in extreme cases, even if they did—they would be like diversities of dietary habits and religious beliefs. Today, racist government practices, or governments that do not intercede in racist practices within their societies, could be accepted by contemporary cosmopolitans. Overall, in contemporary understandings of cosmopolitanism as tolerant pluralism, there is an absence of standards according to which oppressive laws and cultural practices can be criticized or condemned, especially from standpoints outside of the national frameworks in which they occur. In terms of an ethics of race, such tolerance is particularly problematic when those who suffer from the oppression that is "tolerated" are members of nonwhite populations.

One way to make sense of apparent acceptance of injustice by those purporting to be just, in a range of historical contexts, is to identify naturalistic assumptions about differences in social advantage that we can now see are effects of injustice. There was, for example, Aristotle's view that enslavement was a natural response to the natural inferiority of those who were enslaved, at a time when only free aristocrats had opportunities to develop superiority.[5] There was the view in America that black slaves were intellectually inferior to whites, at a time when it was a crime to teach slaves how to read or write. In our own time, we might view disaster victims in a poor country as unfortunate due to unforeseen natural events that are not an instance of injustice but merely an unpredicted effect of the weather. In fact, the extent to which the global poor are victimized by hurricanes or earthquakes may be directly related to histories of exploitation that have resulted in inadequate infrastructure or material capacity to prepare for disaster. (Although even the global rich can be victimized by natural catastrophes if their governments have not fulfilled general expectations of preparation and disclosure of the risk of certain dangers.) In many such cases, socially constructed differences have been accepted as natural, rather than as the result of prior social, political, economic, or military injustice. The question should still be posed of why those purporting to be just have been blind to such prior injustice.

Within their constricted realm of the reach of justice, ancient cosmopolitans did value individual freedom and equality. Such valuations implicitly depended on notions of underlying universal uniformity, because if it is possible to be a citizen of the world, then there must be a sameness of human beings and their cultures in different parts of the world to support the citizenship or belonging of a foreigner. (The alternative would be universal citizenship in a world constructed to support only that, which would not be the existing, real world.) After the collapse of the Greek city-states that were the background against which early cosmopolitans (and cynics) such as Diogenes became famous, the Stoics developed a cosmology based on the implicit cosmopolitan idea of underlying global uniformity. For the Stoics, Universal Reason, the soul of the world, provided a rule of conduct for humankind that was natural law. Roman law, which necessarily had strong cosmopolitan elements over the period of empire (the administration of different legal systems gave rise to a body of *jus gentium*, or law of nations), was based on a contrasting and more down-to-earth idea of the power and authority of the people.[6]

Marcus Tullius Cicero, often cited for his cosmopolitanism, had a concept of human nature as striving for forms of excellence that it was the duty of rulers to fulfill. Thus, for Cicero, good government was coextensive with the authority of the people, although in his Rome "the people" did not include free or enslaved laborers or artisans. Cicero was concerned with the nobility represented and participating in Rome's highly developed militaristic government. Still, Cicero has been hailed as the first to posit a standard according to which positive law could be criticized and opposed. He wrote, "Not all things are necessarily just which are established by the civil laws and institutions of nations."[7] But Cicero was hardly a revolutionary and he posited his standard from the center of an empire, so he could have been referring to Hispania, Gallia, Achaea, Judea, or Carthage, as much as to Rome or Italy. (Although he clearly decried the tyranny of Julius Caesar in *De Officiis*.)[8] That is, progressives today are apt to view cosmopolitanism from the perspective of the open-minded traveler, but there has always been another kind of world-knowledgeable cosmopolitan who begins from a privileged home and always returns there, with critical views of foreign lands, their inhabitants, and practices.

Concerning the epistemology of higher law, if there is a form of law separate from and more binding than positive human law, and if human beings are in some sense obligated to know and follow that law, then this "higher law" is not so much constructed as it is discovered. Demosthenes (who was an almost exact contemporary of Aristotle) held that "every law is a discovery, a gift of God."[9] This ideal of law, or idea of ideal law, as evident through human discovery, rather than human construction or creation, was preserved through medieval scholarship, although it was not put to real political use before its reinterpretation in early modern social contract theory. In 1689, John Locke's *Second Treatise of Government* appeared in support of parliamentary representation for those rich landowners who were in the process of appropriating the commons via "enclosure" in England and land grants in America. Even closer to home, given his own political loyalties, Locke's *Second Treatise* justified the Glorious Revolution that had put William and Mary on the English throne(s).[10] In the course of Locke and others' grand projects of expedient aggrandizement, higher law and/or natural law was reinterpreted as the political derivation of a specifically Christian God's laws to mankind in an original state of nature.

The racist and chauvinist abuses of democratic liberalism as based on modern social contract theory are by now taken for granted by many liberatory scholars. The Christian God gave the law to European man, who he had created in his own image. This godly law was translated directly into the rights of those white European men who were entitled to political representation, private property, and dominion over nature and natural beings, including varied other human beings, such as the inhabitants of Africa and the Americas, and most women in European societies. Few now writing academically about law, race, gender, the environment, or ethics would find this traditional Christian foundation tenable. Neither would contemporary liberatory scholars accept higher laws as objective principles that are "discovered." Many would say that any such process of apparent discovery is at the same time a process of invention or construction and that there is nothing "there" worth discovering outside of conservative or reactionary projects of revision. Nevertheless, in exactly the spirit of liberatory race theory, I think that ancient, medieval, and early modern ideas of higher or natural law bear reexamination for their positive cosmopolitan content and a *theoretical* generality that both predates and postdates Christianity. This chapter offers a critical liberatory interpretation of Cicero's idea of higher law, followed by more general considerations about higher law and the inegalitarian results of philosophical epistemology. I will continue on to medieval and early modern developments of the idea of higher law in chapter 5. Chapter 4 interrupts the historical examination of philosophical ethics to consider slavery as a historical phenomenon.

CICERO'S IDEA OF HIGHER LAW

Cicero flourished as an orator and man of letters, if not as a politician (his career ended in his assassination[11]) in Roman society, when slave labor was a major part of its economy. He did not interpret or apply higher law in what we would take to be egalitarian terms.[12] (When Cicero's own slave, Dionysius, escaped with books from his library in 46 B.C.E., Cicero involved two successive provincial governors in futile efforts to catch him.)[13] Slavery, the exploitation of the laboring poor, conservative property protection, and aggressive property acquisition were all morally, socially, and politically acceptable to Cicero and members of the elite classes who were his contemporary audience. His only interest in reforms or what we would call social justice was to strongly oppose them.[14] Moreover, Cicero has not been taken seriously by philosophers as an original thinker.[15] Nevertheless, Cicero is of historical interest in critical liberatory theory for his explicit and accessible description of several theoretical innovations: the theoretical independence of ethics and political theory, the general idea of higher law as what men universally share based on their reason and speech (*ratio* and *oratio*), and the importance of private property to individuals and the obligation of the state and government to protect it.[16] All of these innovations constitute the beginning of political philosophy as it endured through the medieval period and was more characteristically developed by early modern thinkers, especially John Locke.

For Cicero, ethics and politics bear a sibling relationship, rather than a generative one, because each independently derives from natural law. *On the Commonwealth* is an analysis of ideal Roman republicanism, based on natural law; *On the Laws* is an application of ideal legal theory (based on natural law) to the historical Roman legal system.[17] *On Obligations* (*De Officiis*) presents a system of virtue ethics for an aristocratic or noble man, from that individual's perspective. Cicero's emphasis of the importance to the community of great individuals and his praise of actions that serve the community suggest later utilitarianism, as well as altruism. But the individual's primary virtues derive from natural law and not from political justice as Plato held or from living in a good society as Aristotle required. Thus, at the beginning of *On Obligations*, Cicero writes:

> Our starting point is that all species of living creatures are endowed by nature with the capacity to protect their lives and their persons, to avoid things likely to harm them, and to seek out and procure all life's necessities such as food, hidden lairs, and the like. Again, all living creatures share the instinct to copulate for the procreation of offspring, and once these are begotten, they show a degree of concern to look after them. But between man and beast there is this crucial difference: the beast under sense-impulses applies itself only to what lies immediately before it, with quite minimal awareness of past and future, whereas man is endowed with reason, which enables him to visualize consequences, and to detect the causes of things. . . . Without effort he visualizes the course of his whole life, and prepares the necessities to live it out. . . . Nature also joins individuals together, enabling them by the power of reason to share a common language and life.[18]

Cicero's idea of universal higher law is still cited as an important cosmopolitan inspiration, capable in principle of supporting universal equality. Furthermore, Cicero's rhetorical preeminence fulfills Plato's introduction of Western ethics as a discourse about the good. His focus on Roman aristocratic virtues, while not as psychological as Aristotle's account of virtue development, is a full-blown historical application of Aristotelian virtue ethics. Cicero rose to the highest level of political power from aristocratic but nonnoble and non-Roman origins in Arpinum—he was throughout his life known as a *novus homo*.[19] He is thus striking as someone who was able to become virtuous, according to Aristotle's formula, first through good breeding and education, and second in the course of his own life experience.

But Cicero's combination of practical rhetoric with virtue ethics, in cosmopolitan regard for egalitarian natural law, does little more than suggest why he was such a great inspiration to John Locke, as well as men of letters in the US antebellum South.[20] Cicero's *On Obligations* (*De Officiis*) was written to edify his son Marcus while he was an undisciplined student, living a life of expensive and excessive pleasures. In book 1, Cicero develops the idea of honor as a quartet of the four virtues: eagerness for truth (wisdom), justice in both giving due and keeping compacts, greatness and strength of spirit (magnanimity and courage combined), and moderation and self-control (temperance and fittingness). For every virtue there is a corresponding obligation to act in accordance with it. Although eagerness for truth is the primary virtue, Cicero does not think that knowledge is intrinsically valuable, and throughout *On Obligations* he stresses service to the community. Beneficence and generosity are parts of justice, and Cicero generally upholds the cosmopolitan value of "human fellowship," reminding the reader that we should always give to others when it does not harm us to do so.[21] This is the context in which he introduces the idea leading to a model of a circle with concentric bands:

> There is more than one level of human fellowship. Setting aside that shared by the entire human race without limit, there is the closest link between those of the same race, nation and tongue, which unites men intimately. Within this group lies the closer union of those from the same city-state, for such citizens share many things in common—a city-centre, shrines, colonnades, streets; their laws, rights, courts, and voting privileges; and beyond these, the circles of acquaintances and close friends, and the many who have connections with each other in public affairs and in business. Closer still is the social bond between kindred. Thus we start from the unrestricted fellowship of the whole human race, and arrive at this small and confined group.[22]

Many have tried to reconcile Cicero's professed good will toward the whole of humanity, as a moral ideal, with his indifference to the great inequalities of his day. But it's not as though many of those who write about ethics today are free of a similar inconsistency. We might not *profess* indifference to the global billions who subsist in misery, but neither do we do as much as we could to change their situation. The metaphors of *closeness* and *links* in the passage above offer clues to the magical thinking masking such inconsistency. Everything happens as though beneficence and generosity directly shrink within the *boundaries* (another metaphor) of increasing closeness (intimacy) and more lasting links (familial relations). Not only are we most beneficent and generous to kindred and close friends—not to mention our own selves—but this tendency has been taken to support a positive *normative* assessment of such unequal practices of beneficence and generosity.

The same slippage on the magical ground of what is taken to be natural, between what occurs and what is morally good, can be seen in Cicero's treatment of property. Cicero acknowledges the first obligation of justice to be not to harm anyone who has not already harmed one unjustly. Its second requirement is "communal property should serve communal interests, and private property private interests."[23] Although private property is the result of historical possession, rather than natural private ownership, justice as the law of the community requires respect for such possession. Cicero writes:

> Private property has been endowed not by nature, but by long-standing occupancy in the case of those who settled long ago on empty land; or by victory in the case of those who gained it in war; or by law or bargain or contract or lot. As a result, the territory of Arpinum is said to belong to the Arpinates, and that of Tusculum to the Tusculans; and the allocation of private possessions is of the same order. So since what was by nature common property has passed into the ownership of individuals, each should retain what has accrued to him, and if anyone else seeks any of it for himself, he will transgress the law of the community.[24]

Thus, what was natural has shifted into something unnatural, which is made natural again as "the law of the community" that must be obeyed. For Cicero, the obligations of justice regarding private property are more important than the obligations of justice regarding beneficence and generosity. The laws recognize what has passed from common ownership to private, and respect for the law in regard to private property has become "human fellowship in its broadest sense." What remains in common and is "basically free" can of course be extended to anyone, as circumstances suggest. Cicero is in effect saying that beneficence consists in the recognition of material inequality based on private possession, with a remainder of free and unlimited things that can be passed out as courtesies. Thus:

> This is human fellowship in its broadest sense, uniting all men with each other; within it the common ownership of all things which nature has brought forth for men's joint use must be preserved, in the sense that private possessions as designated by statutes and by civil law are to be retained as the laws themselves have ordained, while the rest is to be regarded, in the words of the Greek proverb, as "all things shared by friends." These possessions common to all men are, it seems of the kind which Ennius applies to a single instance, but which can be extended to many:
>
> > The friendly soul who shows one lost the way,
> > Lights, as it were, another's lamp from his.
> > Though he has lit another's, his own still shines.[25]

Book 2 of *On Obligations* is about what is useful or advantageous, mainly from the perspective of an ambitious politician. Book 3 deals with a topic not addressed as promised by the Greek Stoic philosopher Panaetius: "If an action apparently honourable conflicts with what appears useful, how a decision should be made between them."[26] Cicero declares his answer at the outset:

> For whether, as the stoics maintain, the honourable is the only good, or whether the honourable is the highest good as you Peripatetics argue, since both views lead to the conclusion that all else when put on the opposing scale would scarcely register the slightest weight, there can be no doubt that the useful can never conflict with the honourable. This is why Socrates, so we are told, used to curse those whose views first prised apart these concepts which nature joins together. The stoics agreed with him, arguing that whatever is honourable is useful, and that nothing is useful which is not honourable.[27]

Cicero observes that ordinary life often presents the practical problem of deciding how to behave when what is right according to honor conflicts with what is useful or advantageous. Countless times, through the use of historical examples over which so many have fawned,[28] Cicero simply begs the question through equivocation. He typically begins with an example of a conflict between the practice of a virtue and some immediate advantage and then decides in favor of acting in accordance with the virtue, asserting that is where real advantage lies. Consider these examples. Malicious fraud, such as not revealing the defects of property for sale or lying about advantages that do not exist, is not in fact useful because it is associated with vices and can incur a reputation for being treacherous, wicked, willful, and untrustworthy. That is, "it is never useful to do wrong, because it is always dishonourable; and honesty in a man is always useful because it is always honourable."[29] Cicero's relative, Gratidianus, forestalled his fellow praetors by announcing a resolution to a problem with the currency before all who had drafted it could take credit together. But his ensuing political glory came at the cost of his own virtue, so what he did was not useful.[30] Becoming king is only apparently useful if it is done unjustly. Thus, "if power itself is sought by all possible means, it cannot possibly be useful since notoriety attends it."[31]

In each of these cases and countless others, first we have a common-sense sort of advantage that seems to be at odds with behavior obligated by a virtue. But it turns out that real advantage always lies in acting in accordance with virtue because our ultimate advantage in accord with natural law—even if ideal wisdom and goodness is beyond our abilities[32]—is always located in behaving virtuously. Overall, this is either a tautological moral system or a prudential one: what is best for us is always to behave virtuously because virtuous behavior is what is best for us; the consequences of not behaving virtuously will always negatively outweigh its apparent advantages.

HIGHER LAW AND EPISTEMOLOGY

More still needs to be said about the content of higher law. It is important to recognize that once natural or higher law is taken to be a human construction, the epistemological problems on which philosophers have focused for so long in considering the connection between ethics and religion or any other possible source of higher law dissolve. Thus, the problematic introduced by Socrates as discussed in chapter 1 is no longer particularly perplexing or frustrating. Socrates and Euthyphro part on the question of whether the dictates of God are good to follow because they come from God or whether God issues them because they are good according to some standard higher than or external to God, in which case God can be bypassed. In the history of Western ethics, this problematic has served to sever religion from ethics in conceptual justificatory terms, as a matter of epistemology. But if what is good is a human construction, then it doesn't matter from whence our idea of it originates. What does matter is the content of what is good, and our reasons for considering something good. Returning to the *Euthyphro*, the question of content, of what is good, is whether it was right for Euthyphro to bring his father to trial for having allowed a laborer to die in a ditch. Socrates never even takes this question seriously, except to express shock at Euthyphro's violation of traditional beliefs about honor and loyalty owed to parents:

> Then come, dear Euthyphro, teach me as well, and let me grow more wise. What proof have you that all the gods think that your servant died unjustly, your hireling, who, when he had killed a man, was shackled by the master of the victim, and perished, dying because of his shackles before the man who shackled him could learn from the seers what ought to be done with him? What proof have you that for a man like him it is right for a son to prosecute his father, and indict him on the charge of murder?[33]

Because we are still so awe-struck by Socrates' aplomb in engaging Euthyphro philosophically just before his own trial, and because the effective *epistemological* separation of ethics from religion is so compelling, we are apt to overlook two important elements of this dialogue: one, in expressing shock at Euthyphro's disregard for traditional filial loyalty, Socrates has a chance to establish that he was not the social revolutionary or radical he was about to be prosecuted for being.[34] Two, proof is required, and perhaps even especially stringent proof, that "for a man like him, it is right for a son to prosecute his father, and indict him on the charge of murder." A man like whom? A man like Nexos, who was a laborer on a family's farm. Socrates does not make it clear whether he assigns a questionable moral status to Nexos because he was a laborer or because he committed the criminal act of cutting the throat of a domestic while enraged after drinking. The issue between Socrates and Euthyphro seems to be whether it is right for a son to prosecute his father rather than whether the father was justified in tying Nexos up and leaving him to die. Euthyphro claims that justice and, more than this, holiness requires that his father not be exempt from prosecution.[35] This suggests that according to Euthyphro's idea of holiness, his father acted unjustly and deserves prosecution because even criminals who are laborers ought not be treated unjustly. And that suggests an idea of something like egalitarian higher law, either a principle that positive law should apply to all human beings, regardless of social status, or a principle postulating that all human beings are morally equal, regardless of social status. But if Euthyphro cannot prove to Socrates that his intuition comes from the right source, then the intuition can be rejected and the default mode of traditional loyalties is restored as the proper moral perspective. On the one hand, to interpret Socrates as upholding family loyalty might seem odd given his displacement of the traditional family for the sake of an ideal state in the *Republic*. But on the other hand, Socrates might not have held filial loyalty as a primary value or virtue in the *Euthyphro*, but rather was upholding the tradition of a hierarchical society, in which the life of a laborer such as Nexos was of little account. If Nexos's life doesn't matter, then Euthyphro's prosecution of his father is absurd, as well as morally questionable.

Homicide was a private crime in the ancient world and not a public, legal crime. Except for any pecuniary compensation, which is not emphasized as part of Euthyphro's motive, given the absence of a legal obligation to respond to homicide, Euthyphro's prosecution of his father would have been a moral matter. When Euthyphro justifies the prosecution as a pious act, he asserts that "the holy is what I am now doing, prosecuting the wrongdoer who commits a murder or a sacrilegious robbery, or sins in any point like that, whether it be your father or our mother, or whoever it may be."[36] It is likely that Euthyphro was here referring to the religious laws of Athens that governed procedures of prosecution and punishment when slaves and freemen who were not citizens were killed or defiled.[37] However, in justifying his prosecution of his own father to Socrates, Euthyphro trips himself up by providing examples of patricide among the gods as proof for what he takes to be the power of "the law" to override filial loyalty.[38] Of course, Socrates makes short shrift of Euthyphro's reasoning, but he does not directly address the content of "the law" referred to by Euthyphro.[39]

If by "the law" Euthyphro was referring to a form of natural law that was the foundation of private and civil religious customs, it would provide indirect historical support for the importance of egalitarian natural law as an element of a democratic form of government that Plato rejected. Antiphon the Sophist, who was active in the latter half of the fifth century B.C.E., provided complex dialectical analyses of natural forces. From this metaphysic, he derived a view of human nature as striving for life, sometimes in contrast to actual laws, which were just but worked in opposition to the interests of individuals.[40] Parts of his surviving texts can be interpreted as criticism of distinctions between social classes. Antiphon wrote:

> Those born of illustrious fathers we respect and honor, whereas those who come from an undistinguished house we neither respect nor honor. In this we behave like barbarians towards one another. For by nature we all equally, both barbarians and Greeks, have an entirely similar origin: for it is fitting to fulfill the natural satisfactions which are necessary to all men: all have the ability to fulfill these in the same way, and in all this none of us is different either as barbarian or as Greek; for we all breathe into the air with mouth and nostrils and we all eat with the hands.[41]

The point here is not whether Plato can be put into dialogue with a cosmopolitan sophist such as Antiphon—I think this could be done, although not without scholarly risk[42]—but that the focus on epistemology in the history of philosophical ethics has resulted in a neglect of content. The requirement of egalitarianism in the content of an ethics of race requires a downplaying of the epistemological issues, although the philosophical plausibility of such a turn to content rests on only (relatively) recent expansions in recognition of what has been humanly constructed.

However, when the motive for putting key figures in dialogue is mainly to rescue a thinker from charges of (what we would consider to be) irremedial racism or to create a lineage for an idea, care must be taken to make sure that they are talking about the same things. Here is an example of how certain comparisons appear not to work. Alcidamas of Elaea, writing in the early fourth century B.C.E., claimed that laws were inherently unethical and should be opposed in a return to nature: "God has granted freedom to all, nature has made no man a slave."[43] Some scholars have attempted to make a case that Aristotle referred to Alcidamas' doctrine of universal human freedom.[44] But Aristotle's mention of Alcidamas follows a reference to Empedocles who advocated universal justice and is itself followed by a distinction between wrong actions against individuals (e.g., assault) and those against the community (e.g., avoiding service in the army). Here is the relevant passage from *Rhetoric*, book 1.

> It will now be well to make a complete classification of just and unjust actions. We may begin by observing that they have been defined relatively to two kinds of law, and also relatively to two classes of persons. By the two kinds of law I mean particular law and universal law. Particular law is that

which each community lays down and applies to its own members: this is partly written and partly unwritten. Universal law is the law of nature. For there really is, as everyone to some extent divines, a natural justice and injustice that is binding on all men, even on those who have no association or covenant with each other. It is this that Sophocles' Antigone clearly means when she says that the burial of Polyneices was a just act in spite of the prohibition: she means that it was just by nature.

> Not of to-day or yesterday it is,
> But lives eternal: none can date its birth.

And so Empedocles, when he bids us kill no living creature, says that doing this is not just for some people while unjust for others,

> Nay, but, an all-embracing law, through the realms of the sky
> Unbroken it stretcheth, and over the earth's immensity.
> And as Alcidamas says in his Messeniac Oration . . . [ellipses in Aristotle's text]

The actions that we ought to do or not to do have also been divided into two classes as affecting either the whole community or some of its members. From this point of view we can perform just or unjust acts in either of two ways—towards one definite person, or towards the community. The man who is guilty of adultery or assault is doing wrong to some definite person; the man who avoids service in the army is doing wrong to the community.

Thus the whole class of unjust actions may be divided into two classes, those affecting the community, and those affecting one or more other persons.[45]

Clearly, Empedocles and Alcidamas were talking specifically about how individuals should not be treated, whereas Aristotle was concerned with who or what the subjects of wrongs could be. That is, Empedocles and Alcidamas were talking about the content of right and wrong action, in the sense of what was specifically wrong, while Aristotle was addressing a distinction between wronging individuals and groups, rather than examining specifically what wrongs them. Similarly, in the preceding section Aristotle catalogs the different kinds of circumstances in which wrongs are committed and the kinds of people who are most often wronged, but his tone and analyses are descriptive rather than normative.[46]

The question could be raised of why Plato and Aristotle chose to change the subject: from the content to the epistemology of what was right by Socrates, and from doctrines of universal equality to issues of philosophical syntax by Aristotle. Was each in his own way deliberately using philosophy to protect institutions of class elitism and slavery? If they were, in contexts apart from those in which they directly propounded and defended elitism and slavery, then that would suggest an awareness that elitism and slavery were morally wrong. But given the existence of contexts in which Plato propounded and defended class elitism and Aristotle did the same for slavery, there is no basis for postulating such defenses of conscience. At best it could be suggested that Plato and Aristotle found situations like these, in which they used philosophy to change the subject, irritating, annoying, or necessary to dismiss or defuse. Again, their philosophical discourse on these matters was not normative, but analytically descriptive.

There can be an apparent category mistake in normative readings of Plato, Aristotle, and other figures in the history of philosophy who lived in times when some were enslaved and women were considered lesser human beings than men. Such thinkers often dealt with what later became burning issues of social justice by ignoring them in favor of more abstract levels of thought. The apparent category mistake is to charge the abstract thinkers with racism or sexism or elitism of some kind. This apparent category mistake results in great frustration whenever someone for the first time wants to discuss, on the grounds of moral content, some issue of race or gender. The subject itself is likely to be dismissed by other philosophers as "not philosophical," and the reaction to that is to claim that the other philosophers are racist, sexist, or elitist in their thinking. Perhaps a more precise way of expressing the latter frustration is to point out that the effects of excluding the content of social injustice from philosophy have not supported liberatory thinking in these areas. Also, liberatory thought about matters of social justice seems not to have been an intellectual option before the modern period. Aristotle could give an example of enslavement as a wrong,[47] but was not capable of criticizing the institution itself. He not only thought that some were naturally slaves, but his overall naturalistic approach (which tended to take the status quo to be natural), precluded deep criticism of existing social structures. Plato, because he was not a naturalist, did not face the constraint against criticizing existing social structures, but neither was he opposed to slavery (as we shall see in chapter 4). And Cicero's cosmopolitanism, while it could accept some cultural differences, could not criticize existant culture itself. This ancient blindness to social injustice and the magical thinking in moving from nature to culture, and then to culture-as-nature, became a powerful cognitive mechanism in the service of oppression, for millennia.

NOTES

1. Plato, *Laws*, trans. Taylor, 923a, and Aristotle, *Politics*, trans. Barker, 1227a28–29 (8.1.4.), both cited by Susan Ford Wilshire, *Greece, Rome, and the Bill of Rights* (Norman: University of Oklahoma Press, 1992), 4.

2. From Aristotle, *Politics*, book 3, 15–16, translated by Edward S. Corwin, in his *The "Higher Law" Background of American Constitutional Law* (Ithaca: Cornell University Press, 1955 [1928]), 8 (reprinted from *Harvard Law Review* 42 [1928–1929]: 149–85).

3. Of course, the US Constitution was not initially egalitarian given that a black slave was to be counted as three-fifths of a person for computing taxes and determining the number of representatives for the US House of Representatives. And, of course, just mentioning this overlooks the fact that the number of persons was not then (or now) equal to the number of those eligible to vote. Slaves, women, indentured servants, and Native Americans were ineligible to vote when the Constitution was signed.

4. H. L. A. Hart, *The Concept of Law* (Oxford: Oxford University Press, 1991), 181–89.

5. Aristotle, *Politics*, in *The Basic Works of Aristotle*, ed. Richard McKeon, trans. W. D. Ross (New York: Random House, 1941), 1132–33 (book 1, ch. 5, 1254a15–1255).

6. See Corwin, *The "Higher Law" Background of American Constitutional Law*, 4–9, esp. 9n21.

7. From Marcus Tullius Cicero, *De Legibus*, I, 15, cited by Corwin, *The "Higher Law" Background of American Constitutional Law*, 11. Corwin's citation in support of his interpretation of Cicero as opening up the possibility of criticizing Roman law, specifically, is probably anachronistic because Cicero did not have a theory of individual rights as antecedent to positive law. Legal scholars tend to locate the possibility of a critique of existing government in the official and formal existence of such rights in positive laws, for example, freedom of speech. (See Wilshire, *Greece, Rome, and the Bill of Rights*, 22–29.) But in societies with well-developed doctrines of individual rights, rights are still violated and the identification of their violation and legal action for rectification may proceed on moral intuitions that are based on something more than the rights as specified. This 'something else' could be the higher law foundation of the rights themselves, now used to support criticism of existing practices. At times when the US Constitution has been interpreted in liberatory ways, such as *Brown* (i.e., *Oliver L. Brown et. al v. the Board of Education of Topeka (KS) et. al*, 1954), the grounds for such an interpretation would seem to be something like higher law, even though in legal terms the Constitution alone is referred to as the basis for the reinterpretation.

Corwin's claim that the US Constitution is based on an idea of higher law that can be traced to ancient thinkers has been sharply criticized as a claim about legal intellectual history. See, for instance, Gary L. McDowell, "Coke, Corwin and the Constitution: The 'Higher Law Background' Reconsidered," review of *Corwin on the Constitution*, by Richard Loss, *Law and Social Inquiry* 14, no. 3 (Summer 1989): 603–14. But Corwin may be right about certain conceptual similarities—he would have endured better as a philosopher than a constitutional theorist.

8. See the editor's remarks on Cicero's unmistakable wrath at Julius Caesar in *De Officiis* at book 1, 26, 45, 122; book 2, 27ff.; and book 3, 82ff, in Cicero, *On Obligations (De Officiis)*, ed. and trans. P. G. Walsh (Oxford: Oxford University Press, 2000), ix–x.

9. On Roman law and Demosthenes, see Cicero, *On Obligations*, 4–5. (Aristotle's dates are 384–322 B.C.E., Demosthenes' 383 or 385–322.)

10. Locke used his concept of money as a notational store of value to justify both English enclosure of the commons by large landowners and the appropriation of American land. His reasoning was that labor provides the value of all things including land, that those who improve land are entitled to own it, and that money facilitates the ownership of more than those who provide the labor (either directly or through the labor of their 'servants') can themselves use. The last is because money is a store of value that bypasses the sin of waste—a landowner can sell his surplus and hold it in money. See Naomi Zack, "Lockean Money, Globalism and Indigenism," *Civilization and Oppression*, ed. Catherine Wilson, *Canadian Journal of Philosophy* 25 (1999): 31–53. On the publication of Locke's *Second Treatise* as a exhortation as well as justification for the Glorious Revolution, written over the twenty preceding years, see Peter Laslett, Introduction, in *Two Treatises of Government*, by John Locke, ed. Peter Laslett (Cambridge: Cambridge University Press, 1991), 46–66.

11. From his Roman contemporaries to the 2005–2007 HBO series *Rome*, Cicero is portrayed as having surrendered stoically to his killers, who were sent by Mark Anthony in punishment for having tried to remove him from office. See Plutarch, "Cicero's Death," trans. John Dryden, trans. at intranet.grundel.nl/thinkquest/moord_cicero_plu.html (consulted February 2010).

12. By the time Cicero died, one-third of Italy's population of six million were enslaved. See Neal Wood, *Cicero's Social and Political Thought* (Berkeley: University of California Press, 1988), 20–21; and M. I. Finley, *Ancient Slavery and Modern Ideology* (New York: Penguin, 1980), 80.

13. Finley, *Ancient Slavery and Modern Ideology*, 112. Discussions of slavery in the ancient world are complicated by contrasts with slavery in modern times. Although it was a dire form of bondage, ancient slavery frequently allowed for manumission and was not generally associated with physical characteristics that supported modern ideas of racial difference. These later trait associations required the science of biology for their foundation, which can render equating ancient and modern slavery anachronistic. But there is another basis for comparison. As Wood, Finley, and others point out, there have only been five slave societies in recorded history: classical Athens, Brazil, the West Indies, ancient Italy, and the American South. (Wood, *Cicero's Social and Political Thought*, 19, Finley, *Ancient Slavery and Modern Ideology*, 9). It may be that the broad institutional characteristics shared by these five societies render distinctions based on modern ideas of race beside the point. Modern ideas of race could be viewed as part of the ideology of New World slave-owning groups, useful for justifying and supporting an institution that was fundamentally motivated by economic considerations imbedded in certain divisions of labor. This is the view commonly attributed to Friedrich Engels. (See for instance, Finley's reference to Engels's view that slavery enabled the entire Western world as it was developed economically with "the division of labour between agriculture and industry on a considerable scale," *Ancient Slavery and Modern Ideology*, 12.)

14. On these innovations as new abstractions in the history of thought, see Wood, *Cicero's Social and Political Thought*, 70–90.

15. Cicero is known for having combined rhetoric with philosophy in the service of his humanistic ideal of using knowledge for the betterment of human affairs. He

put philosophy to practical use in his oratory career, and this is perhaps partly why traditional philosophers have slighted him as a political philosopher. See, for instance, P. H. DeLacy, "Cicero," in *The Encyclopedia of Philosophy*, ed. Paul Edwards, 8 vols. (New York: Collier Macmillan, 1967), 1: 112–13. But even without a bias against pragmatism, it turns out that not much can be said in Cicero's defense as a philosopher. Even his innovations in political and moral thought were probably more the result of historical circumstances, that is, the history of Rome intervening between the time of Plato and Aristotle and Cicero's times, than of originality of mind.

16. See Wood, *Cicero's Social and Political Thought*, 122–42.

17. For further characterizations of the generality and specificity of these two works, with further sources for analysis, see Cicero, *On the Commonwealth* and *On the Laws*, ed. James E. G. Zetzel, (Cambridge: Cambridge University Press, 1999), xiv–xxiv.

18. Cicero, *On Obligations*, 6 (book 1, 11).

19. Cicero was a "new man" in the political contexts in which he was influential, which were dominated by the noble elite. But Cicero's origins were aristocratic and his family had many influential connections. Wood, *Cicero's Social and Political Thought*, 42ff.

20. Ancient Stoicism and Cicero's orations in Latin were standard references for educated slave owners in the American South. For a discussion of sources on this subject see Mary L. Haywood, "The Antebellum Library of John Richard Edmunds" (M.S. thesis, University of North Carolina, Chapel Hill, 2006), at etd.ils.unc.edu/dspace/bitstream/1901/323/1/maryhaywood.pdf (consulted March 2010).

21. Cicero, *On Obligations*, 19–20 (book 1, 50–52).

22. Cicero, *On Obligations*, 20 (53).

23. Cicero, *On Obligations*, 9 (21).

24. Cicero, *On Obligations*, 9 (21).

25. Cicero, *On Obligations*, 19 (book 1, 51). It should be noted that Cicero himself was a man of property, relying for his income on multiple houses, including slum dwellings, that he rented out, as well as on political support from those property owners whose interests he continually defended as a barrister, magistrate, senator, consul, and governor of Cilicia. See Wood, *Cicero's Social and Political Thought*, 105–10.

26. Cicero, *On Obligations*, 88 (book 3, 19–20).

27. Cicero, *On Obligations*, 88–89.

28. The fawning literature went well beyond the thought of those who for their day were conservative on issues of social justice. See for instance Robert N. Wilkin's frequently cited *Eternal Lawyer: A Legal Bbiography of Cicero*, (New York, NY: Macillan, 1947).

29. Cicero, *On Obligations*, 102–5, quote from p. 105 (book 3, 53–64).

30. Cicero, *On Obligations*, 111 (80–81).

31. Cicero, *On Obligations*, 112–13, quote on p. 113 (83–86).

32. Cicero, *On Obligations*, 89–90 (10–15).

33. Plato, *Euthyphro*, trans. Hugh Tredennick, in *Collected Dialogues*, ed. Edith Hamilton and Huntington Cairns (New York: Random House, 1964), 177 (9a1–7).

34. Whether Socrates was in fact a traditionalist at heart or whether Plato just wanted to shame some of his contemporaries is moot, given present interests. But I

do find it interesting that, on my reading, Descartes made a similar rhetorical move as Socrates in the *Euthyphro* by dedicating the *Meditations* to his Jesuit presumptive-benefactors and purporting to enforce the church doctrines of the existence of God and the immortality of the human soul. Like Socrates, all that Descartes succeeded in doing was stirring up religious doubt (resulting in initial burial in unhallowed ground and placement of his work on the proscribed "list"). See Naomi Zack, *Bachelors of Science: Seventeenth-Century Identity, Then and Now* (Philadelphia: Temple University Press, 1996), 13–54.

35. Plato, *Euthyphro*, 172 (4d).
36. Plato, *Euthyphro*, 173 (42).
37. See Glenn R. Morrow, "The Murder of Slaves in Attic Law," *Classical Philology* 32, no. 3 (July 1937): 210–27.
38. Morrow, "Murder of Slaves in Attic Law."
39. This reading partly depends on an assumption that Socrates in the *Euthyphro* was the historical Socrates. In the *Gorgias*, 'Socrates,' perhaps speaking more to Plato's idea of how the ideas of the historical Socrates can be developed, vigorously defends seeking punishment for kin guilty of wrongdoing. If the historical Socrates agreed with *Euthyphro* along the lines of the defense of virtue in the *Gorgias*, then his prodding of Euthyphro still expresses his interest in the epistemological issue of how Euthyphro knows what is right, except that Socrates too thinks it's right. However, it seems unusual for Socrates, either as the historical figure or Plato's depiction of him, to engage in spirited dialogue for the purpose of questioning what he already has decided is correct. See, Plato, *Gorgias, Collected Dialogues*, in *Plato: Collected Dialogues*, ed. Edith Hamilton and Huntington Cairns (New York: Random House, 1964), 263–64 (480a–c). Thanks to Jason Jordan for bringing the potential discrepancy to my attention.
40. For an argument that Antiphon was not attempting to redefine justice as understood in law, but to oppose it, see David J. Furley, "Antiophon's Case against Justice," in *The Sophists and Their Legacy: Proceedings of the Fourth International Colloquium on Ancient Philosophy Held in Cooperation with Projektgruppe altertumswissenschaften Der Thyssen stiftung at Bad Homburg, 19th August–1st September, 1978*, ed. G. B. Kerferd (Wiesbaden: Franz Steiner Verlag GMBH, 1981), 81–91.
41. There has been substantial scholarly dispute over whether Antiphon the Sophist was the same person as Antiphon of Ramnus, the orator. In any case, there are different constellations of thought associated with each "Antiphon"; I am following the side that associates cosmopolitan egalitarianism with the person called "Antiphon the Sophist." For fuller discussion of Anthiphon the Sophist's metaphysical thought, see Mario Untersteiner, *The Sophists*, trans. Kathleen Freeman (New York: Philosophical Library, 1954), 228–72, quote in text above from p. 254. Untersteiner's interpretation of Antiphon's fragments as supporting a comprehensive metaphysical system has drawn substantial criticism. See Gerard J. Pendrick, ed. and trans., *Antiphon the Sophist: The Fragments* (Cambridge: Cambridge University Press, 2002), 53–54 passim.
42. See Pendrick, *Antiphon the Sophist*, ibid., pp. 23, 241 for Pendrick's dismissal of any real egalitarianism on the part of Antiphon that would include social class, by Antiphon, based on the discovery of new papyri.
43. Untersteiner, *The Sophists*, 341.

44. See Untersteiner, *The Sophists*, 350n147.

45. Aristotle, *Rhetoric*, book 1, ch. 13, 1373b, 1–25, in *The Basic Works of Aristotle*, ed. Richard McKeon, trans. W. D. Ross (New York: Random House, 1941), 1370.

46. See Aristotle, *Rhetoric*, 1368–70 (1372b22–1373a).

47. See Aristotle's example of Gelon enslaving a town that would have been enslaved by Aenesidemus as an example of "those who are on the point of being wronged by others if we fail to wrong them ourselves." Aristotle, *Rhetoric*, 1369 (ibid., 1373a15–15), p. 1369.

· 4 ·

Moral Law and Slavery

$\mathscr{A}$t present, all legal communities, social communities, religions, and individuals, that is, everyone, except perhaps for those who still buy and sell human beings, recognize that slavery is morally wrong. The perceived wrong of slavery has two aspects that need to be examined: the nature of moral law according to which it is wrong and why exactly it is wrong. The idea of moral law is very untidy philosophically because it is held to be objective and yet depends on universal intuition for its validity. Nevertheless, the idea of moral law merits philosophical attention, if only in terms of its history and the purposes it has served. After such attention, in this chapter, it will be possible to turn to the specifics, both historical and conceptual, of the wrong of slavery.

MORAL LAW

If positive law, that is, actual laws of specific geographical localities, is racially unjust and society is racist, the idea of natural or higher law as an ultimate standard has a strong appeal—as an ideal—in the search for an ethics of race. The ideal of higher law would be imagined and humanly constructed, rather than an objective system of order to be discovered and described, as was believed historically. But once processes of human construction or invention are recognized, it is oxymoronic to call the constructed ideal "natural law." The basis on which such a law would be "higher" is also dubious without reliance on religious belief. What seems to be relevant and defensible as the secular heir to natural law or higher law is something that could be called *moral law*. Moral law, like its predecessors, natural law and higher law, is universal and objective. Its universality means that it applies to every human being (and possibly to other living things as well). Its objectivity means that its principles would be true independently of human assent to them. (That is, human construction or invention does not mean that the end result is dependent on human agreement for its truth—although humans could deconstruct it.) The moral law could not be legitimate if no human beings ever assent to it, as moral law in a secular society would be valid only because it expresses something consonant with broad human intuitions, attitudes, and goals.

In the context of race, moral law would be distinguished from the laws of government in civil society. Without state or government force to respond to failures to follow the moral law, or breaking it, the moral law would not have the legal status of positive law. Neither would the moral law have a legal capacity to generate transmission into positive law, although it could be invoked to create or correct positive law. Overall, the alignment of positive law with moral law would be strived for as a liberatory goal.

If natural law comes from nature and higher law comes from God, one might ask where moral law comes from. Sometimes our awareness of moral law as something preexisting occurs for the first time in an experience of its violation, and that occurrence could be accompanied by an impression or sense of the moral law's existence antecedent to awareness of it. But even a phenomenological experience of moral law as eternally true or always having been there is not the same thing as a long, objective history of the awareness of moral law. The image of Moses bringing the law down from on high, already written in stone, is a powerful and persistent metaphor. But once exposed as a metaphor, the law written in stone loses its credibility as a foundation. (Not that the idea of a foundation isn't itself a metaphor.)

The answer to the question of where moral law comes from is, "It varies." Moral law can "come from" emotions of empathy, reason, common sense, custom, intuition, and even religious teaching or revelation. Wherever it comes from, the moral law always appears in a form that is already normative. This initial normativity relieves us of Hume's burden of deriving an *ought* from an *is*, as discussed in chapter 2. We do not need to derive the moral law from anything. Once it appears, it is already normative and its moral quality is self-justifying. The moral law is, by definition, what everyone is obligated to obey.

The initial normativity of moral law, together with its presumed universality, is what distinguishes it from mores and positive law. Mores are often closely derived from historical realities, as pragmatic ways of dealing with certain otherwise threatening facts or situations. There are reasons for mores that can generate moral intuitions, but insofar as such intuitions are tied to concrete historical contingencies, they are not universal. Someone can always view mores from outside their originating context and not experience their moral force, without incurring blame, such as non-Catholics eating red meat on Fridays. But mores are convincing from within the context of origination. The (normative) first principles of moral law also have to be convincing. What makes the moral law convincing is not that its normativity is a matter of universal acceptance, which it often is not, but that it is an ideal for which we can all plausibly strive. Moral law may result in critical judgments of local mores, and its universality gives it more moral force than normative principles that are mores. The same qualities of universality and greater moral force distinguish moral law from positive law. Moral law can always be used to assess positive law. Speaking from moral law, given human histories of legal oppression, we can say that some positive laws have been morally wrong (e.g., apartheid) and that some things that are morally right have been prohibited by positive law (e.g., teaching American slaves how to read).

Condemnation or criticism on the ground of moral law entails that the mores or positive law in question should be changed. This is a moral *should* as opposed to a practical or instrumental *should*. For example, at this writing the Arizona state legislature is in the process of passing a bill that the governor is expected to sign into law, which will make it a state crime to be in the United States illegally. Police officers will be able to ask anyone for a driver's license or state ID given "reasonable suspicion" that the person may not have such papers. Imprisonment, fines, or deportation may result from such intervention. The view has been voiced that the Arizona law would empower the police to practice a kind of "racial profiling" of Hispanics.[1] The court challenges that are likely to be part of the response to this law will probably derive from moral judgments of unfairness, as well as laws and court decisions prohibiting racial discrimination and matters of state and federal jurisdiction over immigration. But the moral judgments brought to bear will have an extralegal normativity that empowers people to assess the Arizona law and take legal or expressive action against it.

When moral law results in criticism of normative principles derived from mores, there is a similar force in favor of change. As with all social constructions, mores, once identified as such, are presumed possible either to avoid or change. The aspect of cosmopolitanism that counsels leaving home (see chapter 2) entails exactly such avoidance. Those who are normatively ensconced in mores often resist a call for change based on moral law. Loyalty to mores thus creates conservatives and no less so when people are loyal to practices that oppress them. The conservative response to a moral call for change is self-identified as issuing from the side of Hume's *is*. For example, moral law provides a negative assessment of female circumcision. Responses based on mores in defense of female circumcision typically refer to benefits of the practice within the culture in which it is practiced and the right of that culture to preserve itself in immunity from outside criticism as well as physical external intervention.[2]

In contrast to a judgment of moral law against mores and positive law, a judgment from mores against moral law does not have the same normative force. A judgment against moral law from mores would be at best an expression of local opinion or custom, at worst chauvinism. Positive law may push back against moral law when the two are in conflict, especially when government executes positive law, either with the threat of force or with force itself. Thus, if the Arizona state law allowing the police to immediately apprehend those suspected by them of being illegal immigrants is passed and enforced, force will be threatened when a police officer stops a person who looks Hispanic (and probably also appears to be poor) with a request to see her papers. Force may be applied directly if the suspect has no papers and is consequently arrested. This will occur regardless of moral objections to the law and its enforcement. But even legitimate force is not sufficient to show that moral judgments are mistaken or to nullify them. Once a moral judgment is made that a law is unjust, the moral authority of the law is undermined. And even though laws are distinct from morality or ethics, there is a broad presumption in democratic societies that laws will not go against moral or ethical expectations. Thus, in the present example, there may be angry onlookers, sympathetic media coverage, and public demonstrations against the law and the police action, followed by civil lawsuits.

Returning to philosophical expectations, the question of where the moral law "comes from" is not easy to put to rest. However, the idea of fundamental normative principles coming from something may not only be a distracting metaphor but risk getting us lost in epistemology, as discussed in chapter 3. Morality is about the good and the right, not about theories of knowledge; axiology is not epistemology. This is not to say that we should not have a moral epistemology. But even if the approved moral epistemology is followed, the result may not be in accord with moral law. Suppose that our moral principles are required to come from God or the community and either one of these exhorts us to kill children or to deliberately sacrifice a small number of people in order to save many more. In these cases, God may be exhorting in a spirit of vengeance and the community may be proceeding from crude utilitarianism in a crisis. The moral law would enable us to focus on the specific acts in question, with the result that both their reasons and the origins of their design may become morally irrelevant. That is, where our moral principles come from or how we justify them in answer to the epistemological question of how we know they are true is less important than their content.

Of course, reasons can be given for the principles of moral law. But reasons are in the realm of human values and actions, and what counts as a good reason for following a moral principle is not the same thing as how one knows, based on requirements for knowledge that govern nonnormative areas of human life, that the moral principle is true. Moral law is unlike natural law as descriptions of nonnormative regularities, unlike higher law as rules issuing from deities, unlike positive law as rules made by historical governments, and unlike the rules tied to the mores of historical peoples and groups.

Suppose the principle is P: "We should not discriminate based on race." People may have reasons such as the following for acting in accordance with P: practical concern with getting along, concern for the well-being and feelings of others, concern for their own moral virtue, a desire to conform, fear of punishment for not conforming, a conviction that P is true or that the system of which it is a part is right and obligatory. Others may simply follow P because they believe it is the right thing to do, without further qualification. The truth of P may be the result of its logical derivation from more general moral principles, which themselves derive from other general principles, all the way up to the axioms of a moral system. The axioms themselves could be intuitively justified, come from religion, be accepted for the sake of social order, or be accepted arbitrarily. There are no defensible rules for how the derivation or source of P in any epistemological sense does or should line up with different reasons for acting in accordance with P.

Moral law is sui generis—there is nothing else quite like it. Moral law is not the result of human consensus and it does not "come from" assent to it. Nevertheless, an important aspect or indicator of moral law is general human agreement about its content and about whether it applies in any given instance. Not much can be said about moral law apart from its content, to which "we" who are rational and benevolent assent. But always, moral law in its normativity and content cannot be reduced to even the most general and exalted consent. Moral law in all of the foregoing senses would be the standard for an ethics of race.

REQUIREMENTS FOR AN ETHICS OF RACE

Given moral law as a ground and standard, the following question can now be posed. What are the requirements for an ethics of race? At this stage of the inquiry there appear to be six.

1. An ethics of race, like any other ethics, would have to posit the intrinsic value and freedom of each moral unit who acted and was judged according to it and the intrinsic value and freedom of the objects of

such action. That is, ethical subjects would be the agents and other beings with intrinsic value and freedom, the objects. It would need to be assumed that such moral units are autonomous or self-governing in important ways and worthy of respect from one another.

2. An ethics of race would have to be more general than its applications to racial difference or what is experienced as racial liberation or racism. If an ethics of race were derived solely in terms of racism, it would be ad hoc and might not rise above the mores of particular racial identities and their particular histories and phenomenologies of oppression, whether from the standpoint of oppressors or those oppressed. Any such local or ad hoc ethics of race would lack universality. An ethics of race would have to be universal, applying to all of its subjects and objects at all times and in all places. This requirement of universality would impose a certain generality, but not so much as to render the moral principles vacuous.

3. An ethics of race, as applicable to members of all racial groups, would be egalitarian in terms of race, meaning that racial difference would not be sufficient to constitute different moral treatment, including admission to the realm or class of moral agents or beings who were worthy of the highest moral consideration.

4. More specifically than the first three requirements, an ethics of race would have to hold slavery to be a gravely serious moral wrong. The moral wrong of slavery would follow from the general ethical considerations of respect and autonomy for all moral units, regardless of race. Recognition of the wrong of slavery is especially important for an ethics of race in view of the modern history in which race has been so closely associated with slavery. This association is still a live issue in societies with histories of slave-based economies. The specificity of this requirement makes it seem not quite philosophical at first glance. (It isn't philosophical in terms of the historic subject matter of philosophy, because until the twentieth century philosophers in slave-owning societies or societies connected to other slave-owing societies wrote about ethics without addressing slavery as a moral wrong.) But slavery is, from an ethical standpoint, both an abstract and a concrete wrong, given the first and third requirements for an ethics of race.

5. An ethics of race, like ethics in general as invented by Plato (see chapter 1), is understood to be a mode of discourse and practice, as well as principles or rules governing both of these. But unlike Plato and closer to Cicero, an ethics of race would be independent of politics and political theory. This distinction has liberatory powers: it supports the autonomy of those moral subjects and objects who do not

participate in the state or have all of the powers enjoyed by citizens; legal injustice in private life can be normatively addressed; and there can be ethical or moral assessments of laws and government practices, as well as of the state itself.

6. An ethics of race must be possible for human beings to practice by applying its principles and constructing virtues related to those principles (see chapter 1, on Aristotle's technology of virtues). This is simply a form of the common principle of moral theory that *ought* implies *can*.

THE IMPORTANCE OF THE SUBJECT OF SLAVERY

In a philosophical approach to an ethics of race, which proceeds via key moments in the history of moral philosophy, an examination of the connections between slavery and race is a digression. But I consider it necessary because in our contemporary shared imaginary, as part of our legacy from modernity, slavery in the US South is inextricably connected with race and racial difference in the United States. This connection has reverberated in national and international popular understanding, as well as in scholarly treatments of race. The *historical* association of American slavery with black race gives the association of slavery with race its ongoing strength, through official public history, popular public culture, and private intergenerational family culture. Also, the ugliest expressions of antiblack racism continue to invoke slavery. For example, in July 2010, a racially white associate of the political Tea Party movement posted on his website a letter written in the voice of African Americans to President Lincoln, requesting reenslavement. (This letter read in part that African Americans did not want to work or think for themselves.)[3]

In the American South, after the eighteenth century, only individuals of African descent could be enslaved. And it is commonly and ubiquitously believed that they were enslaved because they were black. The inverse was true: the slaves were designated as racially black according to artificial human constructions of what falsely purported to be the natural kind or category of black race so that they could be enslaved with impunity. For example, the idea that black mothers could give birth only to black children, regardless of who their fathers were, gave race a hereditary mechanism that served the economic interests of slave owners. Rather than again make the case here for the socially constructed nature of human racial taxonomy(ies),[4] it is more relevant to the present project to examine the historical institution and practice of slavery from a philosophical perspective. This examination will further substantiate the claim made in the introduction that ancient systems of human hierarchy, which predated biological racial taxonomies, were a fertile and toxic ground for those taxonomies. The history of human hierarchy, beginning in the West with the acceptance of slavery by presumptively morally enlightened philosophers, was the intellectual and emotional foundation for the American enslavement of "blacks." The historical institution of slavery was, of course, specially compatible with modern hierarchical biologistic taxonomies of human race. But, slavery as an institution and the idea of slavery is not reducible to either racial slavery or hierarchical ideas of race. The moral wrong of slavery would not be mitigated by the absence of racial taxonomy (a system of races) and racial hierarchy (a ranking of races). And, racial taxonomy and racial hierarchy are no less inaccurate as descriptions of humankind in the absence of slavery. The intersection of slavery with racial taxonomy and racial hierarchy combined those two wrongs, the first (slavery) moral and the second (race) both conceptual and moral.

At this time in history, there are more slaves in the world than ever existed. Contemporary activists put the figure at between twelve and forty-five million, with a consensus that there are approximately twenty-seven million slaves. Many of these slaves are women and children who are sexually exploited. Most contemporary slaves are kept in bondage, via economic structures that are falsely and unjustly rationalized by debts that are set up to be unpayable, so that others can benefit monetarily from their labor.[5]

People who live in free or relatively free societies find the idea of slavery, as well as its historical and contemporary facts, immediately abhorrent and morally wrong. But neglected in contemporary liberatory theory is an analysis of what slavery is and precisely why it is morally wrong. If moral law is neither teleological natural law nor theological higher law, for this reaction to slavery to be more than an emotional matter, the analysis and reasons are necessary. Slavery limits the freedom of slaves in very bad ways, but in order to understand the myriad forms of slavery in the history of humankind, as well as its present forms in unpaid labor, we have to know what slavery means as a historical institution in the context of Western political theory.

What is it that makes slavery, which has been practiced for millennia all over the world, one of the most serious moral wrongs, if not *the* most serious? Notice that this is not a straightforward moral question. We already know that slavery is wrong and that all legitimate governments at this time have laws against slavery. So the question of why slavery is wrong, or "What's Wrong with Slavery?," the title of a recent article by Kwame Anthony Appiah, is a theoretical question. According to Appiah, slavery is wrong because it gives rise to intergenerational low social status for slaves and their free descendants and it is a form of "heteronomy," which is to say that it violates individual autonomy.[6] I think Appiah is correct here, but we could perhaps say more about what is distinct about slavery in these regards. Poverty and criminal convictions also give rise to intergenerational low status and illness may severely limit individual autonomy. But neither poverty nor illness are deliberately inflicted on people by others (although they may be), so a good part of the distinctive moral wrong of slavery lies in initial acts of enslavement and ongoing practices to keep slaves enslaved. Slavery is a distinctive harm because it inflicts on people, for the apparent benefit of perpetrators, life conditions of being owned and/or not being paid for one's work and having one's actions controlled in support of such ownership and exploitation.

The infliction of enslavement is subsequently experienced by slaves as an affliction. Never in recorded history has there been an account of slavery as an institution in which slaves are honored, advantaged, excellently cared for, and highly respected members of their society, relative to those who are not slaves. Slaves have always been valued for their use, not for their intrinsic qualities as human beings. This complete reduction of human worth to objects used by and for others has been understood by both slaves and free people to be fundamentally demeaning in a way that even undermines basic human species status. For example, in a 1948 interview, Fountain Hughes, a former slave in Virginia, when asked to compare slavery to freedom responded: "If I thought, had any idea that I'd ever be a slave again, I'd take a gun an' jus end it all right away. Because you're nothing but a dog. You're not a thing but a dog."[7] This animal status of slaves is an ancient tradition, not just in how slaves felt but in ways that slave-owning groups referred to them. The ancient Greeks referred to slaves as *andropoda* or "man-footed beings," analogous to *tetrapoda* for "four-footed beings." And slaves in Roman *noxal* or tort actions were treated on the same level as domestic animals.[8]

John Locke justified slavery as the result of victory by the just side in war, otherwise known as "just war." A slave would prefer the condition of slavery to summary execution and if he ever got tired of it, he could run away or forfeit his life "by resisting the Will of his Master, to draw on himself the Death he deserves."[9] We are today more skeptical than Locke was of being able to tell who the just side is in war. There have also been many cases in which people were bred to be slaves or seized to be enslaved from relative conditions of freedom, without war. This suggests that slavery is not only an inflicted kind of imprisonment for the sake of exploitation, but one that is wholly undeserved. It is not merely undeserved by prisoners of war, but undeserved by everyone and anyone. All slaves are innocent, qua slaves. The condition of slavery is a human ill because it impairs or destroys the human good of freedom. Therefore, slavery is always wrong. We should notice that the wrong of slavery is as fundamental a moral wrong as the intrinsic freedom of human beings is a fundamental moral right. And, this is conceptually separate from the wrongness of slavery according to present laws.

The failure of Locke's description of slavery, as just captivity resulting from war, to resonate with us today may be due to the fact that contemporary industrial societies do not practice warfare with the acknowledged result or stated goal of literally imprisoning large numbers of people from the defeated side. We have a concept of "war crimes" but it is applied to actions that violate the international rules for behavior in modern warfare, and war crimes are not in principle limited in application to members of the "unjust" side in war. Furthermore, despite controversy over the treatment of "enemy combatants" during the recent or ongoing War on Terror (2002–2008 or 2002–), there remains in the United States a sufficiently functional distinction between war and crime so that there is no established punitive institution for military prisoners that treats them instrumentally in contexts separate from their military status. And although prisoners in the US criminal justice system may constitute a large source of extremely cheap labor, which some writers have compared to de facto slavery,[10] the official reasons for their incarceration do not include exploitation of their labor. Thus, slavery may be an effect of contemporary imprisonment, but people are not (legally) imprisoned for the purpose of enslaving them.

Slavery and Freedom

As noted, many contemporary theorists of race refer to American black chattel slavery as a race-based moral wrong. However, the moral wrong of chattel slavery was already present in ancient Greek and Roman philosophy, law, and widespread social practice. Once this is explicated, it should be evident that the addition of black race to the predesigned institution of chattel slavery added a fictional but believable genealogical mechanism to a historical system with a strong precedent, independent of race.

On an abstract continuum between autonomy and heteronomy, freedom and slavery are two opposing extremes. But since slavery as an institution is a concrete historical phenomenon, it is necessary to turn to historical examples to understand how freedom and slavery have mutually defined each other in real political contexts. Where instances of slavery are purely private or illegal, to call them "slavery" would seem to draw on the meaning of the word as it has referred to the historical public institution. The subject, then, is slavery as an institution that has been supported by both custom and positive law. This is the historical institution in different forms that one would expect to be highly relative to freedom in any given historical context, with the reverse also true.

SLAVERY IN ANCIENT GREECE

Little is known about slavery in ancient Greece beyond what W. Den Boer calls a "kaleidoscope" from incomplete and fragmentary sources, but certain broad facts are agreed upon by historians. Although slaves were approximately one-third of the population in the fifth and fourth centuries B.C.E., it is not conclusive that the economy would have collapsed without them. Most slaves were foreigners, enslaved after childhood, and the cost of slaves was relatively expensive compared to the wages of free workers. Because slaves interacted regularly with the free population and could remember being free themselves, it is generally assumed that they constantly saw their condition as less desirable than that of freemen and that they sought freedom. It was common for slaves to be resold and relocated. This forced mobility, together with their lack of local ties (as foreigners) and the competition for status among slaves, precluded organization within the slave population. Lack of organization was believed by the slave-owning group to minimize the risk of slave rebellions.

Ancient Greek slaves worked in agriculture, crafts, business, industry, professions such as medicine and teaching, and domestic labor, sometimes alongside free workers, including their owners. Slaves could earn wages and save that money toward emancipation. Upon emancipation, it was possible for them to become *metics*, or freedmen who lacked the legal rights of citizens. In principle, owner-slave relations were governed by custom and religious rules against moral pollution that could harm the entire linage of an offending owner. Slaves could not give testimony in the courts unless they were tortured, and slaves who worked in the silver mines of Laurium were generally unskilled and labored hard, sometimes in shackles. Slaves were controlled by corporal punishment, threats of being sent to the mines, and demotion in status.[11]

In both Greece and Rome, slaves were the only category of human beings who could be subjected to corporal punishment, including torture, except for extreme cases of prosecution for treason or persecution, as in the Roman crucifixion of Christians. Demosthenes said that the main difference between a slave and a free man was that a slave "is answerable with his body for all offenses."[12] The deliberate infliction of physical pain on slaves, but not free people, implied that part of the meaning of freedom was immunity from physical pain deliberately administered by others. Enslavement also distinctively entailed dislocation, special punishments, lack of formal legal rights, and low status relative to freemen. By implication, freedom entailed the ability to determine where to go or remain, the absence of special punishments, having legal rights, and not having a low status compared to others.

Insofar as Greek slaves engaged in a wide variety of occupations that were also the occupations of freemen, slave identity was not tied to the kind of work slaves did. In Plato's description of the second-best (practical) society in *The Laws*, the relations between the occupation of slaves and their identity is even less determined. Plato proposed that the occupations of slaves be limited to occupations appropriate for their owners, which entailed only agricultural work for slaves owned by aristocratic landowners who could not engage in commerce or crafts. Greek slaves in real life could collect and keep their earnings from employers other than their owners, but according to Plato's *Laws*, slaves were not to control their earnings as could the Spartan Helots, who paid fixed rents. Instead, all slave earnings were to be turned over to the owner, who would redistribute them as he chose.

Plato advised the creation of heterogeneous slave populations of different nationalities and origins, who would be regularly dislocated to forestall unification that could breed rebellion.[13] That proposal, combined with lack of control over earnings, seems to present a new formal structure for slavery as an institution. Indeed, concern with control over slaves and the prevention of their unification appears to be associated with the idea that slaves were, in a sense, prisoners of war. War, as taken to be both necessary and honorable, makes slavery associated with it seem less morally bad than slavery in peace. The idea that slavery originates in war also suggests that slaves are a danger to the free population. Indeed, for Plato, the Helots of Sparta, while not slaves, may have represented how slavery could develop. The Helots were tied to the soil, like Roman colonates (coloni) or medieval serfs, except that they were considered to be at war with Spartans.[14] Again, by contrast, individual freedom would entail being surrounded by people with the same origins as oneself and neither presenting an immediate danger to that cohort nor representing a large group who are a danger to them. To be free is not only to be safe for one's own good, but to not constitute a threat to the safety of others in one's community. Thus, stability, familiarity, and peace are characteristics of freedom. Freedom makes security possible for those who are free, while slavery is a condition of double insecurity—for the slave as well as those who are free.

Although war yielded slaves to the victors in the ancient world, this widespread fact is not sufficient to establish war as the origin of slavery as an institutional practice. M. I. Finley argues that in Greece and Rome, the institution of slavery preexisted multiple examples of military captivity. Finley claims that the demand for slaves, and in some cases their specialized training, preceded the supply of slaves. Finley's examples include the use of slaves in the family manufacturing businesses of Demosthenes and the orator Lysias in the late fifth and early fourth centuries B.C.E. in Athens; the need for slaves by wealthy Roman landowners in the fifth and fourth centuries B.C.E.; and the existence in Athens of a police force of several hundred state-owned Scythian slaves, who were expert archers. Given preexisting demand, the military capture of slaves in ancient Greece and Rome merely fed the needs of preexisting economic systems.

In the US South, slaves were not acquired by American military efforts, although there was a need for labor that was fulfilled by slaves. Finley claims that for ancient Greece and Rome and the US South, which were three of the five slave-based societies in Western history, three factors contributed to the demand for slaves: large-scale ownership of property, particularly agrarian property in Rome and the US South; preexisting commodity markets to support a monetary system so that slaves could be bought and sold as commodities; and the lack of a sufficient internal labor supply.[15] Finley does not emphasize the need for a major fourth factor in supporting slavery: the absence of a belief in the moral equality of all humans, which would preclude enslavement and slavery.

However, more important than the three enabling conditions for slavery listed by Finley and the absence of moral egalitarianism would be the enablement of a slave society by laws and customs supporting and protecting the ownership of physical things—property. The ownership of property would have to be held more important than core human equality that all are obligated to protect. Property rights would have to trump other rights, so that no one external to any owner-slave(s) relationship could legally interfere with it. This magnitude of respect for the ownership of property, enforced in law, could account for the coherence of slave societies in which not all free people are slave owners. (If all were slave owners, the respect for property in slaves would merely be something like laws against theft—assuming that everyone owned some property.)

The runaway slave laws in the United States, as well as in ancient Greece and Rome, are examples of legal provisions for the coexistence of slave owners and those who did not own slaves. The Fugitive Slave Law, enacted by the US Congress in April 1850, provided for special commissioners to have concurrent jurisdiction in its enforcement with US circuit and district courts and the courts of territories. Penalties were imposed on those who aided slaves to escape and there was a $10 (equal to about $275 in 2008) reward for returning each slave to an owner. Slave fugitives could not testify on their own behalf and there were to be no trials by jury for runaway slaves.[16] In the Dred Scott case of 1857, it was further stipulated that slaves could not be taken away from their owners without due process.[17]

The importance of the legal enforcement of property rights for maintaining the practice of slavery can probably be extended to other cases of oppression that are related to ideas of ownership as applied to living things, for example violence against wives, child abuse, and animal cruelty. Societies that place a high value on property rights are probably more likely to support mores of privacy and noninterference in ownership relations than societies that do not structure relations among living beings in terms of possession. Before there were laws against oppression within the family, the practice was protected by the idea that what men did with living beings under their authority was a private matter. Liberatory scholarship since the second half of the twentieth century has tended to condemn individualism on the grounds that people flourish in groups of mutual interdependence. However, during the long history of men doing as they wished with and to their dependent living beings, without interference, it was the individuality of those beings that was insufficiently recognized. The idea of individuality in this sense does not yet refer to a political subject of rights, but rather to a human being who is individuated from other human beings so as to have a recognized independent existence.

Strong private property rights have been the major support of slavery as an ongoing practice. There has, of course, been additional normative support. Aristotle, in *Politics*, added to Plato's moral militaristic mitigation of the idea of slavery by stipulating that slavery was natural. He recognized slavery resulting from war to be a matter of convention.[18] But in analyzing the relationship of slavery between different groups within humankind, he likened it to the rule of the body by the soul in an individual. He concluded that analogous to the natural rule of soul over body, it was natural for some men to be masters of slaves and natural for others to be slaves:

> Where then there is such a difference as that between soul and body, or between men and animals (as in the case of those whose business it is to use their body, and who can do nothing better), the lower sort are by nature slaves, and it is better for them as for all inferiors that they should be under the rule of a master. For he who can be, and therefore is, another's and he who participates in rational principle enough to apprehend, but not to have such a principle, is a slave by nature.[19]

Aristotle's association of slavery with physical labor seems obtuse given that slaves in ancient Greece had a great diversity of occupations. But he qualifies this with a distinction between the tendency of nature and factual reality, suggesting that natural slavery is not merely a matter of bodies being suited for a certain kind of work. Rather, the natural difference is located in the presence or absence of reason:

> Nature would like to distinguish between the bodies of freemen and slaves, making the one strong for servile labour, the other upright, and although useless for such services, useful for political life in the arts both of war and

peace. But the opposite often happens—that some have the souls and others have the bodies of freemen. And doubtless if men differed from one another in the mere forms of their bodies as much as the statues of the gods do from men, all would acknowledge that the inferior class should be slaves of the superior. And if this is true of the body, how much more just that a similar distinction should exist in the soul? But the beauty of the body is seen, whereas the beauty of the soul is not seen. It is clear, then, that some men are by nature free, and others slaves, and that for these latter slavery is both expedient and right.[20]

One could ask how or why Aristotle was so confident that there existed a distinction in rationality between natural slaves and freemen, insofar as he acknowledged that the soul was hidden. It would be necessary to assert such a hidden distinction in souls, together with some important distinction in moral status, in order to make slavery appear to be morally acceptable. Otherwise, accounts of slavery based on war or physical capability leave unjustified the fundamental differences in how freemen are permitted to behave toward those who are enslaved, compared to how they are permitted to behave toward other freemen.

Along with this "naturalization" of slavery, Aristotle introduced something close to the idea of the "happy slave" by suggesting that a natural slave and a natural master would or could be "friends": "Hence, where the relation of master and slave between them is natural they are friends and have a common interest, but where it rests merely on law and force the reverse is true."[21] This idea of peaceful coexistence between master and slave would have provided normative support for the institution of slavery that was already established on economic grounds, as described by Finley. Aristotle thereby *normalized* slavery in a way that proceeded from the mores of his time.

SLAVERY IN ANCIENT ROME

There is a better record of slavery as an institution from ancient Rome than ancient Greece. The Roman record reveals not merely the absence of a doctrine of human moral equality, but asserts moral inequality between citizens and slaves. Roman citizens were free forever and generally could not become slaves except for extreme civil punishment or if they sold themselves into slavery. Thus, it was stated in the *Code of Theodosius*:

> If anyone tries to reduce to slavery someone who is free, [the emperor] commands that, on the order of a judge, he is to be led past the populace and through public places in order to find a man to defend his status; and

if he finds such a sponsor, he is to petition the judge in writing, so that his free-born status should not be lost as a result of silence.[22]

However, this passage is not intended to protect the rights of slaves or undermine the institution of slavery, because it is later stated that "if those who are claimed as slaves prove that they are free-born, then he who had unjustly imperiled their free-born status is to be required to pay the same number of slaves of the same age and sex to those whom he tried to reduce to slavery."[23]

Roman slaves had no legal rights to their lives and well-being, they could not choose their occupations, and they were deprived of myriad other entitlements associated with these nonrights. They were not entitled to marry or maintain other social relations of affinity or kinship. Roman slaves were property that could be bought and sold by owners who owned them, as well as other forms of property. In addition to slaves being required to answer bodily for all offenses, they were expected to be available sexually for all desires: Horace famously wrote, "I like my sex easy and ready to hand"; in reference to the passive role in anal intercourse, the elder Seneca wrote, "Unchastity is a crime in the freeborn, a necessity for a slave, a duty for the freedman."[24] Slave names were bestowed by owners, and adult male slaves were addressed as boy (*puer*) in Latin, as they were in Greek (*païs*); slaves were visually represented by "hierarchic scaling."[25]

The *Codex Justinianus*, or *Code of Justinian*, presented a detailed overview of Roman law and its interpretation at the time it was compiled, 529 to 534 C.E. Part V, "On Status," sets out the position of slaves as follows:

3. Gaius *(Institutes)*: Now the main division of the law on persons is this, that all human beings are either free or slaves.
4. Florentinus *(Institutes 9)*: Liberty is the natural power of doing what anyone is disposed to do, save so far as a person is prevented by force or law. 1. Slavery is a creation of the *jus gentium*, [the law of nations] by which a man is subjected, contrary to nature, to ownership on the part of another. . . . .
5. Marclanus *(Institutes 1)*: Now all slaves have one and the same legal condition; of free men some are *ingenui* (born free, never enslaved freemen], some are *libertini* [former slaves who were free, freedmen].[26]

The children of slave mothers were slaves by birth. Nevertheless, Roman law considered the state to have an interest in the welfare of unborn children, so that children born to slave women who had been free either during their conception or at some time during their pregnancy were born free.[27] Unlike the situation in ancient Greece, by the early third century C.E., Roman slaves who were manumitted immediately attained citizenship, albeit limited and always with monetary and service obligations to former owners. But the son of a freedman could attain wealth and political office without strong stigma (although not without resentment and insult).[28] The condition of slavery was a state of complete civil dependence. Roman law held that in accordance with *jus gentium*, "slave-owners have the power of life and death over their slaves, and whatever is acquired through the slave is acquired to the owner."[29] By the same token, crimes or damage committed by the slave were the responsibility of the owner, under civil tort law. However, as Finley points out, this created a problem insofar as the state could not punish the owner who was innocent of wrongdoing and could not punish the slave, which would have amounted to destruction of the owner's property. The solution was to charge the owner with punishing his slave, which was usually done by imprisonment on the owner's premises, while the slave continued to work. Although, the state did respond directly to crimes against itself, as in the 71 B.C.E. revolt led by Spartacus, when six thousand slaves were crucified on the road between Capua and Rome.[30]

Many of the legal constraints on Roman slaves were inverted to become the rights of citizens in democratic societies over the modern period. These rights were explicitly promulgated as universal human rights by the middle of the twentieth century, in the United Nations Declaration of Universal Human Rights. Most such rights are usually considered to be "negative freedoms" from specified harms rather than positive entitlements. In the absence of doctrines of universal moral equality, the connection between slavery and freedom, in ancient Rome and later, emerged in laws that specified the status of slaves, which could be contrasted with what could not be done to citizens. In this strange sense, Western ideas of freedom can be said to have their origins in ancient Roman slave laws. If that is correct on a theoretical level, then it suggests a default condition of human relations before, or in the absence of, specific positive laws as unfortunately more in line with Hobbes' description of the state of nature than Locke's. (This contrast will be considered in chapter 5, following discussion of Christian higher law.)

Ancient Slavery and Modern Race

The discussion of ancient slavery serves to establish certain distinct subjects that are often conflated in both discussions of race and discussions of slavery. The condition of slavery needs to be distinguished from the underlying causes of slavery and from the nature of initial acts of enslavement. The condition of slavery is also distinct from the process by which slaves can be freed or not and from the status of former slaves after they are freed. However, acts of enslavement, the condition or treatment of slaves, emancipation, and the status of freed slaves could all be strongly connected to the identities of those enslaved. Relative to any specific society that practiced slavery, this question can be asked: who could become a slave? We know that the answer for eighteenth- and nineteenth-century America was "members of the black/African/Negro race." But we would expect the answer to differ in historical periods that came before the establishment and acceptance of a racial human taxonomy based on early modern biology and biological anthropology.

Who could become a slave in Greece and Rome? A small number of slaves were Greek and Roman, and at different times citizens feared being kidnapped into slavery.[31] Practices of infant exposure and child abandonment generated slaves because the rescuer of an infant or child in those circumstances became its legal owner.[32] However, the majority of slaves in ancient Greece and Rome were imported as the result of military capture or piracy. Foreign sources of slaves in Greece included what William Westermann referred to as the "then-barbarian" lands of Phyrgia, Lydia, Caria, Pathlagonia, and Thrace, in addition to Syria, Thebes, Illyria, Scythia, and Malta. Rome at different times obtained slaves from Brittania, Germania, Gallia, Hispania, Etruria, Syria, and Carthage.[33] Jews were regarded as "born slaves" by Cicero.[34] It has already been noted that slaves in the ancient world were not limited to specific occupations and, indeed, some were highly skilled, not only as craftsmen but as doctors, tutors, writers, and scientists.[35]

The diversity in occupation, geographical origins, religion, and age among ancient Greek and Roman slave populations precludes anything antecedent to slavery or independent of it being shared by all slaves. Slave identity was thus limited to the brute facts of being enslaved, which together with the sanctification of property was sufficient to justify attitudes of contempt for slaves, as well as treatment ranging from instrumental to punitive. This is perhaps not surprising in the absence of what came to be widespread egalitarian ideals in the Enlightenment, although there is an ironic historical effect. After the Enlightenment there was a perceived need to justify slavery with elaborate pseudoscientific and moral biological taxonomies about the inferiority of blacks who were enslaved. This made black chattel slavery more intergenerationally lasting, less amenable to emancipation, and more inherently dehumanizing than slavery in ancient Greece and Rome. Black American slaves could be freed—although they infrequently were—but emancipation, either before or after the Civil War, did not relieve them of their black racial identity, which symbolized their ancestors' low status as slaves. (That American blacks continue to suffer from ancestral slavery shows how deep hereditary social class is in the United States, still masked by recalcitrant biologically unfounded racial taxonomy.)

US BLACK CHATTEL SLAVERY

Much more is known about black chattel slavery in the United States than about ancient slavery, including comprehensive detail, based on primary records of births, deaths, bills of sale of slaves, treatment of slaves, and so forth.

However, specialized historical information is not required to compare the US institution with slavery in ancient Greece and Rome. Overall, as noted, US slavery contrasts with ancient slavery in its absence of direct military conquest as a source of slaves. Slave breeding became an established practice after 1830, when it became illegal to import new slaves. Like its Roman antecedent, the US institution of slavery fit a need for labor, especially agricultural, that could not be met by free residents. Unlike ancient slaves, US slaves were restricted to low-status work and the population was less diverse insofar as US slaves were all designated racially black by the time the institution was well established. The emancipation of slaves by owners was a less frequent occurrence than in the ancient world, and the low status of slaves was attached to identities of racial blackness, both for those who had been emancipated and among free blacks who had never been enslaved.

The mechanism of hereditary racial blackness allowed the institution of US slavery to continue with less fear of slave revolt, a caste-type inheritance of low status, and ongoing contempt from nonblacks for blacks. As in the ancient world, constructions of freedom existed in contrasts between citizens and slaves. But in the case of the United States, these different constructions have been historically mediated by ideas of race. Racial blackness became more or less socially synonymous with the effects of being enslaved: illiteracy, lack of stable family structure, extreme poverty, and overall moral inferiority compared to nonblacks. Mythical theories of racial identity and inheritance accomplished much of this work. Americans were considered black if they had any black ancestry. Black identities were held to proceed from black "essences" that caused not only physical racial traits, but moral failures, undeveloped reason, and lack of aesthetic taste. Even into the early twenty-first century, American black people who do not have slave forebears accept the identity of the members of the group that do—and may cherish it—sometimes using it for political purposes and other times honoring and expressing solidarity with those who directly suffer the legacy. Nevertheless, it is theoretically important to distinguish the part of this legacy that belongs to the real practice of slavery and the part attached to false blackness.

SLAVERY, PROPERTY, AND
REQUIREMENTS FOR AN ETHICS OF RACE

We can now see that slavery is wrong not primarily because it singles out certain groups for enslavement. US slavery would be a historical wrong if the country had begun with a black majority and whites had been enslaved. The construction and restriction of special identities for those enslaved enables discrimination, which is also a wrong, but such discrimination, invidious as it is in being tied to racial identities, is not the primary wrong of slavery. If it were, then slavery by lottery would not be wrong. The primary moral wrong of slavery is based on the permissibility and/or legality of some human beings owning other human beings as property. The effect of slavery is radical interference with the autonomy of those enslaved, together with a lack of respect for them. But the primary or pivotal wrong of slavery lies not in those effects but in the fact of ownership. Slavery in a system of property entails physical ownership of entire human beings and, along with that, control over all aspects of their lives. Ownership of the labor of another, under conditions that are forced or coerced, may for a while share certain characteristics of slavery. But such appropriation and exploitation is not the ultimate wrong of slavery because oppressed workers have over time been successful in improving their working conditions and pay and, with that, their autonomy.

Still, there are oppressive human conditions that share aspects of slavery insofar as they are based on some having property in parts of the persons or labor of others. The category of morally impermissible acts that are impermissible on account of what they share with the ultimate wrong of slavery include not only forced, coerced, or exploitative employment but corporal punishment, torture, and particularly brutal forms of warfare. Finley notes that by the second century C.E. in Rome, corporal punishment and torture became legally permissible treatment for the lower classes of citizens, and he calls this "a qualitative transformation in social values and behavior."[36] We should note that this Roman institutional extension of violence against slaves to other groups continued unabated through medieval and early modern Western history, on through the colonial period into the Third Reich, and it is now evident in more recent local events such as the 1994 Rwandan genocide in which eight hundred thousand were killed without serious intervention by the international community.[37] The torture of prisoners by the United States and its allies in the War on Terror (or the Long War), as well as punitive corporal treatment of inmates in US prisons, may be further examples.[38]

Historically, Western institutionalized inhumane treatment and large-scale cruelty can be understood as part of the legacy of radical moral wrong, based on an almost sacred status of the institution of property in human beings, first fully expressed in ancient Greek and Roman slavery. Returning to the fourth requirement for an ethics of race, earlier postulated as the prohibition of slavery, it is now possible to state the more fundamental, general, and abstract moral wrong that enables slavery, namely the wrong of complete ownership of some human beings by others. The fourth requirement prohibiting slavery should now be rephrased as follows:

(4) Ownership of entire human beings is absolutely forbidden and any ownership of their labor should be limited to practices that do not interfere with their overall autonomy, respect from others, and opportunities to further their own well-being. It is in addition required that the governments, institutions, corporations, and individual members of society interfere with such ownership of human beings and their labor, regardless of whether the ownership is based on otherwise legal rights and entitlements to property.

NOTES

1. Bill Whitaker, "Arizona Lawmakers to Crack Down on Immigration," *CBS Evening News*, April 16, 2010, at www.cbsnews.com/stories/2010/04/16/eveningnews/main6403983.shtml (consulted July 2010).

2. For a pragmatic defense voiced by an individual, see "In Defense of Female Circumcision," at www.rjgeib.com/thoughts/circumcision/response.html (consulted April 2010). For a defense of the rights of cultures to preserve themselves without external interference, see Leslye Amede Oboria, "Bridges and Barricades: Rethinking Polemics and Intransigence in the Campaign against Female Circumcision," in *Global Critical Race Feminism: An International Reader*, ed. Adrien Katherine Wing (New York: New York University Press, 2000), 260–74.

3. See "Tea Party Ousts Official over Incendiary Letter . . . over an Incendiary Blog Post in which He Wrote a Fictitious Letter to Abraham Lincoln," *Detroit News*, July 19, 2010.

4. See Naomi Zack, *Philosophy of Science and Race* (New York: Routledge, 2002).

5. See www.freetheslaves.com (consulted April 2010), which became www.freetheslaves.net/ (consulted March 2011).

6. Kwame Anthony Appiah, "What's Wrong with Slavery?" in *Buying Freedom: The Ethics and Economics of Slave Redemption*, ed. Kwame Anthony Appiah and Martin Bunzl (Princeton, NJ: Princeton University Press, 2007), 249–58.

7. Fountain Hughes, interview by Hermond Norwood, Baltimore, Maryland, June 11, 1949, as part of a WPA project, at www.xroads.virginia.edu/~hyper/wpa/hughes1.html (consulted March 2010).

8. M. I. Finley, *Ancient Slavery and Modern Ideology* (New York: Penguin, 1983), 99.

9. John Locke, *Two Treatises of Government*, ed. Peter Laslett (Cambridge: Cambridge University Press, 1991), 283–84 (II, ch. 4), quote from p. 284 (S. 23).

10. See Asatar P. Bair, *Prison Labor in the United States: An Economic Analysis* (New York: Routledge, 2008).

11. W. Den Boer, *Private Morality in Greece and Rome: Some Historical Aspects* (Leiden, The Netherlands: E. J. Brill, 1979), 205–41.

12. Citation by Finley in *Ancient Slavery and Modern Ideology*, 93, from Demosthenes, *Against Androition*, sec. 22, 55.

13. Glenn R. Morrow, *Plato's Law of Slavery* (New York: Arno, 1976), 17–25; references to *The Laws* for the work permitted slaves based on owner's class are VII, 805e, 806d.

14. See Thomas Wiedemann, *Greek and Roman Slavery* (Baltimore, MD: Johns Hopkins University Press, 1981), 11.

15. Finley, *Ancient Slavery and Modern Ideology*, 82–86.

16. The complete text of the 1850 Fugitive Slave Law is available online at www .usconstitution.net/fslave.html (consulted May 2010).

17. See John Vishneski, "What the Court Decided in Dred Scott v. Sandford," *American Journal of Legal History* 32, no. 4 (1988): 373–90.

18. Aristotle, *Politics*, in *The Basic Works of Aristotle*, ed. Richard McKeon, trans. W. D. Ross (New York: Random House, 1941), 1133–34 (5, 1255a).

19. Aristotle, *Politics*, 1132–33 (5, 1254b, 15–23).

20. Aristotle, *Politics*, 1133 (1254b25–1255a3).

21. Aristotle, *Politics*, 1134–35 (1255b13–4).

22. *Code of Theodosius*, 4, 8, 5. Wiedemann, *Greek and Roman Slavery*, 35.

23. *Code of Theodosius*, 4, 8, 5.

24. Quotes from Finley, *Ancient Slavery and Modern Ideology*, 96: Horace, *Satires* 1.2/116–19; Seneca, *Controversies*, 4, praef. 10.

25. Finley, *Ancient Slavery and Modern Ideology*, 96.

26. Quoted from *The Digest of Justinian*, trans. Charles Henry Monro (Cambridge: Cambridge at the University Press, 1904), at www.archive.org/details/digestofjustinia 025178mbp (consulted May 2010).

27. See *The Digest of Justinian*, 5, nos. 2–3.

28. See Finley, *Ancient Slavery and Modern Ideology*, 97–98.

29. *The Digest of Justinian*, part 6. *On Persons Sui juris and alieni juris*, 1. Gaius (*Institutes* 1) 1, 28.

30. Finley, *Ancient Slavery and Modern Ideology*, 98.

31. Suetonius, *Augustus*, 32. In Wiedemann, *Greek and Roman Slavery*, 113.

32. See Aelien, *Different Stories*, 2, 7; Suetonius, *Grammarians*, 5; *Code of Theodosius*, 5.10.1: "Persons who buy New-born children, or Take Them to bring Them up"; and *Code of Theodosius*, 3.3.1: "Fathers who have Sold their children." In Wiedemann, *Greek and Roman Slavery*, 117, 117, 118, and 118, respectively.

33. See William Linn Westermann, *The Slave Systems of Greek and Roman Antiquity* (Philadelphia: American Philosophical Society, 1955), 8–12.

34. In *On the Consular Provinces* 10, Cicero wrote: "And as for the miserable farmers of the revenue, (miserable man that I also am, when I see the miseries and sufferings of those men who have deserved so well at my hands) he handed them over as slaves to the Jews and Syrian nations, themselves born for slavery." Referred to by Finley, *Ancient Slavery and Modern Ideology*, 177–78n99. Quotation from M. Tullius Cicero, *The Orations of Marcus Tullius Cicero*, literally translated by C. D. Yonge (London: George Bell & Sons, 1891), www.archive.org/details/orationsofmarcus01ciceuoft (consulted March 2011).

35. Finley notes that Rome did not have physicians until slaves and freemen together, who were from "the Hellenistic East," began to practice in the second century

B.C.E. See Finley, *Ancient Slavery and Modern Ideology*, 106. Slaves were also often employed as tutors for children. See Quintilian, *Educating an Orator*, 1.1, in Wiedemann, *Greek and Roman Slavery*, 125. See also Pliny the Elder, *Natural History*, 35, 58, in reference to the enslavement of Publilius Syrus, who collected sayings, and Manilius, an astrologer from Antioch, in Wiedemann, *Greek and Roman Slavery*, 111.

36. Finley, *Ancient Slavery and Modern Ideology*, 95.

37. See BBC News/Africa/Rwanda for stories and pictures at webcache.google usercontent.com/search?q=cache:0fRy2YRJrEQJ www.bbc.co.uk/2/hi/africa/35941 (consulted March 2011).

38. Contemporary analyses of the abuse of prisoners during the Iraq war have included information that those employed in setting up and running military prisons abroad often have work experience in correctional institutions within the United States. See Deborah LaBelle, "Ensuring Human Rights for All: Realizing Human Rights for Prisoners," in *Bringing Human Rights Home: Portraits of the Movement*, ed. Cynthia Soohoo, Catherine Albisa, and Martha F. Davis, 3 vols, (Santa Barbara, CA: Praeger, 2007), 1: 121–49.

· 5 ·

Christian Metaphysics and Inequality

$\mathcal{N}$atural law purports to describe the order of things. Within that order, living things are teleological, with inherent natures that they "ought" to fulfill. From a contemporary empiricist perspective, teleology is a mistaken conflation of how things are with how they should be. We saw in chapter 4 that Greek and Roman ideas of natural law were used to rationalize inegalitarian social arrangements. Aristotle, for example, thought that slaves were naturally inferior to freemen. We also saw that cosmopolitan ideas of human commonality could coexist with great social inequality, including slavery, by shrinking that commonality to fellow citizens and kin. Ideas of cosmopolitan commonality could also be expanded to encompass all humans based on their shared biological needs and attributes, but in a way that became vacuous in contexts of legitimate or legal unequal ownership of property.

During the medieval and early modern periods, natural law underwent a Christian transformation into higher law. Although it was still often called "natural law," higher law was theoretically constructed in both theology and philosophy as an expression of God's rules for how Christians should organize their societies, as well as conduct their individual lives. Indeed, the uses of Christian higher law by John Locke, in particular, represent its transition into historical political reality, alongside abstract political philosophy. Unfortunately, the Christian base of such transition, while it portends universality, was limited to universality within Christendom, and in Locke's case, Protestant Christendom at that.[1] So the universality of both Christianity and Protestant representative democracy never was genuinely universal, which means that it did not rise above mores. During the medieval European hegemony of Christianity, despite the overreaching cosmology constructed by Christians, no allowance was or could be made for the spiritual or even earthly well-being of Jews, much less, later on, Muslims. Also, slavery was a common practice.

More is at stake here than ethical inconsistency or contradiction if it can be shown that the unequal and oppressive historical practices that accompanied higher law's contexts of origin and application were compatible with the idea of higher law. They were, because the ethical problem with Christianity stemmed from its metaphysics. This chapter has two theses. First, the metaphysics of Christianity enables the compatibility of Christian doctrine with extreme inequality, including slavery. Second, the Neoplatonic idea of unity not only inspired the Christian idea of God but has the continuing ability to mask political injustice.

THE ETHICS AND METAPHYSICS OF CHRISTIANITY

That the prescriptions of Christianity were, from the beginning, ethical, cosmopolitan, benevolent, compassionate, and peace loving almost goes without saying. Jesus publicly defends his disciples for breaking with the tradition of their elders by not washing their hands before eating bread, with the words, "Not that which goeth into the mouth defileth a man; but that which cometh out of the mouth, this defileth a man."[2] Like Socrates, Jesus implies that what makes behavior correct or right is independent of tradition or mores. Jesus as described by Paul presents a transnational, supratribal, cosmopolitan message. Indeed, Jason Hill (see chapter 2) finds a foundation for contemporary universal identity in Galatians:

> For you are all children of God through faith in Christ Jesus. For as many of you who were baptized into Christ have put on Christ. There is neither Jew nor Greek; there is neither slave nor freeman; there is no male and female: for you are all one in Jesus Christ. And if you belong to Christ, then you are Abraham's offspring, heirs according to the promise. (Gal 3:26–29)[3]

The benevolence, compassion, and peacefulness of Christian ethics is evident in several parts of Jesus' Sermon on the Mount:

> 5. Blessed *are* the meek: for they shall inherit the earth.
> 7. Blessed *are* the merciful: for they shall obtain mercy.
> 38. Ye have heard that it hath been said, An eye for an eye, and a tooth for a tooth:
> 39. But I say unto you, That ye resist not evil: but whosoever shall smite thee on thy right cheek, turn to him the other also.
> 42. Give to him that asketh thee, and from him that would borrow of thee turn not thou away.

44. Love your enemies, bless them that curse you, do good to
     them that hate you, and pray for them which despitefully use
     you, and persecute you;

45. That ye may be the children of your Father which is in heaven: for
     he maketh his sun to rise on the evil and on the good, and sendeth rain
     on the just and on the unjust.[4]

Not only are meekness and mercy upheld as virtues in these passages, but God
does not discriminate between his good and evil or just and unjust 'children.'

Christian ethics developed in concert with European political and social
systems that allowed for slavery, the subordination of women, rigid class hierarchies, war, and all manner of violence and cruelty. There was and still is
no contradiction in this combination because the ethics of Christianity were
welded to a metaphysics and cosmology that divided what is most important
from what could be experienced by the human senses. The mind and its ratio
nality, as originally prized by ancient Greeks and Romans, acquired a spiritual
dimension that could connect the individual to an imagined realm that was
posited as real, consisting of God, heaven, and hell. How an individual fared
after death was tied to the individual's loyalty to God while alive.

The Christian imagined realm, posited as real, was a radical ontological
expansion of the universe, of what could be considered to exist. Before Christianity, the cosmos consisted of the earth, the physical heavens, and geographical Hades, with a number of competing deities, who could act in all these
spheres. Christianity, as Judaism before and Islam after it, posited the existence
of one omnipotent and all-good God who had created the universe and mankind and imposed certain absolute rules on individuals. The connection of
Christian divine rules to an individual's position in heaven or hell after death
created a new concern for mankind: the religious relationship between man
and deity. The Christian break with Judaism involved more than differences
in religious content because Christianity projected into the human world the
presence of the one God, which is to say, the whole of what could be meant
by any word for God. Before then, God had spoken and indirectly appeared to
Jews and some of the gods were at different times present to humans in Greek
accounts. But Jesus, as the son of God and himself part of God, iconographically represented God on earth. Martin Buber, addressing Christians as a Jew,
sums up the metaphysical religious difference as follows:

> Your expectation is directed toward a second coming, ours to a coming
> which has not been anticipated by a first. To you the phrasing of world his-
> tory is determined by one absolute midpoint, the year one; to us, it is an un-
> broken flow of tones following each other without a pause from their origin
> to their consummation. But we can wait for the advent of the One together,
> and there are moments when we may prepare the way before him together.

Pre-messianically, our destinies are divided. Now to the Christian, the Jew is the incomprehensibly obdurate man, who declines to see what has happened; and to the Jew, the Christian is the incomprehensibly daring man, who affirms in an unredeemed world that its redemption has been accomplished. This is a gulf which no human power can bridge.[5]

Judaism structured the religious relationship primarily between the community of Jews and God, whereas Christianity insisted on the cultivation of an individual's direct, individual relationship to God. This is not to say that individual faith is lacking in Judaism or a sense of community lacking in Christianity, but that Christianity admits of a more solitary individual relationship to God, along with renunciation of many things, even of the entire world.[6]

The Christian relationship to God had to be maintained through prayer, various prescribed rituals, and, above all, a state of the new Christian mind-soul that aimed for purity from sin. The new mind-soul was the human term in the religious relationship. In the process of individual development as a Christian, the introspective, self-reflective, prototypical modern human mind was born. Christianity, like Judaism and Islam, is a "religion of the book." The power of reading to create certain kinds of minds through nonsynchronous meditation with authors was from the beginning emphasized in Christianity, sometimes most compellingly beyond the pages of the New Testament. St. Augustine through his *Confessions* contributed as much or more to Christian self-creation as St. Paul did. Augustine, like Paul and Jesus, preached and led Christians in prayer, both before and during his tenure as bishop of Hippo, but what Augustine "wrote down" became the source of the (Latin) Christian tradition in a special holy way that privileged the act or process of reading.

Both Paul and Augustine separated the Christian mind from the Christian body as a condition for being able to resist sin in this life and achieve heaven in the next. The physical human body with its desires and lusts was in the part of the overall cosmology consisting of the physical world; the human mind-soul was nonmaterial and if not itself divine, at least immortal. Thus, consider Paul in his Epistle to the Romans, chapter 7.

14. For we know that the law is spiritual: but I am carnal, sold under sin.
15. For that which I do, I allow not: for what I would, that do I not; but what I hate, that do I.
16. If then I do that which I would not, I consent onto the law that *it is* good.
17. Now then it is no more I that do it, but sin that dwelleth in me.
22. For I delight in the law of God after the inward man:
23. But I see another law in my members, warring against the law of my mind, and bringing me into captivity to the law of sin which is in my members.

24. Oh wretched man that I am! Who shall deliver me from the body
of this death?
25. I thank God through Jesus Christ our Lord. So then with the mind
I myself serve the law of God; but with the flesh the law of sin.

Paul's distinction between the law of God and the law of sin that is obedience
to the body thus results in a change in identity. Paul is not his body but his
mind, which is not sinful thanks to Jesus. Thus, Romans 8 immediately begins:

> There is therefore now no condemnation to them which are in Christ
> Jesus, who walk not after the flesh, but after the Spirit.

And then, Paul suggests that even God is helpless to direct the body:

6. For to be carnally minded *is* death: but to be spiritually minded *is*
life and peace.
7. Because the carnal mind *is* enmity against God: for it is not subject
to the law of God, neither indeed can be.[7]

Augustine in his *Confessions* unites the presence of God in reality with a Christian repudiation of, and disassociation from, the physical body. The power and
urgency of his teaching is presented through the literary form of an autobio-
graphical account of his struggles in becoming a spiritual Christian. He writes:

> Being admonished by all this [Christ's teachings of humility and the un-
> godliness of idolatry[8]] to return to myself, I entered into my own depths,
> with You as guide; and I was able to do it because You were my helper. I
> entered and with the eye of my soul, such as it was, I saw Your unchange-
> able Light shining over that same eye of my soul, over my mind. It was not
> the light of everyday that the eye of flesh can see, nor some greater light of
> the same order, such as might be if the brightness of our daily light should
> be sent shining with a more intense brightness and filling all things with its
> greatness. . . . And I knew that I was far from Thee in the region of unlike-
> ness, as if I heard Thy voice from on high: "I am the food of grown men:
> grow and you shall eat Me. And you shall not change Me into yourself as
> bodily food but into Me you shall be changed."[9]

We see here not only the repudiation of sin but a transformation, through the
religious relationship, of a part of a mere mortal into divine material. Most
Christian theologians and philosophers did not take the religious relationship
to this extreme, although the mind-body distinction of course endured.

Thomas Aquinas was exceptionally skillful at juggling ideas of justice for
the Christian mind-soul with acceptance of oppression for its accompanying
body in contexts of social and political hierarchy. He quotes Seneca, "It is

wrong to suppose that slavery falls upon the whole man, for the better part of
him is excepted. His body is subjected and assigned to his master, but his soul
is his own."[10] Aquinas explains that man does not have to obey other men but
God alone in matters "touching the internal movement of the will." Obedience is obligatory in external bodily action, but "since by nature all men are
equal," obedience is not required in terms of the nature of the body, such
as sustenance or reproduction. Furthermore, according to Aquinas, a slave's
obedience is not obligatory in contracting marriage or remaining "in the state
of virginity or the like."[11] Aquinas continues:

> But in matters concerning the disposal of actions and human affairs, a sub-
> ject is bound to obey his superior within the sphere of his authority; for
> instance, a soldier must obey his general in matters relating to war, a slave
> his master in matters touching the execution of the duties of his service, a
> son his father in matters relating to the conduct of his life and the care of
> the household, and so forth.[12]

It is interesting to note that for Aquinas, there is a tripartite split: the religious
mind-soul, the sphere of action, and the individual body. Only in the sphere
of external action is the body subject to enslavement because the individual is
entitled to autonomy in bodily movements and decisions that concern his biological processes. This is a curious respect for human physical integrity when
medieval slave owners, like later modern ones, had the authority to feed and
breed their slaves as they saw fit, as well as the discretion to inflict on them
corporal punishment and in some cases death. Although Aquinas may have
had in mind the domestic or agricultural slaves of his time, who were closer to
servants while the institution of slavery was giving way to serfdom in Europe.[13]

For some reason—perhaps a deliberate ignorance of history as well as religion?—philosophers and other humanists are inclined to blame Descartes for
creating the mind-body problem that still afflicts us today. Descartes merely cod-
ified and presented in theoretical form a live distinction from Christendom that
was more than one thousand years old. Because the metaphysics of Christianity
is often neglected by philosophers, it is worth a slight digression to underscore
the Christian metaphysical tradition that grounded Descartes' presumed mind-
body split. In his dedicatory letter of the *Meditations* to priests of the Sorbonne,
Descartes states that his aim is to use natural reason to prove "that the human
soul does not die with the body, and that God exists."[14] Descartes presents the
existence of God as an unquestionable matter of belief based on Scripture: "It is
of course quite true that we must believe in the existence of God because it is a
doctrine of Holy Scripture, and conversely, that we must believe Holy Scripture
because it comes from God." And he refers to the Lateran council of 1513 that
condemned the Averroist heresy denying personal immortality.[15] Descartes has
thus set himself the academic exercise of providing philosophical proofs for what

is already known and accepted by the Catholic Church. In his "Preface to the Reader" of the *Meditations* he immediately takes up an objection to his claim that the human mind is only a thinking thing, based on his perception that it is that. Descartes answers the objection that perception of the mind as only a thinking thing is not sufficient to establish it as that, by stating that in the passage in question he was only talking about his perception.[16] Descartes's claim, the objection, and his reply are but philosophically technical aspects of a truth that everyone already took for granted on religious grounds.

In fact, Descartes himself, as an avid anatomist, follower of the scientific revolution, and extremely subtle thinker and observer, did not think that the human mind was in reality distinct from the human body, as some bit of stuff that could be identified separately from the body. His separation of mind from body was a theoretical point based on introspection, or what would today be called a "phenomenological experience" of thinking:

> Nature also teaches me, by these sensations of pain, hunger, thirst and so on, that I am not merely present in my body as a sailor is present in a ship, but that I am very closely joined and, as it were, intermingled with it, so that I and the body form a unit. If this were not so, I, who am nothing but a thinking thing, would not feel pain when the body was hurt, but would perceive the damage purely by the intellect, just as a sailor perceives by sight if anything in his ship is broken.[17]

Unlike Paul, Descartes rejects an attitude of dissociation of mind-soul from body, and unlike Augustine, he nowhere claims that his knowledge of God amounts to the part of him that knows God itself becoming divine. To blame Descartes for what we now condemn as Cartesianism is anachronistic, because, as noted, the mind-body split existed before he recreated it in meditations that invited the reader to retrace his steps.[18] Our contemporary view of the mind that many strive to reunite with the body—in various multidisciplinary projects of "embodiment"—is a reality and idea of mind that only came into being with the metaphysical concerns of medieval Christian constructions of the self. That is, our mind-body problem is more securely based on pseudoconstructions of a religious soul in the place of "mind" than on a (relatively straightforward) theoretical separation of first-person cognitive experience from physicality.

CHRISTIANITY AND SOCIAL JUSTICE

The metaphysics of Christianity allowed for human inequalities that would otherwise appear to be excluded by its egalitarian ethics. To put it abruptly, social justice is not an urgent matter if the chances for individual human salvation, that is, eternal life in heaven, are not diminished but may even be enhanced by the misery of oppression in the here and now. Nietzsche, in bitter declamation of the Christian devaluation of healthy, noble, and ancient human virtues and values, described the success of the Christian priest thus:

> For two millennia now we have been condemned to the sight of this new type of invalid, "the sinner"—shall it always be so?—everywhere one looks there is the hypnotic gaze of the sinner, always fixed on the same object (on "guilt" as the *sole* cause of suffering); everywhere the bad conscience, that "abominable beast," as Luther called it; everywhere the past regurgitated, the fact distorted, the "jaundiced eye" for all action; everywhere the *will* to misunderstand suffering made the content of life; the reinterpretation of suffering as feelings of guilt, fear, and punishment; everywhere the scourge, the hair shirt, the starving body, contrition; everywhere the sinner breaking himself on the cruel wheel of a restless, morbidly lascivious conscience; everywhere dumb torment, extreme fear, the agony of the tortured heart, convulsions of an unknown happiness, the cry for "redemption." The old depression, heaviness, and weariness were indeed *overcome* through this system of procedures; life again became *very* interesting: awake, everlastingly awake, sleepless, glowing, charred, spent and yet not weary—this was the man, "the sinner," initiated into *this* mystery. This ancient mighty sorcerer in his struggle with displeasure, the ascetic priest—he had obviously won, *his* kingdom had come: one no longer protested *against* pain, one *thirsted* for pain; "*more* pain! *more* pain!" the desire of his disciples and initiates has cried for centuries. Every painful orgy of feeling, everything that shattered, bowled over, crushed, enraptured, transported; the secrets of the torture chamber, the inventiveness of hell itself—all were hence-forth discovered, divined, and exploited, all stood in the service of the sorcerer, all served henceforward to promote the victory of his ideal, the ascetic ideal.—"My kingdom is not of *this* world"—he continued to say, as before: but did he still have the right to say it?[19]

Nietzsche was not concerned with human groups who encountered Christianity as slaves but with the effect of Christian asceticism on ancient noble ideals of strength, solitude, and great physical power. The impression left by the foregoing passage is not an exhortation of those disadvantaged or oppressed to rise up in anger, but rather concern for the otherwise robust and advantaged who had been enervated by the hegemony of Christian values. Nietzsche thought that the kingdom that was "not of *this* world" had already fully informed this world. Outright rebellion by the oppressed did not occur to Nietzsche and neither did he care about the injustice of oppressive social and political structures. Nevertheless, his address of Christian glorification of pain and suffering, as both caused by original sin and instrumental for its redemption, is an effective rhetorical summation of how Christianity, in philosophical moral terms, is neither universally deontological nor utilitarian. It is not universally deontological because it accepts the effects of some oppressing others; it is not utilitarian because its greatest good is not the well-being on earth of everyone, including oppressed multitudes.

None of the foregoing is to deny that some oppressed peoples have found solidarity, hope, and consolation in Christian doctrine. Neither is it meant to negate the coherence of liberation theology or the inspiration of prophetic tradition. The point is merely that classic Christian doctrine is not incompatible with oppression. As already suggested, the reason for that is metaphysical rather than ethical. Paul said male and female, slave and free, Greek and Jew—the sweep includes all human beings—are "one" in Christ. Let's assume here that Paul's "one" means "equal to one another" rather than "united." We have also seen that, according to Christian doctrine, Jesus and God are not of this earthly realm, and neither is the mind-soul of a human being who becomes a Christian. Therefore, great inequality and injustice in the earthly realm are compatible with the Christian God and widespread salvation. We could all be saved for heaven but remain wretched and miserable on earth. It has never on earth reached the extreme where all human beings are wretched and miserable, but inequality and injustice have been and still are present where Christianity is the dominant religion and worldview. Medieval, early modern, and modern history are replete with this paradoxical combination, not only theoretically and philosophically but in real life.

The official positions of the Catholic Church on slavery, before and after the New World slave trade in Africans became a major enterprise, document the practical aspects of the paradox. In his controversial 1993 article, "Development in Moral Doctrine," John Noonan considers changes in the moral teachings of the Catholic Church on usury, marriage, slavery, and religious freedom. Noonan's account of the history of church doctrine regarding slavery, from Paul to Leo XIII, whose papacy ended in 1903, can be chronologically compressed as follows:

Catholic moral doctrine considered the institution of slavery acceptable. St. Paul had accepted it, returning Onesimus to his master (Phlm 11–19) and instructing the Christian slaves of Corinth to obey their masters (1 Cor 7:21). St. Augustine said succinctly that Christ "did not make men free from being slaves." . . . The greatest of reforming popes, Gregory I, accepted a young boy as a slave and gave him as a gift to another bishop; his famous decision to send missionaries to England is said to have arisen from his musings as he browsed in a slave market in Rome.

The greatest of Catholic jurisprudents, Henri de Bracton, thought slavery was contrary to natural law, but accepted it as an institution of the law of nations; he merely copied the great Catholic lawgiver, Justinian. St. Antoninus of Florence followed St. Thomas in acquiescing in the civil law permitting slave status to follow birth to a slave woman. Paul III praised the benevolent effects of slavery on agriculture while approving the traffic in slaves in Rome. The eminent Jesuit moralist Cardinal Juan De Lugo was in harmony with the moralists' tradition when he found slavery "beyond the intention of nature," but "introduced to prevent greater evils." Near the end of the seventeenth century, the master French theologian, Bishop Bossuet, declared that to condemn slavery would be "to condemn the Holy Spirit, who by the mouth of St. Paul orders slaves to remain in their state."

In 1839 Gregory XVI condemned the slave trade, but not so explicitly that the condemnation covered occasional sales by owners of surplus stock. In the first treatise on moral theology written for Americans, Bishop Francis Kenrick in 1841 declared it no sin against nature to own slaves treated in a humane way and added that, even if Africans had been brought to America unjustly, long lapse of time had cured any defect in title on the part of those who had inherited them. . . . As late as 1860, the Church taught that it was no sin for a Catholic to own another human being. . . . Leading Catholic jurist, Chief Justice Roger Taney, wrote Dred Scott. Beginning with Leo XIII, on the rights of labor, uncompensated slave labor [was] seen as a moral outrage.[20]

Beyond its doctrinal acceptance of slavery, the church actively participated in the practice of slavery. Throughout the medieval period, slaves owned by the church and individual clergy worked as domestic and agricultural laborers. The early church forbade the enslavement of Christians by non-Christians, particularly Jews; during the seventh century, all of the Jews in Spain were enslaved, to be freed only when the Muslims decisively defeated the Visogothic kings in 711.[21] Slavery tapered off into serfdom by the twelfth century in northern Europe, but it persisted until the Renaissance in the Mediterranean and Constantinople. The church also used enslavement as a weapon in its own political struggles: in 1303, Pope Boniface VIII enslaved the Colonna family; in 1309, Pope Clement V threatened Venice, Italy, Bologna, and Florence with enslavement; Pope Paul III in opposition to Henry VIII threatened his English supporters with enslavement and promised them as a reward to crusaders who would defeat Henry.[22]

Portugal was authorized to enslave heathens by a papal bull in 1455, and in ensuing decades Portuguese traders began to engage in an African slave trade to work the sugar plantations of Madeira and the Cape Verde Islands. The Spanish conquest of the Caribbean eventually led to the prominence of the slave trade in Africans when it became obvious that the local "Indians" could not furnish desired slave labor for the New World. Before then, Pope Alexander VI had divided the spoils of the New World between Spain and Portugal.[23]

CHRISTIAN ETHICS AND THE
INVENTION OF HUMANITARIANISM

Contemporary writers disagree on the kindness and cruelty toward slaves owned by the church and its officials, but the historiography of the medieval period generally presumes relative kindness.[24] Although the metaphysics of Christianity did not make it obligatory to extend Christian ethical egalitarianism to human material life, the teachings of early Christianity, particularly Jesus' Sermon on the Mount, do advocate compassion toward those who are disadvantaged from those who are able to help them. Insofar as such compassion and the actions motivated by or expressing it address human suffering on earth, in the here and now, Christianity invented *humanitarianism*. Humanitarianism endures as an attitude and type of action that seeks to alleviate suffering. Humanitarian ideals should therefore be one of the requirements for an ethics of race. Returning to the six requirements proposed in chapter 4, we can add the following:

> (7) An ethics of race should posit humanitarian goals of alleviating human suffering, particularly suffering that distinctively accompanies the circumstances of people with disadvantaged racial identities.

But such kind humanitarianism does nothing to address the underlying causes of the suffering that evokes it. Of course we should be kind. But in a moral framework that posits ideals which are neither rooted in reality nor required to be practically instantiated, kindness is more of a social grace than a deep moral act or disposition. It is like providing medical services to those who have had their hands amputated for thievery or requiring the presence of doctors when torture is a form of legal interrogation or the state executes a prisoner on death row. Of course, humane practices are morally required, but they are not a substitute for addressing the human practices and constructed conditions that distort and destroy lives. To address those ills, something like *egalitarian humanism* would be required.

SOCIAL BODIES AND NEOPLATONISM

The modern world has developed with three major "religions of the book": Judaism, Christianity, and Islam. Christianity arose from and built on Judaism, and Islam, the youngest of these religions, has always recognized predecessor doctrines in Judaism and Christianity. These three monotheisms, with their different interpretations of a shared history, could be viewed as variations or sects of the same monotheism. Nonetheless, of course, there have been major historical, geographical, and political differences. Christianity, as the dominant Euro-American religion, divided into Catholicism and Protestantism. Protestant political theorists constructed the ideal of the modern state that shaped the US Constitution, as well as ongoing American economic, social, and political values.

In terms of human inequality, the shift from Catholicism to Protestantism was a case of things remaining the same the more they changed. The ontology of Christianity represented an expansion of the cosmos to include one omnipotent God. Christian political Protestantism itself posited new entities, particularly new fictive social bodies or "corporations," the most important of which was the new nation-state—think of Hobbes' *Leviathan*. The development of corporatism could facilitate new forms of oppression in a very simple way: those who constituted themselves within new legitimate "bodies" could legally oppress or do whatever they wanted to those who were outside. The legality of the new exclusive Protestant state has been especially formidable because of its presentation as democratic and representative.

It has become a mainstay of radical and progressive critique since the last quarter of the twentieth century to criticize the liberal state, or liberalism, for the inequalities and oppression with which it is compatible. As in the case of the early Christian church, one may ask how it is possible for democratic ideals to coexist with oppression both within and without the borders of nations that purport to be founded on these ideals. Part of the answer concerns the remarkable persistence of Neoplatonism. Early Christians posited fictive realms and used their new ontological categories as receptacles for different "tranches" of human privilege—slave, free, saved, damned, Christian, infidel, and so forth. Democratic nations have posited citizenship as an entitlement to freedom, using a similar methodology: first construct the important underlying political categories and then relegate different groups of human beings to them in ways that seem natural and obvious. For example, consider the category "US citizen" and how individuals enter it. Some are born US citizens, while others require special processes of admission and approval to become citizens. There are no distinctive important individual traits that accompany citizen or noncitizen status.

The Christian methodology of constructing underlying social categories has never been a taxonomy directly applied to individuals. Group membership mediates the relationship between the category and individual. The categories are not formed by the traits of individuals but by the metaphysical nature of the social universe. As such, these categories are already hierarchical and carry with them normative rules for behavior, reflecting the function and status of different human groups as determined by their category membership, for instance, medieval guilds with both a place in an overall social hierarchy and specific productive functions. We can consider in this regard the deeply contested medieval architectonic of the categories of state and church. The present term of art for those categories is "institutions," but to view church and state in that way depends on their prior naturalization within a society. It seems to us that all societies inevitably have institutions, but not all human societies are sufficiently complex to have what we would call "institutions." Neither are all societies structured on ideas of church and state. Before the medieval period, issues of competition within this pair were not salient because "the church" had not yet been imagined and constructed.

The late nineteenth- and early twentieth-century legal history scholar Otto Gierke delineated three perspectives on the state-church relationship that preoccupied medieval Christian scholars and political activists for centuries: the ancient view that the state was all-encompassing and the church a part of it; the medieval view, preferred by the church, that God created the church, which delegates part of its authority to the state; and the "ancient-modern" view that God created church and state as independent entities.[25]

It did not occur to advocates and critics working within the medieval architectonic that they were talking about fictive entities and wholly human constructions that they wanted to obstruct or further—the state, the church, God. As a result, they did not realize the extent to which their worldview was metaphysical—they thought their subject was objective, already-existing reality. It also seemed obvious to them that reality was composed of "bodies," and awareness of the fictive nature of these "bodies" did not develop in political philosophy before Hobbes in the seventeenth century. Gierke notes that by the modern period, such bodies or corporations that were intermediate between individuals and the state had passed:

> A combat it was in which the Sovereign State and the Sovereign Individual contended over the delimitation of the provinces assigned to them by Natural Law, and in the course of that struggle all intermediate groups were first degraded into the position of the more or less arbitrarily fashioned creates of mere Positive Law, and in the end were obliterated.[26]

This passage reads as though Gierke thought that the intermediate groups were in reality obliterated. Frederic Maitland, his English translator, emphasizes that what was in fact destroyed was a theoretical tradition that sought to account for such intermediate bodies. He cites examples of a general English inflexibility to recognize and adapt to such corporations in policies concerning the government of India, the American colonies, and Ireland.[27]

We could add to Maitland's list the apparently ungovernable activities of contemporary global corporations that have been presumed at the peril of many to be merely private fictitious persons, existing by the permission of sovereign states and subject to the powers of those states. It should be noted, however, that the depredations of global business corporations are not the same kind of avoidance of central government as former colonies. In the business case, what has escaped control constitutes a danger to others exceeding the interests of the fictive body of the state, whereas former European colonies escaped central control for the legitimate purpose of their own self-determination and freedom. Global business corporations may justify their actions in terms of an inviolate motive for profit, but their profit often comes through the exploitation of consumers and suppliers. Former colonies, by contrast, rarely have interests predicated on exploitation external to themselves. The undertheorized ontological status of global corporations that exceed the political power of the governments that legalize them is becoming increasingly ominous in the early twenty-first century. The investment banking crisis of 2008 and the BP oil spill in the Gulf of Mexico in 2010 are two examples of external depredation protected by political ideas about fictive entities, which inadequately comprehend those entities.

Not only were many of the bodies or corporations posited by medieval political scholars abandoned in favor of modern ideas of the nation-state with its centralized powers, but the literally embodied view of society as a whole presumably was also abandoned. Late twentieth-century feminist scholars in critiques of masculinist constructions of reason and the objectification of nature instigated by the scientific revolution have expressed a degree of nostalgia about the medieval view of the entire earth as an integral female organism—a mother.[28] However, this maternal metaphor was part of a more comprehensive metaphysical animism about the parts of human society. The Christian medieval world view held God, omnipotent and omniscient, to be the head of the body of the human world. The entire human community was another unity, a *universitatas* that was a partial whole of the entire creation, under one law. Every group within this community had its own final cause, as well as a unique place as a component of the whole creation. Each particular being within a partial whole was a *microcosmus* that mirrored the whole creation. All of the "manys" were subordinate to the One and order was the result of the primacy of that One.[29]

The organic view of human society, with hierarchical divisions of labor and function corresponding to the human body, persisted until the Reformation in England and the French Revolution in some parts of Europe.[30] In the twelfth century, although John of Salisbury in *Policraticus* posited the church as the soul of society and the king as its head, he emphasized the importance of mutual interdependence: "Remove from the fittest body the aid of feet, it does not proceed under its own power but either crawls shamefully, uselessly and offensively on its hands or else is moved with the assistance of brute animals."[31] John Walters refers to the pre-Reformation celebration of Corpus Christi Day, consisting of a public procession of clergy and laity followed by the celebration of the Mass. Such English processions were arranged to represent the hierarchy and interdependence of society based on the structure and function of the human body: the ruler was the head, the people were the feet or belly, craftsmen arms, knights the ankles, and so forth.[32]

Robert Darnton in *The Great Cat Massacre* presents the perspective of those of the great stage of history during the half century leading up to the French Revolution. Darnton summarizes a bourgeois townsman's description of a procession in Monpellier in 1768:

> A general morphology stood out. The ranks mounted as the procession passed, progressing from the confraternities to the regular clergy, the secular clergy, and the bishop with the canons of the cathedral accompanying the Host—that is, the living presence of Christ. At this point, the most sacred in the procession, the ecclesiastical order shaded off into civil society, for the canopy over the host was carried by the six Consuls or principal officials of the municipal government. They in turn were divided, the first three coming from the patriciate of noblemen and *rentiers*, the second from the upper ranks of guild masters. In this way the three traditional estates of the realm—clergy, nobility, and commoners—came together in the heart of the procession. And then the procession wound down through a suite of municipal corps, which passed by in descending order of importance. . . . Instead of dividing into classes, the social order rippled past the onlooker in graduated degrees of *dignités*.[33]

The medieval organic view of society as an integral human whole never really expired. Its underlying Neoplatonic principle and ideal of unity passed largely uncriticized into modern ideas of the state and central government: one nation, one country united under one God. When populations within a nation have diverse customs and interests, unity as imposed by dominant groups has been Procrustean. There is no grand rational secular justification for such political ideas of overarching unity, apart from contingent pragmatic considerations such as the interest of those who control the central government and their requirement for an ideology that will support the continued submission of less powerful groups, perceived needs for a mighty military force to defend or expand geographical areas, or a need for a central source of services and benefits for an entire population—public infrastructure, emergency response, education, medical care, old-age pensions. The justification of unity so that a central government can provide services and benefits is probably the most morally defensible justification for ideas and structures of unity. But it is the most contested site and consequence of unity in the United States, where unity has often been stressed for the sake of wealthy groups that directly benefit from central governance and military power and do not need government services and benefits.

Political plurality or decentralization is not necessarily the moral corrective to inequalities that endure within unities, because local mores can be more oppressive than the unifying force. For instance, the church was particularly open toward cultural contributions from Jewish philosophers, doctors, translators, and theologians during the twelfth century. In 1179 the Third Lateran Council called for toleration of the Jews *pro sola humanitate*. The scientific thought of Avencebrol (Ibn Gabirol) was accepted by the Franciscans, and Maimonides was highly regarded by Aquinas and subsequent Thomists and Dominicans. But in the thirteenth century, Jews were expelled from England and over the next two hundred years from France, Lithuania, Spain, and Portugal. In France and the Rhineland, synagogues were burned, killing entire communities. The instruments of medieval European anti-Semitism were fanatical crusading groups who reignited ancient superstitions among peasants and workers in response to individual accidents and epidemics, such as the plague of 1348 to 1350. Although the Dominicans were originally optimistic about converting Jews to Christianity, they became virulent anti-Semites when this did not happen. The Crusades themselves had energized xenophobia in many rural localities, and insofar as the mendicant orders generally were dependent on Crusade funding from the people, they had developed the ability to motivate mobs beyond the control of papal authorities.[34]

THE CATHECTIC NEOPLATONIC IDEA OF UNITY

The medieval metaphoric model of one God, one church, and one social body was not successful insofar as the church itself was continually embattled, beginning with initial persecution under the Roman Empire. Viking invasions, Islamic wars, the Reformation, morally recalcitrant local populations, persecution of Catholics in Protestant countries, and the scientific revolution all took their toll. But the Catholic Church was only one historical instantiation of Neoplatonic cosmology, a set of ideas more general, profound, and psychically compelling than Christianity. A brief reminder of Neoplatonic teachings is therefore useful toward understanding the foundation of the metaphysics of Christianity, which has endured in underlying political ideology and rhetoric for secular as well as religious publics through the Renaissance, the modern period, and to the present.

Specifically at issue is the Neoplatonic idea of *unity*, which not only grounded fictive medieval social bodies but the modern nation-state. It is pertinent to distinguish between "Neoplatonism," identified as a distinct school of thought in seventeenth-century English and nineteenth-century German scholarship,[35] and Neoplatonic metaphysical ideas that persisted in medieval and modern ideologies. The four most prominent Neoplatonists were active through the third to fifth centuries: Plotinus (204/5–270 C.E.) was the most famous Neoplatonist; Porphyry (234–c. 305 C.E.) systematized Plotinus' work; Iamblichus (c. 245–325 C.E.) contributed to Pythagorian and Aristotelian dimensions of Neoplatonism; and Proclus (412–485 C.E.) wrote the most comprehensive account of ancient Platonism, which was influential throughout the medieval period. Neoplatonic thought emphasized at times a Pythagorian religious tradition that predated Plato. Neoplatonists sought to resolve disagreements in the philosophies of Plato and Aristotle by using Aristotle as a "guide" to Plato.[36]

The Neoplatonic posit of "the One" is usually understood to be based on Plato's form of the Good, which was beyond being or everything that existed. Second to the One was Intelligence, the cause of the world of forms, and third was Soul, the cause of the sensible world. Plato had inconclusively discussed the nature of the One in his dialogue *Parmenides*, suggesting that if it existed, it could not be known.[37] Plotinus developed a comprehensive metaphysical system of the One, Intelligence, and Soul, which explained what these entities were, how they related to one another, and how they caused sensible reality; intertwined with this metaphysics was an ethical system that outlined the best human life.

According to Plotinus, the One is the first principle in the intelligible realm, the cause of everything else, which is many. The One is ultimately simple and unified; it is unaware of itself because awareness of itself would have divided it within itself, and it has no qualities. Intelligence is the effect of the One through its overflow, emanation, or "effulguration." Intelligence, or what Aristotle called "nous," is also One, but it contains numbers, which are its emanation in the form of Soul. Soul is the principle of the sensible world. There is a soul of the world and souls of living individuals—plants, animals, human beings. These individual souls take on bodies out of a desire to rule or assert themselves. They first reflect themselves and, in "identifying"—an anachronistic term, here—with the reflections of themselves, become temporarily united to those bodies. The One is without desire, but everything else desires the One: "It is in a way, borne to its interior, in a way, loving itself, the 'pure radiance,' being itself that which it loved. This means that it causes itself to exist, if, in fact, it is an abiding activity and most loved."[38]

Because the One is ultimate Good and the individual human soul is contaminated and unhappy in its union with its body, that is, in life, the ultimate goal of human existence is a reascension of the soul to the One, through Intelligence—both Intelligence as the source of the world soul and all individual souls, and Intelligence as the divine part of the individual soul. When Intelligence left the One and the individual soul left Intelligence, both remained with their originating sources while also becoming something different from them. The result is that the individual soul is always already in Intelligence, although most are not aware of this: "Someone has, indeed, himself become Intellect, when letting go of the other things that are his, he looks at Intellect with Intellect; he then looks at himself with himself. Then it is indeed as Intellect that he sees himself."[39]

Reascension can be achieved by contemplation and a cultivation of individual intelligence, as well as the development of virtue and specific abstemious practices. Evil is generally a privation, an absence of virtue, besides the fallen nature of the soul's original descent into a union with a body that it has imagined.[40] Plotinus assumes that when the soul through contemplation reunites with Intelligence, its motivating force is love of the One:

> Then, when someone sees this light, he is at that moment moved towards them [Intellect and its life] and, longing for the light that glimmers on them, he is delighted, just as, also, in the case of bodies here, love is not for their underlying substrata but for the beauty shining on these.[41]

Proclus later relates Neoplatonic love to the Chaldean virtues:

> If the auditor has united in himself all three qualities under the direction of his intellect—if he has familiarized himself with the dialectical method of Plato, if he has immersed himself in activities that are immaterial and transcend corporeal powers, and if he has striven to contemplate true reality by thought with the aid of reasoning—then let him apply himself avidly to the explication of the divine and blessed doctrines, "unfolding through love the depths of his soul," in the words of the Oracle, since one cannot have any better helper than Love for the acquisition of this insight, as indeed is asserted in the text of Plato.[42]

Speaking generally, and in a way that could only be fully supported with a body of scholarship that exceeds the present project, the tenth- to fifteenth-century Scholastic concentration on reconciling Aristotle's philosophy with Christian doctrine mirrored the Neoplatonic project of reconciling its religious interpretation of Plato's philosophy with an Aristotelian approach to the temporal world. However, insofar as Plotinus valorized a life dedicated to intellectual activity that allowed the individual soul to ascend and save itself as what it was, uncontaminated by the body that had fascinated it, Neoplatonism was a rigorous practice for a select few. Porphyry described Plotinus as continually focused on his philosophical ideas throughout his engagements with students, colleagues, friends, and local political figures who became his followers. He lived ascetically as a strict vegetarian and served as the guardian of a number of orphans with property that he scrupulously managed for them. Porphyry claims that Plotinus was able to spiritually ascend four times over his life (compared to once for Porphyry himself):

> For the term, the one end, of his life was to become Uniate, to approach
> to the God over all; and four times, during the period I passed with him,
> he achieved this Term, by no mere latent fitness but by the ineffable Act.[43]

By contrast, religious Christianity was suspicious of free intellectual activity
and offered salvation only after death. The unavoidable intellectual elitism of
Neoplatonism qualifies it as a philosopher's religion par excellence; Christianity was more egalitarian in its outreach for the faith of multitudes.

In the history of ideas, and in history itself, because of its metaphysical
emphasis on unity, Neoplatonism inaugurated an enduring tradition of individual emotional attachment to powerful fictive entities. For instance, the
fictive entity of the state has been a major motif in the political imagination of
the United States as a nation, as well as a rhetorical flashpoint for evocations of
emotional patriotism. That is, political unity has not merely been an idea in a
cognitive sense, but at times a highly charged emotional and spiritual motivating principle. Examples of this cathexsis of political unity in American history
could fill several volumes, but consider just these few: *E Pluribus Unum* (out
of many, one) was adopted as the motto of the Great Seal of the United States
in 1782 and ever since reproduced on American money.[44] President Lincoln
evoked national unity in his 1863 proclamation that established Thanksgiving
Day (as a day of fasting!).[45] President George W. Bush's convocation of the
leaders of religion, government, and the military in the National Cathedral for
a national ceremony on September 14, 2001, following the attacks of 9-11,
iconographically displayed American unity to galvanize popular imagination
in support of war in Afghanistan, as well as Iraq.[46] The McCain campaign
displayed mordant brilliance in an August 2008 ad that mockingly depicted
Barack Obama as "The One."[47]

The cathexis of unity can be used for internal oppressive aims, for instance, early twentieth-century antiblack and anti-immigrant ideas of American nationality based on "nativism,"[48] but it can also be used for liberatory
aims, for example, Lincoln's desire to preserve "the union" during the Civil
War. The ongoing US battle between the strength of the federal government
and the rights of states is a paramount example of how ideas of unity compete.
Those who oppose the unitary legal power of "big government" often wish to
preserve their own spiritual conceptions of unity on local levels, for example
through the culture of private gun ownership and Christian teachings in public
education. The point is that unity, as a highly speculative metaphysical principle with a powerful emotional and spiritual motivational force, often passes
unexamined as an accurate representation of the ultimate nature or structure of
things, in order to serve this or that particular system of mores. This occasions
an eighth requirement for an ethics of race.

(8) Ideas of unity over groups and individuals, whether physical or spiritual, should be subject to critical empirical examination before acceptance and application: do they symbolize the interests of all in an egalitarian way? Or, do they impose the interests of some on others through mighty fictive "wholes" that are used to mediate the interests of those who are not being served?

NOTES

1. See Locke's famous exclusion from toleration of Catholics because they owed allegiance to a "foreign prince," and atheists because they cannot be trusted if they take oaths. John Locke, *A Letter concerning Toleration,* Latin and English texts revised and edited by Mario Montuori (The Hague: Martinus Nijhoff, 1963), 91 and 93, respectively. Locke's foreign prince exclusion of Catholics endured until John F. Kennedy was elected president in 1960. I remember public argument about whether he would obey the pope over the US Constitution.

2. Matthew 15:11 (KJV).

3. Galatians 3:26–29, cited in Jason D. Hill, *Beyond Blood Identities: Posthumanity in the Twenty-First Century* (Lanham, MD: Rowman and Littlefield, 2009), 206.

4. Matthew 5 (KJV).

5. Martin Buber, "The Two Foci of the Jewish Soul," pp. 266–76, in *The Writings of Martin Buber,* ed. Will Herberg (New York: World Publishing, 1956): 275–76.

6. For Buber's existential sense of Jewish community, see "I and Thou," excerpted from *I and Thou*; for Buber on religious solitude and renunciation of the world, see "The Question to the Single One," excerpted from *Between Man and Man*; both in *The Writings of Martin Buber,* ed. Will Herberg (New York: World Publishing, 1956), 43–62 and 63–88.

7. Romans 8:6, 7 (KJV). There have been complex controversies concerning what Paul meant by "slavery," insofar as he also refers to being a Christian as being a slave of God. However, most secular historians appear to agree on two points: that Paul accepted slavery and that he thought those who were slaves were being justly punished by God for their sins. Neither what Paul means by slavery nor his position on the justice of slavery as ownership of human beings is relevant to what I have emphasized in this text; namely, that any Cosmopolitan human equality endorsed by Paul referred only to the spiritual realm and that such spiritual equality was not logically incompatible with an acceptance of secular slavery. For contemporary controversy on the Catholic Church's views and actions concerning secular slavery, see John T. Noonan Jr., "Development in Moral Doctrine," *Theological Studies* 54 (December 1993): 662–78. A characteristic response to Noonan's claim that Catholic moral doctrine did not explicitly and decisively repudiate slavery until 1890 is Joel S. Panzer, "The Popes and Slavery," The Church in History Information Center, at www.churchinhistory .org (consulted June 2010). I take up Noonan's article later in this chapter section.

8. See Augustine, *Confessions: Books I–XIII,* trans. F. J. Sheed (Indianapolis, IN: Hackett, 1993), 116–17 (book 7, IX).

9. Augustine, *Confessions,* 117–18 (X).

10. Saint Thomas Aquinas, *On Law, Morality, and Politics*, ed. William P. Baumgarth and Richard J. Regan, S.J. (Indianapolis, IN: Hackett, 1988), 243 (Thomas Aquinas, *Summa Theologica*, II–IIQ. 104, "Of Obedience," Fifth Article). The reference to Seneca is *De Beneficiis*, III, 20.

11. Thomas Aquinas, *On Law, Morality, and Politics*, 243.

12. Thomas Aquinas, *On Law, Morality, and Politics*, 242–44.

13. It seems commonplace that such control always *accompanied* the institution of slavery. To allay any doubt concerning an anachronistic reading of Aquinas, see Milton Melzer, *Slavery: A World History*, 2 vols. (New York: Da Capo Press, 1993), 1: 209–27 ("Medieval Slaves").

14. Descartes, *Meditations on First Philosophy*, in *The Philosophical Writings of Descartes*, ed. John Cottingham, Robert Stroothoff, and Dugald Murdoch, 3 vols. (Cambridge: Cambridge University Press), 2: 3.

15. Descartes, *Meditations on First Philosophy*, 1: 4n1.

16. Descartes, *Meditations on First Philosophy*, "Preface to the Reader," 1: 7.

17. Descartes, *Meditations on First Philosophy*, Sixth Meditation, 1: 56.

18. In "Preface to the Reader," Descartes refers to scarce readers "who are able and willing to meditate seriously with me, and to withdraw their minds from the senses and from all preconceived opinions" (*Meditations on First Philosophy*, 1: 8).

19. Friedrich Nietzsche, *Genealogy of Morals*, in *The Basic Writings of Nietzsche*, ed. Walter Kaufmann (New York: Random House, 1968), 577 (third essay, sec. 20).

20. Noonan, "Development in Moral Doctrine," 665–66.

21. Melzer, *Slavery*, 1: 223–24.

22. Melzer, *Slavery*, 1: 230.

23. Melzer, *Slavery*, 2: 8.

24. See for example, Agnes Mathilde Wergeland, *Slavery in Germanic Society during the Middle Ages* (Chicago: University of Chicago Press, 1916), 60–63. Wergeland wrote, "There is no doubt that, but for the constant good offices of the church through her ministers, the improvement in the condition of the slave would have been of far slower growth. . . . On the other hand, it is true that the church did not abolish slavery within her own precincts; she seemed far more eager to have slaves given her than to give them away herself" (60, 62).

25. Otto Gierke, *Political Theories of the Middle Ages*, trans. Frederic William Maitland (Boston: Beacon, 1958), 30–37.

26. Gierke, *Political Theories of the Middle Ages*, 100.

27. Gierke, *Political Theories of the Middle Ages*, x–xi.

28. See Naomi Zack, *Bachelors of Science: Twentieth Century Identity, Then and Now* (Philadelphia: Temple University Press, 1997), ch. 1.

29. Gierke, *Political Theories of the Middle Ages*, 9–11ff.

30. John Walters, "The Commons and Their Mental Worlds," in *The Oxford Illustrated History of Tudor and Stuart*, ed. John Stephen Morrill (Cambridge: Oxford University Press, 1990), 191–218, refer. 200–21.

31. John of Salisbury, *Policraticus*, ed. Cary J. Nederman (Cambridge: Cambridge University Press, 1990), 66–67.

32. See note 30, above.

33. Robert Darnton, "A Bourgeois Puts His World in Order: The City as a Text," pp. 107–44, in *The Great Cat Massacre and Other Episodes in French Cultural History* (New York: Vintage Books, 1985): 123.

34. See *Antisemitism: An Historical Encyclopedia of Prejudice and Persecution*, ed. Richard S. Levy (Santa Barbara, CA: ABC-CLIO, 2005), s.v. "Dominicans"; Friedrich Heer, *The Medieval World*, trans. Janet Sondheimer (New York: New American Library, 1961), 309–13.

35. John Dillon and Lloyd P. Gerson, eds., *Neoplatonic Philosophy: Introductory Readings* (Indianapolis, IN: Hackett: Indianapolis, IN, 2004), xiii.

36. Dillon and Gerson, *Neoplatonic Philosophy*, xiii–xx.

37. Philip Merlan, "Plotinus," in *The Encyclopedia of Philosophy*, ed. Paul Edwards (New York: Macmillan, 1967), 343. Throughout this article (351–59), Merlan provides comprehensive textual citations for the main ideas in Plotinus' *Enneads* (keyed into the Ennead number and its chapters and lines).

38. Plotinus, *Enneads*, VI, 8, S. 16, in *Neoplatonic Philosophy: Introductory Readings*, ed. John Dillon and Lloyd P. Gerson (Indianapolis, IN: Hackett, 2004), 176.

39. Plotinus, *Enneads*, 91 (V, 3 S. 4).

40. Plotinus, *Enneads*, 56–61 (IV, 8, S. 1–4).

41. Plotinus, *Enneads*, 150 (VI, 7, S. 22).

42. Proclus, *Platonic Theology*, book 1, 2, in *Neoplatonic Philosophy: Introductory Readings*, ed. John Dillon and Lloyd P. Gerson (Indianapolis, IN: Hackett, 2004), 286.

43. Porphyry, *On the Life of Plotinus and the Arrangement of His Work*, trans. Stephen McKenna (Sequim, WA: Holmes, 2001), 28. The biographical information about Plotinus appears in the initial pages of this short volume.

44. On the meaning of the US Great Seal and its history, see www.greatseal.com (consulted June 2010). It is an interesting coincidence that Plotinus' student Amelius of Tuscany preferred to call himself "Amerius," because, Porphyry writes, "as he explained, it suited him better to be named from Amereia, Unification, than from Ameleia, Indifference." Porphyry, *On the Life of Plotinus*, 12.

45. Lincoln proclaimed in part: "All this being done, in sincerity and truth, let us then rest humbly in the hope authorized by the Divine teachings, that the united cry of the Nation will be heard on high, and answered with blessings, no less than the pardon of our national sins, and the restoration of our now divided and suffering Country, to its former happy condition of unity and peace." Text in full available at www.freerepublic.com/focus/f-news/2495406/posts (consulted June 2010).

46. See "President George W. Bush's Comments about 9/11/01," *USA Patriotism!*, at www.usa-patriotism.com/speeches/gwbush_911.htm (consulted June 2010).

47. See Kate Phillips, "McCain Ad Mocks Obama as the One," NewYorkTimes.com, August 1, 2008, at thecaucus.blogs.nytimes.com/2008/08/01/mccain-ad-mocks-obama-as-the-one/ (consulted June 2010).

48. See Walter Ben Michaels, *Our America: Nativism, Modernism, and Pluralism* (Charlotte, NC: Duke University Press, 1995).

· 6 ·

Social Contract Theory and
the Sovereign Nation-State

$\mathcal{S}$ocial contract theory is a method and tradition in political philosophy. It consists of a speculative discourse about how nation-states have been formed and normative accounts of how they should be formed. In political philosophy a 'should' applied to such a historically big-stage subject needs justification. It has been usual in Christian-Judaic contexts for a political-philosophical 'should' of this magnitude to be based on an understanding of God's rules. But that is no longer necessary. The 'should' can be understood to come from any supernatural force, a particular human group(s), prudence, custom, the good of humanity, human reason, human empathy, intuition, and so on. But what is a nation-state? Most definitions specify the political independence of a government and a people; there is a connotation of "integral whole" in "nation-state." But the term also refers to a type of government that is a government over a people or a nation. A third possibility is that a nation-state is the people as a political unit, apart from the government. Fourth, the entities we call nation-states might be sufficiently diverse so that none of their political structures, if explained in depth, would apply to all nation-states. This last could be resolved with an ostensive definition listing concrete nation-states; once we got used to that definition, we could refer to all or some of the countries of the world in practical discourse, restricting the abstract referent of "nation-state" to theoretical usage. But nation-state, as an abstraction, cannot be a purely theoretical subject in a specialized intellectual mode because it has life in the real world, via terms such as "motherland," "fatherland," "country," and "homeland." All of these terms presuppose some version of Neoplatonic unity, as it was discussed in chapter 5.

Most nations and many smaller units of social organization have founding myths, some purely fictive; others, particularly in the modern era, have been based on historical events. Such myths are not static cultural information but are reconfigured as circumstances change, to edify a populace, motivate it for war, win votes, and so forth. Most founding myths are about events that occurred in the past or the exploits of heroes in earlier times that resulted in the origination of a people as they see themselves at some later time. Seventeenth-century social contract theorists successfully changed this temporal convention by first imagining a condition of human life without government that for rhetorical purposes was a very distant time in human history, before the existence of government. They then used the conditions of human life in that imaginary "state of nature" to justify the creation in the future of the kind of nation-state they preferred. There was intellectual precedent for this project of creating new political and social entities in the medieval construction of social bodies and in Christian ideas of unity, which in real life resulted in the institution of the Catholic Church (as discussed in chapter 5). Christianity also allowed individuals to imagine a better future in an "afterlife."

The early modern political innovation invoked the Christian God, but its practical aims of founding new nation-states were strongly connected to real politics: Hobbes published *Leviathan* in 1651, a year after Charles I was executed, during intense discussion about the best kind of government; Locke published the *Second Treatise* in 1669, a year after the Glorious Whig Revolution when parliament restored a Protestant king to the throne; later, Rousseau took up the tradition in ways that inspired the French Revolution. Otto Gierke surveys the early modern innovation in political theory thus:

> In opposition to positive jurisprudence, which still continued to show a Conservative trend, the natural-law theory of the State was Radical to the very core of its being. Unhistorical in the foundations on which it was built, it was also directed, in its efforts and its results, not to the purpose of scientific explanation of the past, but to that of the exposition and justification of a new future which was to be called into existence.[1]

Gierke further observes that the development of natural law political theory dispensed with *ius gentium*, or the laws of nations, and dismissed existing law, to focus wholly on the laws that should regulate the new sovereign state. Some groups of free humans were imagined as coming together to fulfill mutual needs, and their first free political act was to establish themselves as a political collective that would create a sovereign state. That is, whatever form of government resulted, the state would be inherently sovereign, and all other associations, such as the church, would exist within the state.[2] This was a very decisive break with the medieval tradition in which either the church was the sole sovereign or church and state coexisted as sovereignties. It was not an idea that could coherently accommodate empire, from either the perspective of the state or that of its colonies, and it did not emphasize federations of states or permanent peaceful coexistence among states. Gierke, writing in the 1920s, remains relevant:

> If the theory of Natural Law were to remain true to its conception of sovereignty, it could never admit a federal combination of particular States [any more than it could admit a general society of all States] to the position of a Super-State. . . . The conception of the federal state . . . could not grow on natural-law soil; indeed we may even say that it has only maintained its existence in modern thought by dint of a constant and bitter struggle with Natural Law.[3]

Early modern social contract theorists plied extraordinary sleights of mind by using a fictive idea of the past to shape the future into the form of a newly imagined sovereign nation-state. This trick of positing an imaginary situation from which to derive a preferred type of political structure endured through John Rawls's 1971 *A Theory of Justice*.[4] While the earlier social contract theorists depended on ideas of natural law to use what they imagined about the past to justify what they imagined and wanted to see develop in the future, Rawls simply began with a general normative principle of justice and a more specific principle of justice as fairness (that is, a *concept* and a *conception* of justice).[5]

While presenting itself as universally normative, seventeenth-century social contract theory developed political and economic structures that were highly advantageous for some groups to the exclusion of others. By definition, its universal normativity could be operative only within a single nation-state, and in calling forth the new nation-state out of an existing population, it was not the case that all members of that population were to be citizens, despite proclamations of equality. In this sense, even with the abstraction of foundational normative principles, the different versions of social contract theory have not expanded beyond mores, the beliefs and ideals of specific peoples, the inhabitants of particular sovereign nations—England, France, the United States. Conquest cannot expand a social contract in a practical sense because the social contract is supposed to be voluntarily undertaken by a specific people. Nevertheless, rights and freedoms attributed to social contract societies have been rhetorically invoked to justify changes imposed on societies taken over by social contract nation-states.

Rawls, in restricting his discussion of the principles of justice to "a well-ordered society," in which "everyone is presumed to act justly and to do his part in upholding just institutions,"[6] would have to assume, for his discussion to be relevant, that he was referring to the society or societies of his audience. Insofar as such *ideal theory* is only relevant to a few states, which given modern history are likely to be dominated by whites according to a received taxonomy of human races, even Rawls's discussion of justice does not expand from mores into ethics. (In *The Law of Peoples* Rawls does formulate ethical principles for international relations, but without a critique of the *sovereignty* of existing nation-states.)[7]

This chapter will proceed as a critical examination from an egalitarian perspective of the social contract theories of Hobbes, Locke, Hume, Rousseau, and Rawls. In beginning with a premise of human equality, Rawls is surprisingly close to Hobbes. Because the state of civil society or society under legitimate government is not that different from the state of nature for Locke, the rhetoric propounding Locke's state of nature is more historical than hypothetical. Hume, however, provides the most naturalistic historical account and ends up with an endorsement of Enlightenment ideas of secular progress in a well-ordered society, which is, of course, eighteenth-century England. Rousseau also makes use of a historical account, but his métier is more speculative-anthropology and psychology than politics, and for a principle of government, Rousseau departs from social science to posit a completely fictive entity, the general will. I will now consider them in turn.

HOBBES' LEGAL POSITIVISM CONCERNING RIGHTS

It is quite a paradox that Hobbes' version of social contract theory results in the most oppressive version of the state in the history of Western philosophy, while Hobbes remains one of the most sophisticated social constructivists of the tradition. Contemporary social constructivists tend to emphasize individual or group freedom in a generally progressive project based on the possibility of social change. Hobbes' social constructivist insights require no apology, but his oppressive portrait of the state does require an explanation. Hobbes' writing style is uniformly declarative and confident, and he was involved in dangerous intellectual controversies over most of his adult life, to the extreme that his enemies in the Roman Catholic Church and Oxford University banned and wanted to burn his books. Hobbes himself burned his writings to avoid imprisonment when Parliament passed a bill to suppress atheism following the Great Plague of 1665 and the Great Fire of London in 1666. Some members of Parliament wanted to burn Hobbes himself, which they did in effigy.[8] Despite his appetite for controversy, or talent for attracting it, Hobbes described himself as a timid man. In his autobiography that was written in verse, he claimed that the approaching Spanish Armada had caused his premature birth:

> And hereupon it was my mother dear
> Did bring forth twins at once, both me and fear.[9]

Indeed, both *De Cive* and *Leviathan* in places read as exercises in primal fear. Men can think, they are rational, but the first rule of reason is self-preservation in the avoidance of sudden violent death. In the dedication of *De Cive*, Hobbes claims that the rational part of every man provides a maxim "to fly a contra-natural dissolution, as the greatest mischief that can arrive to nature."[10] All great and lasting societies originate "not in the mutual good will men had towards each other, but in the mutual fear that they had of each other." Hobbes explains in a footnote that this fear is not limited to instant fright but extends to precautions taken against "a certain foresight of future evil."[11]

In *Leviathan*, chapter 13, Hobbes begins his description of "the natural condition of mankind," or the state of nature, which is not a historical past but any condition without government, by positing human equality in physical strength as well as "faculties of the mind." On that basis men compete and "endeavor to destroy or subdue one another," which leads to diffidence (self-defense) and a desire for glory (the high opinion of others).[12] The state of nature is thus a condition of war, "a tract of time wherein the will to contend by battle is sufficiently known"—war, like fear, is an ongoing condition.[13] The result is a lack of industry, trade, agriculture, knowledge, arts, letters, and society, "and which is worst of all, continual fear and danger of violent death, and the life of man, solitary, poor, nasty, brutish, and short."[14] The cause of this constant insecurity of a condition of war is the same as what defines the situation, the lack of government. "Where there is no common power there is no law." In the absence of law, no actions are unjust; there are no property rights (i.e., "no mine and thine distinct"). But there is a desire for peace, and reason reveals the Laws of Nature.[15]

The Right of Nature is the liberty each has to preserve his own life, and a Law of Nature is a general rule, found out by reason "by which a man is forbidden to do that which is destructive of his life or taketh away the means of preserving the same, and to omit that by which he thinketh it may be best preserved."[16] The first Rule of Nature is to seek peace and the second is "to defend ourselves."[17] There can be no peace so long as everyone has a right to everything, but peace can be attained if some rights are transferred. Only those rights can be transferred that are reciprocally transferred back by another, and the transfer must be voluntary and of benefit to whoever gives up his rights; the right to resist physical force against one's life and imprisonment cannot be transferred. The mutual transference of rights is Contract.[18] However, contracts or covenants are easily rendered void in the state of nature because there is no "common power" to enforce the performance of a second party after the first party has performed his part of the agreement. Besides the Rule of Seeking Peace, there are other rules of nature against injustice, ingratitude, arrogance, pride, and inequity, as well as obligations that facilitate obedience to all of the rules of nature. But although these rules are immutable and eternal, they are not effective laws in the absence of a common power to enforce them.[19]

Because "covenants without the sword are but words, and of no strength to secure a man at all,"[20] and men do not naturally agree, the solution to the condition of war in the state of nature is for men to erect a higher power. They do this by conferring all of their power and strength to one man or an assembly of men that will unite them in the same artificial person who will express their common will. This unity is achieved by

> covenant of every man with everyman, as though every man should say to every man *I authorize and give up my right of governing myself to this man, or to this assembly of men, on this condition, that thou give up thy right to him, and authorize all his actions in like manner.* . . . . This is the generation of that great *Leviathan* or rather (to speak more reverently) of that *Mortal God* to which we owe, under the *Immortal God* our peace and defense.[21]

Once the Leviathan has been generated, the subjects cannot change the form of government, the sovereign power cannot be forfeited, and the sovereign is the sole judge of what is required to keep the peace and defend his/their subjects. The sovereign thereby has indivisible rights to form the government, make war and peace, make laws, and settle disputes, as well as to decide what doctrines may be published and taught and to determine the nature of property rights.[22]

There are a number of obvious problems with Hobbes' account. It is debatable whether without government all groups of people represent such great internal danger to their members. It is debatable that if people could not trust one another, they would, while still in the state of nature, agree to give up their right to harm and loot each other. If people are as fractious as Hobbes asserts, then the possibility of forming the political body that gives the rights of all to the sovereign is foreclosed—there can be no social contract, not because it is unenforceable but because it requires for its origination a degree of peace and good will. This problem of origins applies to Plato's *Republic* and other utopias, but in those cases, it is a problem external to the political entities described—however they get together, once they get together there is no impediment arising from their natures to prevent founders from setting up the ideal society. The problem is internal for Hobbes' social contract theory because the fractious nature of the parties to the social contract could make the creation of the social contract impossible.[23]

A second psychological problem is that some, and perhaps enough to block the original political agreement, might prefer freedom of thought and speech more than safety under censorship. (This would include Hobbes himself.) The issue is not whether the gift of rights would fail to get sufficient "votes," but of whether foregoing civil freedom for security is a good bargain. Although life preserved is a condition for having values, this does not mean that being alive is the highest value. Also, it is debatable that the goods of collective civilized life would be forthcoming under conditions of absolute political repression, as many of those goods depend on free development of human capabilities. And finally, the idea of an absolute secular ruler, in perpetuity, posits a fictive entity similar to the omnipotent Christian God, and it is, for all practical purposes, all good as well, so that there is something mystical about the Leviathan.

Left unanswered in Hobbes' account are the questions of whether all national governments are supposed to strive for the totalitarian ideal of absolute sovereignty of a nation-state, and of how sovereign nations in the state of nature or state of war in which they will exist are to keep the peace. As Gierke implies in the passage quoted earlier, sovereignty implies that there is no higher power, so there is in principle no possible entity that could keep the peace among nations. (Again, the similarity to arguments for monotheism is uncanny, for instance, God is the greatest, there can only be one greatest, and so on.) History since Hobbes has been replete with wars between nation-states, which probably have greater capacities for destruction than nonsovereign states. On a global level, the realization of Hobbes' *Leviathan* might therefore contradict or disobey the natural law principle, "keep the peace." If the only peace worth keeping is internal national peace, then the nation does not transcend tribalism.

Hobbes' social constructivism is a direct consequence of his view that all the goods in complex human life are the result of social organization. He did not spend much time trying to figure out how diversities in human culture could result in different specific forms of human social goods, because he was not interested in diversity in culture, values, or social interaction. For Hobbes, the state of nature seems to have been universally the same, just as life under an absolute sovereign would be the same everywhere. Therefore, Hobbes was not a proper social constructivist, in our sense, because his focus on monolithic abstractions precluded paying attention to their contexts of instantiation in any comparative way—there is nothing to compare if every state of nature is the same as every other in occasioning primal fear and if all absolute rulers are the same in their complete sovereignty.

Hobbes was nonetheless a strong social constructivist in attributing social causes to certain things that many other thinkers accepted as natural. First among these was Hobbes' acknowledged construction of the state as an artificial and thereby fictive entity. *Leviathan*, chapter 16, which immediately precedes his description of the commonwealth at the beginning of part 2, is titled, "Of Persons, Authors, and Things Personated." According to Hobbes, a "feigned or artificial person" is he whose words "are considered as represent-ing the words and actions of another."[24] Hobbes anticipates his construction of the *Leviathan* in his definition of representation:

> A multitude of men are made *one* person, when they are by one man, or one person, represented so that it be done with the consent of every one of that multitude in particular. For it is the *unity* of the represented, that maketh the person *one*. And it is the representer that beareth the person and but one per-son, and *unity* cannot otherwise be understood in multitude . . . every man giving their common representer authority from himself in particular, and owning all the actions the representer doth, in case they give him authority without stint.[25]

Hobbes expressed the required view that God existed and had told man how he should behave in the state of nature. That man was incapable of following God's rules necessitated not a state with government that was created by God or that required God's ongoing participation (even though Hobbes is willing to posit God as blessing it), but a secular state constructed by men and wholly run by them. This constructed state was the locus of protection for what we would call human rights. That Hobbes in the form of government he advocated was willing to bargain away the greater part of such rights is beside the point that the rights themselves, insofar as they were to be taken seriously, would have to become political, which is to say that they required expression in actual law and protec-tion by an effective executive. In this sense, Hobbes is an early theorist of human rights who is a legal positivist concerning political human rights. And, his con-struction of rights fits into his construction of the secular sovereign nation state.

RAWLS AND THE TRANSITION FROM MORAL TO LEGAL RIGHTS

Hobbes and Locke are usually contrasted as seventeenth-century social contract theorists and it is usual to follow a discussion of Hobbes with one of Locke. However, Hobbes' assertion of human equality, together with his transition from a condition without government to humanly constructed civil society, has a striking twentieth-century counterpart in Rawls's political theory—even though Rawls does not count Hobbes as one of his antecedents.[26] Rawls can be viewed as talking about distributive justice under democratic forms of government that are concretely and historically the governments of some con-temporary nation-states. Thus, "a conception of social justice, then, is to be regarded as providing in the first instance a standard whereby the distributive

aspects of the basic structure of society are to be assessed."[27] Commensurate
to Hobbes, Rawls draws on an idea of human nature as rational. In positing
a hypothetical state of nature that yields a conception of justice as fairness, he
relies on the background condition of a shared concept of justice—'men' share
a concept of justice, from which they derive different conceptions of justice.

> Existing societies are of course seldom well-ordered. . . . Men disagree
> about which principles should define the basic terms of their association.
> Yet we may still say, despite this disagreement, that they each have a
> conception of justice. That is, they understand the need for, and they are
> prepared to affirm, a characteristic set of principles for assigning basic rights
> and duties and for determining what they take to be the proper distribution
> of the benefits and burdens of social cooperation.[28]

Based on this shared concept of justice, Rawls proposes his conception of justice as fairness, which is to be instantiated as a deliberative process in which the
participants do not know how they are already advantaged or disadvantaged
in existing society:

> No one knows his place in society, his class position or social status, nor
> does any one know his fortune in the distribution of natural assets and
> abilities, his intelligence, strength and the like. I shall even assume that the
> parties do not know their conceptions of the good or their special psycho-
> logical propensities. The principles of justice are chosen behind a veil of
> ignorance.[29]

Rawls's requirement of ignorance imposes equality during deliberation and the
constructed equality is comparable to Hobbes' starting point of equality based
on roughly equal mental and physical abilities among men in the state of nature.
Rawls expects his constructed equality to yield principles "that free and rational
persons concerned to further their own interests would accept in an initial position of equality as defining the fundamental terms of their association."[30] And
he claims that they would arrive at these two principles of justice:

> First: each person is to have an equal right to the most extensive basic
> liberty compatible with a similar liberty for others.
> Second: social and economic inequalities are to be arranged so that they
> are both (a) reasonably expected to be to everyone's advantage, and (b) at-
> tached to positions and offices open to all.[31]

Rawls thinks inequalities should be arranged to benefit those already disadvantaged, according to the difference principle, which is "a strongly egalitarian conception in the sense that unless there is a distribution that makes both

persons better off (limiting ourselves to the two-person case for simplicity), an equal distribution is to be preferred."[32]

Rawls is confident that by continually referring to justice as fairness and changing the conditions of the original position, *reflective equilibrium*, or the closest possible approximation to intuitive ideas of justice, will be achieved by participants.[33] Rawls assumes that out of good will and self-interest, it will be possible to arrive at the right structure of the basic institutions of a society, using the original position as a test. He also assumes that agreement will be possible in the original position, just as Hobbes assumes that men in the state of nature will agree not to harm one another and to transfer their powers to a sovereign.

The main difference between Hobbes and Rawls is this: Hobbes' notion of equality is based on an empirical claim concerning human sameness, whereas Rawls first constructs equality as an imagined situation and then uses that situation to posit liberty as a normative ideal. Both Hobbes and Rawls are working with an idea that, given a background sense of justice (natural law for Hobbes and the general rules of a well-ordered society for Rawls), it will be possible to translate that background sense into a better system of social organization. Despite the flaws in the structure of Hobbes' solution to what is intolerable in the state of nature, the transfer of powers to a greater power is not unfair. Rawls's solution is altogether more comfortable for at least the privileged members of a well-ordered society, who have the leisure to deliberate, and Rawls says little that is disturbing about human nature. But there is nothing in Rawls's structure of the original condition to prevent a consensus about basic institutions that fairly results in less freedom for all in cases where the participants cannot agree on the specific structures that will preserve more freedom. Thus, it is not clear how Rawls's setup prevents the kind of repression embraced by Hobbes.

Hobbes places his faith in the ability of the sovereign to create security and Rawls places his faith in the ability of abstract individuals to construct fair institutions. Both theorists are in Gierke's sense "calling forth" unknowns based on new formal procedures: absolute rule for Hobbes and consensus based on hypothetical self-ignorance for Rawls. For all we know, the absolute rule of a Leviathan could be very just, if the Leviathan were very smart and knew enough. Consensus reached in self-ignorance could be very unjust, if what participants willed themselves not to know about their social identities and circumstances were more important than they assumed.

Various science fiction scenarios (e.g., the computer, HAL, in the movie *2001: A Space Odyssey*) can be used to effectively dispense with the Leviathan. However, Rawls's veil of ignorance needs to be taken more seriously, for example in terms of US black racial identities. Charles Mills has forcefully argued against Rawls that if people pretend not to know their racial identities, they will be unable to correct racial injustice because the unjust distribution of social goods resulting from preexisting institutional racism cannot be corrected solely by measures that are based on principles of fairness, from any present time onward. Mills revises Rawls's conception of fairness to include an option for correcting past injustice, behind the veil. Thus, justice as fairness, in a situation where deliberators do not know their own race, would include an option to choose reparations for past racial injustice, particularly slavery, among the basic social institutions.[34] I think that Mills's suggestion opens the door to corrections of a multiplicity of historical wrongs, such as historical harm done to Asians, Mexicans, Native Americans, and also some white groups. This would create a new economic, political, and social historical project that would defy many intuitive and procedural principles of justice.[35] The problem is that an option to choose reparations behind the veil makes reparations too abstract and general an issue in designing the basic institutions of society.

However, Mills's objection is cogent for showing that the willed self-ignorance in Rawls's original position, insofar as it includes an ignorance of injustice in the past, may in some situations defeat both its goal of fairness and its raison d'être as an actualization of fairness. To anticipate a little the discussion of deontology in the next chapter, it is assumed that all human beings have equal intrinsic value. This is their dignity. Racism is a violation of such dignity and it can occur in at least three kinds or applications of justice/injustice: retributional, distributive, and procedural. Rawls is mainly concerned with procedural justice, although in a thick sense that does not directly violate shared principles of distributive justice. It is something like the universal dignity of human subjects that grounds justice as fairness. Still, the recognition of human dignity may or may not lead to retributional and distributive justice, depending on circumstances. Racial egalitarianism on that ground of human dignity should preclude racist obstructions to retributional and distributive justice, but it cannot require a specific kind of retribution or distribution because racism can always sabotage even the most just practices and dignity can be maintained and recognized in even the most oppressive and unjust circumstances. That racism can obstruct the best human practices does not entail that specific remedies for racism, such as reparations for past slavery, are part of the fundamental considerations of what counts as procedural justice. (More about this in chapter 7.)

A NOTE ON MORAL AND LEGAL RIGHTS

The transition between moral human rights and legal human rights rests on an idea that human beings are equal in some core sense: moral equality that results in equal entitlements to some good, such as respect from others; sameness in origins ranging from a common creator to a common evolutionary history that becomes a foundation for empathy and/or justice; sameness in abilities or capabilities that evokes ideas of justice in treating equals equally; sameness in needs that becomes a foundation for mutual obligations. Hobbes, of course, recognized human equality on the grounds that motivated fear (i.e., "the weakest has strength enough to kill the strongest"[36]), but the importance of his contribution lies not in that, but in his use of human equality to motivate a transition from a condition without govern- ment to a condition with it. Later theorists such as Locke posited human rights in the condition without government so that it became the duty of government to protect such rights without having to create them. (Unlike Hobbes, Locke was not a legal positivist concerning human rights.)

If we can retain a distinction between moral human rights, which are a matter of ethics, and political human rights, which are a matter of living in the right kind of political unity, then much of the current disagreement about whether contemporary rights doctrines are egalitarian on a global level can be resolved: moral rights are universal, but political rights require positive law. It is easy to conflate moral and legal rights because there have been politi- cal promulgations of moral rights before they have had support in positive law. This has led to an apparent failure of human rights doctrines as they are generally understood, when the failure can be more accurately pinpointed as a failure to effect a transition from moral human rights to legal human rights.

At this time, the political entities in which rights are supported and protected are not limited to nation-states but include international humanitar- ian organizations that protect specific rights, such as Amnesty International, Oxfam, and Médicins Sans Frontières, and also NGOs (nongovernmental organizations) that promote interests of specific groups whose moral rights are unprotected on political levels or only protected within political unities to which their constituents do not belong, such as PEN (Poets, Essayists, and Novelists), EZLN (Zapatista Army of National Liberation, Mexico), and ILGHRC (International Lesbian and Gay Human Rights Commission). The need for such organizations, as well as their effectiveness, is symptomatic not so much of the failure of rights doctrines that are expressed in law but of the fact that the rights they seek to protect are not yet legal rights.

LOCKE'S LEGAL NATURALISM CONCERNING PROPERTY RIGHTS AND INEQUALITY

Because the legal rights posited by Locke were the same (natural) moral rights that existed in the state of nature as he conceived it, Locke blurred the distinction between moral and legal rights. Much more than Hobbes' *Leviathan*, Locke's *Second Treatise* was influential for the founding documents of the United States, and the supremely high value he placed on the ownership of private property is a primary tenet of most, if not all, liberal nation-states today. Such liberal nation-states have not been egalitarian concerning racial minorities, immigrants, or indigenous populations. It is therefore important to clarify what is distinctive about Locke's political thought in the way he combined an acceptance of inequality with ideas of natural and legal human rights. Locke's attempt to justify slavery with ideas of just war has already been noted in chapter 4, and the connection of the permissibility of chattel slavery with strong property rights was also examined there. The focus here will be not so much on rights of ownership after ownership is established but on rights to appropriation that result in ownership. If there is something ethically wrong with Locke's ideas of appropriation, then what blocks that general wrong should also make enslavement impermissible and preclude the construction of political entities that support slavery as an institution.

Locke perfected the conflation of moral and political thinking from which Hobbes, as (what we would call) a social constructivist, had moved away. He presented distributive human inequality as morally just in the state of nature, so that legitimate government had to protect it, both within the European nation-state and beyond. Locke began by using a benign description of human nature in the state of nature:

> The *State of Nature* has a Law of Nature to govern it, which obliges every one: And Reason, which is that law, teaches all Mankind, who will but consult it, that being all equal and independent, no one ought to harm another in his Life, Health, Liberty or Possessions.[37]
>
> And here we have the plain *difference between the State of Nature, and the State of War,* which however some Men have confounded, are as far distant, as a State of Peace, Good Will, Mutual Assistance, and Preservation, and a State of Enmity, Malice, Violence, and Mutual Destruction are one from another.[38]

Still, Locke allowed that not everyone keeps the peace in the state of nature and thus to settle disputes fairly, as well as to protect inhabitants from external enemies, men form a commonwealth, or government, as a convenience: "For where there is an Authority, a Power on Earth, from which relief can be had by *appeal*, there the continuance of the State of war is excluded, and the controversie is decided by that power."[39]

However, Locke had two pictures of the state of nature. His apologists and champions have focused on the one drawn in chapter 4, "Of Property," in the *Second Treatise*, in which cooperative industrious humans thrive: "God, who hath given the World to Men in common, hath also given them reason to make use of it to the best advantage of Life, and convenience."[40] To make use of the world, men need to individuate parts of it for their consumption. This is accomplished by a mixing of labor with certain items, which results in owning them: every man already owns his own person, so he owns his labor, and what he labors on becomes exclusively his, his *property*—especially when land is labored on.[41] Others have no reason to object to such ownership, so long as "there is enough and as good left in common"[42] for them to labor on. Furthermore, God gave the world "to the use of the Industrious and Rational,"[43] so the entire process of appropriation or coming to own something is divinely blessed.

The condition of peaceful coexistence and industrious labor rewarded by ownership are perfected by the instauration of minimal representative government that protects preexisting natural rights, plus the right to request that protection:

> But because no *Political Society* can be, nor subsist without having in it self the Power to preserve the Property, and in order thereunto punish the Offenses of all those of that Society; there, and there only is *Political Society*, where every one of the Members hath quitted this natural Power, resign'd it up into the hands of the Community in all cases that exclude him not from appealing for Protection to the Law established by it.[44]

This first picture of the state of nature relies on a simplistic "just desserts" theory, as not all who labor become property owners and many property owners have never labored. Nevertheless, its intuitive attractiveness has made it easy for some, especially those property owners who can identify with the subjects in the picture, to overlook the inequalities that can coexist with Lockean natural rights as the result of fair appropriation.

Locke's second picture of the state of nature depicts the conditions of contemporary Indians in America in contrast to Europeans, so that the Indians are referred to as a living record of European history. This picture superficially resembles what Hobbes wrote about America, namely: "For the savage people in many places of *America* (except the government of small families, the concord whereof dependeth on natural lust) have no government at all, and live at this day in that brutish manner as I said before."[45] However, Locke departs from a comparison based on social, political, or military relations among men, which could elicit comparisons of savagery versus civility, to one based on economics, thus:

> The greatest part of *things really useful* to the Life of Man, and such as the necessity of subsisting made the first commoners of the World look after,

as it doth the *Americans* now, *are* generally things *of short duration*; such as if they are not consumed by use, will decay and perish of themselves.[46]

Thus in the beginning all the World was *America*, and more so than that is now; for no such thing as *Money* was anywhere known.[47]

Given the potential to have money in Locke's European past state of nature and its absence in America, his two pictures of the state of nature as the European past and the American present merge into one. The image resulting from this stereoscope is a global meritocracy, where industriousness is the primary merit. Because the Europeans have money as a sign of their greater industry, the advantages they can gain over indigenous people would be just. But the Lockean sense of justice is strained by equivocation in what Locke means by "money" and "trade," in transferring property rights from the European state of nature to contemporary society under civil government.

Locke uses money in three different senses throughout his writing: precious objects in the state of nature, money in circulation, and money as itself a commodity in seventeenth-century England. Only the first two senses are directly relevant to this discussion.[48] As precious objects in the state of nature, Locke views money as a store of value for an industrious person, which is in compliance with the proviso against waste concerning accumulation through labor:

> If he would give his Nuts for a piece of Metal, pleased with its color; or exchange his Sheep for shells, or Wool for a sparkling Pebble or a Diamond, and keep those by him all his Life, he invaded not the Right of others, he might heap up as much of these durable things as he pleased; the *exceeding of the bounds of his just Property* not lying in the largeness of his Possession, but the perishing of any thing uselessly in it.[49]

Locke must have been aware of bartering among Native Americans and between Native Americans and Europeans, and there is no evidence that he thought all Native Americans had the same amount of property. Native Americans, like Europeans in the state of nature, would have participated in an economy where precious objects were a store of value; they should have been included in Locke's broad descriptions of unequal property and money, which is as follows:

> This partage of things, in an inequality of private possessions, men have made practicable out of the bounds of Societie, and without compact, only by putting a value on gold and silver and tacitly agreeing on the use of Money.[50]

But Native Americans were not part of this description, according to Locke. Locke described Native Americans as lacking money and the kind of trade that went with it based on his second sense of money, where money was coin in circulation in an economic system, which could be "exchanged for," that is, used to buy, a wide variety of objects. Locke believed that money within an economic system was an incentive to labor, particularly in that improvement of land which removed specific parts of it from the great commons of humanity to become private property:

> For I ask, What would a Man value Ten Thousand, or an Hundred Thousand Acres of excellent *Land*, ready cultivated, and well stocked too with Cattle, in the middle of the in-land Parts of *America*, where he had no hopes of commerce with other Parts of the World, to draw *Money* to him by the Sale of the Product? It would not be worth the inclosing, and we should see him give up again to the wild Common of Nature, whatever was more than would supply the Conveniences of Life to be had there for him and his Family.[51]

Not only is money in this sense valuable as an individual incentive to labor, but it is required to support continued ownership of land, because otherwise those who inhabit land that they do not wholly use forfeit it. The land goes back into the commons from which the industrious, who do participate in a monetary system, can come to own and keep it. Thus:

> Yet there are still *great Tracts of Ground* to be found, which (the Inhabitants thereof not having joined with the rest of Mankind, in the consent of the Use of their common Money) *lie waste*, and are more that the People who dwell on it, do or can make use of, and so still lie in common. Tho' this can scarce happen amongst that part of Mankind, that have consented to the Use of Money.[52]

The Lockean 'doctrine' of tying labor to ownership through continuous use and commerce would have cleared the way for European appropriations of indigenous land all over the world (the question of Locke's intent constituting a separate subject). There were other grounds for such appropriation, such as possession through conquest. Carole Pateman points out that in Australia, the designation of *terra nullius* was used for property that settlers considered uninhabited, despite its occupation by Aborigines. Pateman suggests that European settlers of newly discovered lands could, drawing on Locke, view themselves as in a state of nature from which they constructed new political societies based on their own founding social contracts.[53] This, however, would require new sovereignties from the beginning, which were not common during the colonial period. The high value placed on wealth calculated according to the existing European monetary system was a common incentive, although few have extolled the moral value of money to the degree that Locke did. Whether

European settlers formed new sovereign states or mere colonies would not matter in terms of their property rights, according to Locke. Given his use of labor and money to justify unequal property ownership in the state of nature and the protection of existing property ownership as the main justification for legitimate government, inequalities of wealth and disregard of those who did not place the same value on accumulation would be morally good in either the state of nature or under civil society, although civil society would afford more force to protect accumulations.

HUME'S AND ROUSSEAU'S USES OF HISTORY

Hume and Rousseau both made extensive use of history in their political philosophy. The difference in their approaches and the inegalitarian results of each of their projects is cautionary for any attempt to use the past in attempting to shape the future. Of course, political theorists need to understand the past, but there are as yet no clear rules for how not to misuse the past, except for negative examples such as these: Rousseau imagined a golden age vastly different from his present and resolved the discrepancy by positing an untenable utopia; Hume gave a narrow, property-interest historical account of justice and prized commerce in a way similar to Locke, but with higher regard for its social and cultural benefits. Rousseau was the more original and romantic thinker, Hume somewhat pedestrian and bourgeois in contrast.

Rousseau provided a grand narrative of human history in three works, each of which stemmed from his dissatisfaction with eighteenth-century French society, particularly the Parisian elite. In his prize-winning *Discourse on the Sciences and Arts*, his answer to the contest question, "Has the revival of sciences and arts contributed to improving morality?" was scathingly negative. Where Enlightenment intellectuals, scientists, and artists saw themselves as engaged in a rational project toward human progress, Rousseau saw decadence, corruption, hypocrisy, and a neglect of real human virtues and values. His comparative ideal was Spartan self-sacrifice, austerity, strength, and civic duty, at a time when outward appearance directly revealed inner character instead of being a mere façade:

> Now we see how luxury, licentiousness, and slavery have always been the punishment for the presumptuous efforts man has made to escape from blissful ignorance in which eternal Wisdom had placed us. . . . A taste for luxury and a taste for probity do not cohabit in the same souls.[54]

There was cause for hope in a few men who could surpass the greatness of Bacon, Descartes, and Newton, but only if kings would but welcome "into their councils people who are most able to give them good advice" and realize that enlightening nations is more difficult than governing them.[55]

In his *Discourse on the Origin and Foundations of Inequality among Mankind,* Rousseau posited stages in human history, beginning with solitary life in the state of nature, followed by happy family life and limited exchange. The discoveries of agriculture and metallurgy then led to the institution of private property. "The first man, who after enclosing a piece of ground, took it into his head to say, *this is mine,* and found people simple enough to believe him, was the real founder of civil society."[56] People distorted their healthy self-love into pride based on how others regarded them. Competition, appropriation by the rich, and unjust social divisions made life sufficiently unbearable so that one rich person offered everyone else a social contract. Freedom would be exchanged for security, peace, and justice. The result was enslavement of the people to the ruler, motivated by personal ambition, desire for luxury, vanity, and fear of the opinions of others. Leadership became increasingly corrupt, resulting in despotism, with the people less free, more miserable, and again solitary. Revolution is not only inevitable in such a situation, but not unjust:

> The insurrection, which ends in the death or deposition of a sultan, is as juridical an act as any by which the day before he disposed of the lives and fortunes of his subjects. Force alone upheld him, force alone overturns him. Thus all things take place and succeed in their natural order; and whatever may be the result of these hasty and frequent revolutions, no one man has reason to complain of another's injustice, but only of his own indiscretion or bad fortune.[57]

In the *Social Contract,* after dismissing the legitimacy of government based on natural right or force, Rousseau accepts convention as its foundation. Unlike other social contract theorists, he argues that any exchange of freedom for peace or prosperity is likely to benefit the ruler at the people's expense. Beyond these pragmatics, freedom is an absolute value:

> To renounce one's liberty is to renounce one's essence as a human being, the rights and also the duties of humanity. For the person who renounces everything there is no possible compensation. Such a renunciation is incompatible with human nature, for to take away all freedom from one's will is to take away all morality from one's actions.[58]

Before a people can give itself to a king, it must become a people, an act which is "the real foundation of the society."[59] Because people in the state of nature need to cooperate for survival, they form a contract consisting of "the total alienation to the whole community of each associate with all his rights."[60] This results in a perfect union. "Each of us puts in common his person and all his power under the supreme direction of the general will; and in return each member becomes an indivisible part of the whole."[61] The resulting public person is the sovereign, or state, which cannot do anything to violate how it was formed, submit to another sovereign, or act contrary to the interests of its parts.[62]

Rousseau thus posits a communitarian nation-state. The property of its members belongs to their sovereign to re-allot as private property.[63] (This is a marked departure from both Hobbes and Locke: Hobbes did not think that there could be property before the state; Locke believed that the state merely preserved preexisting property rights.) Other rights, such as the right to one's own life, may be determined by the sovereign, and both censorship and a civic religion may be imposed. "Whoever refuses to obey the general will shall be constrained to do so by the whole body: which means nothing else than that he shall be forced to be free."[64] The general will is always right but the will of the people can err; the expression of the general will depends on the legislator, but his particular will is tested by the votes of the people.[65] However, the executive power concerns particular acts "not within the province of the law," and this power is carried out by the prince or government on a "commission" from the sovereign, although "sooner or later the prince oppresses the sovereign and violates the social treaty."[66]

In striking contrast to Rousseau, Hume's treatment of social contract theory in book 3 of *A Treatise of Human Nature* is neither motivated by dissatisfaction nor does it embrace abstract ideals. Hume's account is comfortable, historical, subtle, and reductively empirical. Justice is a necessary virtue, which like all virtues must have a motive that is distinct from a sense of obligation to practice the virtue: "no action can be virtuous, or morally good, unless there be in human nature some motive to produce it, distinct from the sense of its morality."[67] There are no universal human motives of justice, so justice is not a natural but an artificial virtue. In nature, men require the assistance of others for bare survival through conjunction of forces, division of labor, and mutual assistance. Society is therefore beneficial, but men do not know this. Instead, they are motivated by sexual desire to form the societies of families. Families require movable goods, but movable goods are insecure, there is a scarcity of them, and people are not generous to strangers. The remedy is a promise: "I observe, that it will be for my interest to leave another in the possession of his goods, *provided* he will act in the same manner with regard to me."[68] A convention of the stability of possessions gradually arises (as does human language and the use of money). With this convention come ideas of justice, property, right, and obligation.[69] "'Tis only from the selfishness and confin'd generosity of men, along with the scanty provision nature has made for his wants, that justice derives its origins."[70] Because men come to view society as beneficial, they are not only willing to submit to its rules, but develop a sympathy with public interest that is the source of the moral approbation attending the virtue of justice.[71]

According to Hume, property is caused by the relation, external to an object, of occupation or first possession. This relation gives rise to duties to abstain from the object, which are "properly what we call justice."[72] Justice as a principle that orders society is often difficult for individuals with immediate interests to follow. Therefore, its administration is placed in the hands of those making up the government, for whom justice is their immediate interest. That is the origin of government. Magistrates also have an immediate interest in the interest of any considerable part of their subjects and are able to promote that interest by public works, and that is the benefit of government.[73] Moreover, as Hume wrote in his *Essays Moral, Political, and Literary*, security of property enables commerce, which contributes to collective greatness:

> The greatness of a state, and the happiness of its subjects, how independent soever they may be supposed in some respects, are commonly allowed to be inseparable with regard to commerce; and as private men receive greater security in the possession of their trade and riches, from the power of the public, so the public becomes powerful in proportion to the opulence and extensive commerce of private men.[74]

F. A. Hayek observes that Hume's contribution to the Enlightenment in political and legal theory was distinctively British in its emphasis on the importance of the historical development of liberal legal institutions.[75] However, unlike other social contract theorists (to the extent that he can be included in that tradition), Hume characterized these institutions as "advantageous to the public though . . . not intended for that purpose by the inventors."[76] Hayek notes that Hume's insight about societal institutions predates Darwinian evolutionary accounts of the development of living things. Long periods of intense struggle for survival reach a stage of development that is conducive to functioning in a certain environment.[77] Hume, like his friend Adam Smith, wrote at a time when Britain was liberal and prosperous. Both could support the freedom of the marketplace, although Hume, more than Smith, would have recognized that the "unseen hand" was a fiction and that changes in circumstances could alter the goodness of the effects of social evolution.

Hume and Rousseau represented extremes of planning and the lack of planning in a transition from moral principles to legal principles. The main difference between them was that Rousseau's descriptions of society were normative, and Hume's, like Aristotle's, descriptive. The danger ensuing from Rousseau's ideas was the French Revolution and Robespierre's reign of terror. Based on Rousseau's *Social Contract*, Robespierre appointed himself the ultimate authority on the general will. He was killed and replaced by the Thermidorians, Rousseau's next legitimate heirs, who could not agree on what the general will was.[78] (Of course, Rousseau's support of revolutionary democracy can be discerned in less horrendous liberatory efforts, and as chapters 7 and 8 will show, his claims about human freedom and equality inspired moral philosophers who would have repudiated his view of the social contract and the nation-state issuing from it.) Hume's confidence in the justice of British institutions was contemporaneous with the British colonial role in the African slave trade,[79] and his influences can be discerned in the theory of capitalism as well as nineteenth-century social evolutionary (e.g., social Darwinian) justifications for its injustices. That broad speculations such as the foregoing are plausible is consistent with the conclusion that neither Rousseau nor Hume has clear implications for a just and egalitarian ethics.

EQUALITY AND FREEDOM

The idea that governments are for the benefit of those governed and not for the benefit of rulers was an important democratic insight of all the social contract theorists. The problem is that this premise leaves out how governments may behave toward those they do not govern, especially noncitizens, or those who do not fully participate in civil life. Thus, an ideal of beneficial government is not the same thing as an ideal of universally beneficial government. The idea that all who will be governed are equal is another important democratic insight but more needs to be said about what it is that makes them equal, and what is said has to take ideals of freedom into account or else the result could be oppressive government. These problems will be pursued in chapter 7, "Deontology, Utilitarianism, and Rights."

The great innovation of social contract theory was the idea that government could be created according to ethical principles rather than conquest or the overwhelming use of force, even though, as we have seen, theorists differ on how legitimate government should be created. Any new government or revision of an existing one is likely to proceed from situations in which all are not equal materially and socially. This was Rawls's insight and he was enough of a realist about power not to require the creation of complete equality by foundings or revisions of government. A utopian theorist might insist on complete equality, but even if a starting or reset condition of complete equality could be achieved, luck alone would result in inequality over time. However, realists and utopians alike who are committed to an ideal of equality (in some sense) would accept Rawls's difference principle. I'm going to add a revised version of it now as a requirement for an ethics of race.

(9) New governments or revisions of existing governments should not intentionally cause those who are disadvantaged to become worse off, either in material well-being or civil status; if the disadvantaged do become worse off as the result of government founding or revision, those actions should be revised.

The three-fifths person rule, applying to how slaves were to be counted relative to free men, entails that the US Constitution, as a founding document, violated such a Rawlsian difference principle, even though, or because, issues of taxation and state representation were at the forefront of discussion and not either the status of slaves or the institution of slavery.[80] It was not merely the fractional counting rule that rendered those disadvantaged worse off (because they counted for less and were to have less political power and status than those counted as full units), but that a sovereign nation-state was founded in which the institution of slavery was included as a legitimate institution that could be taken into account in deciding how to count the population for the purposes of representative democracy. The legitimacy of slavery was a subject of debate in Europe before the American Revolution, and Northern US states outlawed slavery, as did Canada, in the early 1800s. The recognition of slavery as legitimate in the US Constitution was a virtually uncontested victory for the proslavery side of that debate, mainly because abolitionary voices were dispersed and weak in political debate during the founding process.[81] Although in his first draft of the Declaration of Independence Thomas Jefferson included a condemnation of King George III for his support of the African slave trade, the Continental Congress omitted it from the Declaration. And although the Pennsylvania Abolition Society asked Benjamin Franklin, its president, to deliver a memorial urging the Constitutional Convention to abolish the African slave trade, Franklin said nothing about slavery as a delegate.[82]

There are at least three distinct issues in considering the ethics of the three-fifths rule: that some will count for less than others, that slaves will be those who count for less than others, that slavery is a practice that is worthy of legalization by its acceptance in a new nation-state. Those who were enslaved during the colonial period were worse off after they became slaves according to the US Constitution, because their enslavement was extended from accepted facts of ownership to a legal institution in a new sovereign state. If ratification of the US Constitution was the social contract for the passage of Americans from a state of nature to civil society, then uncontested slave ownership was thereby naturalized along with other rights.

NOTES

1. Otto Gierke, *Natural Law and the Theory of Society 1500–1800*, trans. Ernest Barker (London: Cambridge University Press, 1934), 35–36.

2. Gierke, *Natural Law and the Theory of Society*, 36–42.

3. Gierke, *Natural Law and the Theory of Society*, 86.

4. One could argue that Plato and Aristotle set the precedent for this maneuver. Plato began his description of the ideal society by imagining simple conditions of collective human life and then asking what would be the best way to organize a more complex society. Aristotle simply assumed that city-states had naturally resulted from historical developments of smaller associations, such as the household and village. But Plato did not claim to derive his ideals of the republic from its simpler antecedents and Aristotle was not advocating a new form of government that would be radically different from what had already developed.

5. John Rawls, *A Theory of Justice* (Cambridge, MA: Harvard University Press, 1971). Rawls's social contract roots are sometimes neglected, but he writes, "My aim is to present a conception of justice which generalizes and carries to a higher level of abstraction the familiar theory of the social contract as found, say, in Locke, Rousseau, and Kant" (11).

6. Rawls, *Theory of Justice*, 8.

7. John Rawls, *The Law of Peoples* (Cambridge, MA: Harvard University Press, 1999).

8. See the account of Hobbes' contemporary in John Aubrey, *Brief Lives, Chiefly of Contemporaries, set down by John Aubrey, between the years 1669 and 1696*, ed. Andrew Clark, 2 vols. (Oxford: Clarendon Press, 1898, 322–401, facsimile available at books .google.com (consulted June 2010).

9. See "Hobbes Verse Autobiography," in Thomas Hobbes, *Leviathan*, ed. Edwin Curley (Indianapolis, IN: Hackett, 1994), line 27, liv.

10. Thomas Hobbes, *De Cive*, ed. Bernard Gert (Indianapolis, IN: Hackett, 1991), 93.

11. Hobbes, *De Cive*, ch. 1, 113.

12. Hobbes, *Leviathan*, 74–76 (XIII, 1–8). This natural condition without government may very well have been England itself, as Hobbes, during the 1630s from the safe distance of Paris, reflected on the turmoil that included the assassination of Charles I. See R. S. Peters, "Hobbes," s.v., in *The Encyclopedia of Philosophy*, ed. Paul Edwards (New York: Macmillan, 1967), 4: 33.

13. Hobbes, *Leviathan*, 76 (XIII, 8).

14. Hobbes, *Leviathan*, 76 (XIII, 9).

15. Hobbes, *Leviathan*, 78 (XIII, 13, 14).

16. Hobbes, *Leviathan*, 70 (XIV, 1–3).

17. Hobbes, *Leviathan*, 71 (XIV, 4).

18. Hobbes, *Leviathan*, 82 (XIV, 8, 9).

19. Hobbes, *Leviathan*, 83–100 (XIV, 10, XV).

20. Hobbes, *Leviathan*, 108 (XVII, 2).

21. Hobbes, *Leviathan*, 109 (XVII, 13).

22. Hobbes, *Leviathan*, 100–17 (XVIII).

23. Curley finesses this point in his introduction to the *Leviathan* by claiming that only a minority need agree to serve the sovereign as his "enforcers." But this would turn the rule of the sovereign into a form of conquest over the majority of the population. Curley also notes that in his review and conclusion to *Leviathan*, Hobbes claims that most governments are founded by conquest and concludes that the origin of sovereignty is

less important than its power. (See Hobbes, *Leviathan*, 34, in reference to "Review and Conclusion," 8, which is found on 491–92.) However, if we are to take social contract seriously as requiring the consent of those governed, then if the sovereign rules by internal conquest or widescale conquest from without, the sovereignty in question is not legitimate.

24. Hobbes, *Leviathan*, 101 (XVI, 1, 2).

25. Hobbes, *Leviathan*, 104 (XVI, 13, 14).

26. Rawls, *Theory of Justice*, 3, 11n4.

27. Rawls, *Theory of Justice*, 2, 9.

28. Rawls, *Theory of Justice*, 1, 5.

29. Rawls, *Theory of Justice*, 3, 12.

30. Rawls, *Theory of Justice*, 3, 11.

31. Rawls, *Theory of Justice*, 11, 60–61.

32. Rawls, *Theory of Justice*, 13, 76.

33. Rawls, *Theory of Justice*, 20, 48–51.

34. Charles Mills in Carole Pateman and Charles W. Mills, *Contract and Domination* (Malden, MA: Polity Press, 2007), 106–33.

35. See Naomi Zack, "*Contract and Domination*, Carole Pateman and Charles Mills," *Ethnic and Racial Studies* 32, no. 8 (November 2008): 1506–7.

36. Hobbes, *Leviathan*, XIII, 1, p. 74.

37. John Locke, *Second Treatise*, in *Two Treatises of Government*, ed. Peter Laslett (Cambridge: Cambridge University Press, 1991), 271 (II, S. 6).

38. Locke, *Second Treatise*, 280 (III, S. 19).

39. Locke, *Second Treatise*, 282 (III, S. 21).

40. Locke, *Second Treatise*, 286 (V, S. 26).

41. Locke, *Second Treatise*, 290 (V, S. 32), 296 (V, S. 36).

42. Locke, *Second Treatise*, 288 S. (V, S. 27) and 291 (V, S. 33), p. 288 and 291.

43. Locke, *Second Treatise*, 291 (V, S. V, 33), p. 291.

44. Locke, *Second Treatise*, 324 (VIII, S. 87).

45. Hobbes, *Leviathan*, 77 (XIII, 11).

46. Locke, *Second Treatise*, V, S. 47, pp. 299–300.

47. Locke, *Second Treatise*, 299–300 (V, S. 47). Locke, *Second Treatise*, 301 (V, S. 49).

48. Locke treats money as a commodity, the price of which is relative to interest rates that are like rent paid for land, in *Some Considerations of the Consequences of the Lowering of Interest and Raising the Value of Money* and *Further Considerations concerning Raising the Value of Money Wherein Mr. Lowndes's Arguments for it concerning an Essay for the Amendment of the Silver Coins, are particularly Examined, 1865*, both in John Locke, *Locke on Money*, ed. Patrick Hyde Kelly (Oxford: Oxford Clarendon Press, 1991). For comparison of Locke's commodity view of money with his precious-objects and exchange-function views of it, see Naomi Zack, "Lockean Money, Indigenism and Globalism," in *Civilization and Oppression*, ed. Catherine Wilson, supplementary volume 25 of *Canadian Journal of Philosophy* (1999): 31–54.

49. Locke, *Second Treatise*, 300 (V, S. 46).

50. Locke, *Second Treatise*, 300 (V, S. 46).

51. Locke, *Second Treatise*, 301 (V, S. 48).

52. Locke, *Second Treatise*, 299 (V, S. 45).

53. See Carole Pateman, "The Settler Contract," in *Contract and Domination*, by Carole Pateman and Charles W. Mills (Malden, MA: Polity Press, 2007), 35–78. Pateman discusses the importance Locke placed on money on p. 52.

54. Rousseau, *Discourse on the Sciences and Arts*, in *The Social Contract and the First and Second Discourses*, by Jean-Jacques Rousseau, ed. Susan Dunn (New Haven, CT: Yale University Press, 2002), 43–68, quotes 55 and 59.

55. Rousseau, *Discourse on the Sciences and Arts*, 66.

56. Rousseau, *Discourse on the Origin and Foundations of Inequality among Mankind*, in *The Social Contract and the First and Second Discourses*, by Jean-Jacques Rousseau, ed. Susan Dunn (New Haven, CT: Yale University Press, 2002), Part II, p. 113.

57. Rousseau, *Discourse on the Origin and Foundations of Inequality*, 136.

58. Jean-Jacques Rousseau, *The Social Contract and the First and Second Discourses*, ed. Susan Dunn (New Haven, CT: Yale University Press, 2002), 159 (book I, ch. IV).

59. Rousseau, *Social Contract*, 162 (ch. V).

60. Rousseau, *Social Contract*, 163 (ch. VI).

61. Rousseau, *Social Contract*, 164.

62. Rousseau, *Social Contract*, 165–66 (ch. VII).

63. Rousseau, *Social Contract*, 167–69 (ch. VIII).

64. See Rousseau, *Social Contract*, 166 (ch. VIII), for the "forced to be free" quote, and 244–54 (book III, chs. VII and VIII), for Rousseau's provisions for censorship and a civil religion.

65. See Rousseau, *Social Contract*, 170–82 (book II, chs. I–VII).

66. Rousseau, *Social Contract*, 193–94 (book III, ch. I). See p. 214 (ch. X) for "sooner or later."

67. David Hume, *A Treatise of Human Nature*, ed. L. A. Selby-Bigge (London: Oxford University Press, 1964), Bk. III, Part II, S. I, p. 479.

68. Hume, *Treatise of Human Nature*, 490 (S. II).

69. Hume, *Treatise of Human Nature*, 490–91.

70. Hume, *Treatise of Human Nature*, 495.

71. Hume, *Treatise of Human Nature*, 499–500.

72. Hume, *Treatise of Human Nature*, 527 (S. VI).

73. Hume, *Treatise of Human Nature*, 538–39 (S. VII).

74. David Hume, "Of Commerce," in *Essays Moral, Political, and Literary*, ed. Stuart D. Warner and Donald W. Livingston (Indianapolis, IN: Hackett, 1994), 220–21 (essay VII).

75. F. A. Hayek, "The Legal and Political Philosophy of David Hume," in *Hume*, ed. C. V. Chappell (New York: Doubleday, 1966), 335–60.

76. Quoted by Hayek, "Legal and Political Philosophy of David Hume," 344, from *The Philosophical Works of David Hume*, ed. T. H. Green and T. H. Grose, 4 vols. (London, 1874–1875), 2: 235, and at Hume, *A Treatise of Human Nature*, 529 (book III, part II, S. VI).

77. Hayek draws a parallel between Hume's idea of liberal institutions and his description of apparent design in nature in *Dialogues concerning Natural Religion*, and he claims a line of transmission through Charles Darwin's grandfather, who was strongly

influenced by Hume's ideas. See Hayek, "Legal and Political Philosophy of David Hume," 356–57.

78. On Rousseau's immediate political influence, see Conor Cruise O'Brien, "Rousseau, Robespierre, Burke, Jefferson, and the French Revolution," in *The Social Contract and the First and Second Discourses*, by Jean-Jacques Rousseau, ed. Susan Dunn (New Haven, CT: Yale University Press, 2002), 301–15.

79. On the inability of common law to effectively deal with colonial slavery, see Seymour Drescher, *Abolition: A History of Slavery and Antislavery* (Cambridge: Cambridge University Press, 2009), 78–79, 96–101.

80. Slave-owning states would have favored counting slaves for less for purposes of taxation and equally for representation. The three-fifths rule was a compromise on the taxation issue that was adopted for the representation issue. See Drescher, *Abolition*, 130–31.

81. For an overview of the slavery debate in Europe during the late eighteenth century, see Mary C. Jacob, *The Enlightenment: A Brief History with Documents* (Boston: Bedford/St. Martin's, 2001), 62–68. For the ways in which the slavery debate became shaped by the politics of the American Revolution, see Drescher, *Abolition*, 115–46.

82. Drescher, *Abolition*, see p. 124 and p. 132 for the references to Jefferson and Franklin.

• 7 •

Deontology, Utilitarianism, and Rights

It is clear by now that a significant number of key figures in the history of moral philosophy have had little interest in universal human equality. Despite this, from its critical perspective the present inquiry has thus far been successful. The difference between ethics and mores has been retrieved from the history of philosophy, beginning with Plato's and Aristotle's inventions of ethics. A focus on the compatibility with inequality of cosmopolitanism, ancient natural law, and Christianity has generated a number of compelling requirements for an ethics of race. Even with the relatively new idea of equality across humanity as an avowedly important presumption, early modern social contract theorists continued with the philosophical tradition of accepting slavery. (Had seventeenth-century social contract theorists been egalitarian across humanity in greater depth than rhetoric, race-based slavery would have been ruled out on a more general prohibition of slavery.)

HOW RAWLS AND ROUSSEAU MAY FALL SHORT

Rawls and his followers are well known to have assumed that all members of well ordered societies, that is, ideal societies, will be guaranteed the minimal goods for both survival and the ability to choose further goods. However, Rawls's acceptance of unequal distribution is disappointing in the context of global conditions of poverty that make human life materially dysfunctional to an extent that precludes work, creativity, sociality, and personal and civil respect. The global face of poverty is nonwhite. In terms of an ethics of race, global disadvantage cannot be avoided. Racial categories purport to be universal and are generally applied across national borders (even though specific racial

137

taxonomies may be culturally and geographically relative). Besides internal taxonomies of race, members of societies with salient racial taxonomies tend to apply them to other nations, so that even if members of a culture do not see themselves in racial terms, their racial perception by those outside with whom they have trade, depend on for aid, or are in conflict, are important. Projections of privileged racial identities may go hand in hand with projections of devalued ones, for example in immigration policies that favor whites.

A minimum condition of material well-being seems to be a requirement for many nonmaterial minimal goods.[1] But, if we look closer at this, it is evident that a global "social minimum" which goes beyond issues of material distributive justice has to do not with universal human dignity in any grounding moral sense, but with recognition of that dignity. The extreme poor and unfortunate can be and frequently are helped by charitable or humanitarian measures that do not recognize their dignity. Still, the dignity of the extreme poor can be respected independently of material assistance. Furthermore, there are conditions of economic exploitation, low status, and poverty that may deprive some groups of moral respect from other groups, within the best candidates for those Rawlsian well-ordered societies, where justice can be conceived as fairness. The combination of global unfairness, the possibility of universal human dignity, and recalcitrant injustice within rich democratic nations suggests that the Rawlsian conception of justice as fairness, with reasonable unequal distribution, is a complacent ideal, likely to inspire only those who are already treated fairly and have material ease. Missing from the Rawlsian ideal is the notion of universal moral respect.

Moral respect is the recognition of another as a being with intrinsic value to whom certain things may not be done. When members of some groups are deprived of moral respect, members of groups that are not so deprived have less moral restraint in harming them or refusing to help them. This was the situation of African Americans before the civil rights movements and it is the present moral condition in the United States of undocumented immigrants from Mexico (as of this writing in June 2010). Racial segregation and exclusion of African Americans from goods and opportunities enjoyed by whites, together with unjust violence against them, over generations, constituted and resulted in a deficit of moral respect for members of that group. Because undocumented immigrants do not have the full civil rights of citizens or legal residents and are not ethnically white, their lower legal and racial status evokes abusive and exploitative behavior that is both morally wrong and largely unrecognized as such; violation of their international legal rights incurs neither censure nor punishment. Undocumented immigrants are denied moral respect.

Insofar as the lack of moral respect as an ongoing condition of life is accepted as an initial condition of inequality from which Rawls's conception of justice as fairness could proceed, it is difficult to see how the situation could be corrected by any measure of fairness—or even by distributive justice according to implementations of some social minimum.[2] What is required, first, is a conception of justice as *moral* human equality.

Rousseau was an exception to the social contract neglect of an ideal of moral equality in the real world. His chapter on slavery in the *Social Contract* introduces an absolute ideal of moral equality that is an important intervention for the exclusionary nature of the entire social contract tradition. Still, it is not clear what "man was born free" means literally, as Rousseau knew that some people were born into slavery when he wrote it and that all infants have neither liberty nor freedom. Rousseau uses "man was born free" to emphasize the artificial nature of human nature under bondage. He writes of Aristotle's idea that some are natural slaves, "he mistook the effect for the cause," thereby implying that no human beings are born with or inherit the traits of slaves and that such traits are therefore artificial or imposed by society.[3]

If no one should be enslaved, then everyone is entitled to freedom as a condition that requires valid reasons to remove. Rousseau's idea of universal moral freedom is implied in his critique of Grotius' just war theory justification of slavery (the theory also used by Locke). Rousseau claims that war is not a relation between human individuals but between states, so that soldiers fulfill a special role distinct from their roles as citizens. Human rights are prior to the rights of rulers, soldiers, and citizens, so justice requires that civilians not be killed. The so-called right of conquest is only the might-makes-right law of the stronger party and it does not confer the right to kill civilians. If civilians may not be killed, then they may not be enslaved as an alternative to being killed. It is nonsense to suggest that the slave agrees to obey in exchange for being spared his or her life:

> These words, *slavery* and *right* are contradictory and mutually exclusive. Whether spoken by a man to a man, or by a man to a nation, such speech as this will always be equally aberrant: "I make an agreement with you wholly at your expense and wholly for my benefit, and I shall observe it as long as I please, while you also shall observe it as long as I please."[4]

Rousseau is here assuming that a natural condition of human freedom is the basis of a right to remain free. It is also a natural right of all human beings that they not be killed. Therefore, enslavement has no justification as an alternative to killing. (That no one can agree to be a slave because it has no advantages for which the person facing slavery can contract is another issue, relating to promises and contracts.)

Why, if there is a natural right to remain free, doesn't Rousseau assert that enslavement is absolutely wrong? It seems that for Rousseau, the right not to be killed is a more fundamental right than the right to be free, so that the right to remain free could be given up in appropriate circumstances to save one's life. But the right not to be killed is still not an absolute right, according to Rousseau. First, the foregoing passage implies that although civilians may not justifiably or legally be killed in war, soldiers, qua soldiers, do not have the same right. Second, under the social contract, each member of society is prepared to give up that right should it be required by the general will: "Now, the citizen is not a judge of the peril to which the law requires that he expose himself; and when the prince has said to him, 'It is expedient for the State that you should die,' he ought to die."[5] Thus, Rousseau starts from a principle of equality and an assertion of rights that support moral equality—like Hobbes, he is not unfair—but his idea of the general will compromises individual *moral authority*. This is because the sovereign is the ultimate moral authority as the representative of the general will, and he or they can override every individual's will.

MORAL AUTHORITY AND KANT

Moral authority is the ability to act. It encompasses what subjects who have dignity are able to do and it is a consequence of dignity that connects with material conditions. Moral authority in this sense is at stake in the way that Rawls's conception of justice as fairness, together with his difference principle, fails to address the conditions of the deeply disadvantaged. Moral authority, as effective moral standing that can generate rights and corresponding obligations on the part of others, itself has certain requirements—some absolute, others relative. In an absolute sense, control over the basic wherewithal to plan one's life is part of moral authority and that capacity usually requires some security concerning the material necessities for biological survival. In a relative sense, moral authority would require having enough social status to be recognized as a bearer of rights. Members of minority racial groups in racist societies may have absolute minimal life-sustaining material requirements for moral authority, but the contempt of dominant group members toward them would diminish their overall relative moral authority. It is moral authority, and not dignity as the ground for justice as fairness, that directly leads to consideration of the *social minimum* (of bare requirements for survival in society). But such consideration is distinct from material values, distributive justice, or utilitarian maximizations.[6] There is now a tenth requirement for an ethics of race:

> (10) Human equality must include an equality of moral authority. This may require redistribution of material and social resources so that the disadvantaged can be recognized as moral equals by the advantaged.

Returning now to the discussion of Charles Mills's critique of Rawls in chapter 6, the idea of dignity motivates a Rawlsian conception of justice as fairness. Reparations for past racial injustice in racist societies is too specific an option for deliberation behind the veil of ignorance because it would lead to too many group candidates for reparations and constitute too radical a reorientation of the social order, from facing the future to trying to correct the past. What can be done behind the veil is to emphasize the moral authority of all participants equally so that deliberation about distributive justice might include reparations when the veil is removed.

For philosophical understanding of egalitarian moral authority, it's now necessary to turn to Kant. Despite the intensely abstract and exclusive nature of Kant's moral system, it introduces a core idea of the moral subject, capable of supporting contemporary egalitarian rights doctrines. Because Kant is not primarily interested in the happiness of the human subject, utilitarianism's focus on happiness, together with its egalitarianism, offers a promising development for practical ethics beyond Kant. However, utilitarianism alone does not directly address deep inequalities, and it neglects equality of moral authority. Contemporary global moral perspectives therefore require a combination of Kantian deontology and utilitarianism or consequentialism. This combination has been expressed in twentieth-century human rights doctrines, centered on the United Nations Universal Declaration of Human Rights (1948). After considering Kantian deontology, this chapter proceeds to compare it with utilitiarianism, concluding with a brief examination of contemporary international rights doctrine.

KANTIAN DEONTOLOGY

The procedural emphasis on moral decisions to which classic Kantian "deontology" refers is not of primary importance for the nature of the moral subject who will have moral authority in an egalitarian totality of moral subjects. Even Kant's most ardent defenders recognize his excessive legalism and inflexibility concerning applications of "the moral law." His requirement that the moral subject be rational in the form of detached cognition exceeds requirements for effective goal-directed behavior (for animals, as well as humans). Nevertheless, we can look to Kant for a well-developed idea of the intrinsic value of human individuals and the fundamental requirement that they each be treated as ends rather than means. Despite his Eurocentrism, unfounded belief in human races, overt racism, and ultimately religious moral metaphysics,[7] Kant is the premier theorist of secular human dignity.

First, to make good on the claim that the cognitive emphasis in Kant's moral theory is untenable, neither Kant's restriction of moral worth to rational beings nor the cognitive burden he places on what may count as moral reasons accord with a principle of human equality or with what the majority of humanity would recognize as moral goodness. Morality for Kant is a matter of reason because "the only thing at all in the world, or even out of it, which can be regarded as good without qualification" is a *good will*, the development of which is the task of reason.[8] By "good will," Kant does not mean something like "benevolent intent" but a will that determines action in accordance with moral principle—the exercise of the will is *practical reason*. Kant's good will is a will that logically follows certain principles. A good will in Kant's sense results in actions that fulfill duties, where the fulfillment of duty is the primary motive, in an almost mechanical way. Motives in response to compulsion, for gain, or that are mere inclinations or desires do not count morally. Kant is here inverting Hume's claim (see chapter 6) that "no action can be virtuous, or morally good, unless there be in human nature some motive to produce it, distinct from the sense of its morality."[9]

Kant holds that although we have a duty to be beneficent and contribute to the joy of others, the pleasure that some naturally sympathetic people take in fulfilling that duty has no moral worth. Rather, the highest moral worth accords to those who help others with no desire and even an antipathy to charitable or philanthropic deeds. The moral worth of an action is dependent neither on the emotions associated with its intent nor on its success in achieving some end, but on the "principle of volition" according to which it has been done.[10] The action must be done as *duty*, which is "the necessity of an action done out of respect for the law."[11] Objectively, or from the perspective of others, the moral law determines the will; subjectively, the will is determined by the *maxim* of a person's action, which represents the law as a rational being's reason for action.[12]

The test for whether a maxim is in accord with the moral law is whether I can will it to become a universal law, which I cannot do if becoming a universal law would defeat it: "I should never act except in such a way that I can also will that my maxim should become a universal law." This is Kant's first formulation of the categorical imperative in *Grounding for the Metaphysics of Morals*. He gives as an example the self-destructive quality of willing that everyone should lie to get out of a difficult situation, because if everyone lied, no one would tell the truth and lies could serve no purpose insofar as their success depends on a widespread belief that almost everyone tells the truth.[13] Although the categorical imperative is in accord with ordinary practical reason, ordinary life is full of distractions in the form of needs, desires for happiness and pleasure, and interests, so it is necessary to develop a philosophical understanding of how practical reason is distinct from experience. The upshot of this is that morality is not a matter of experience:

In fact there is absolutely no possibility by means of experience to make out with complete certainty a single case in which the maxim of an action that may in other respects conform to duty has rested solely on moral grounds and on the representation of one's duty. . . . [W]e can never, even by the strictest examination, completely plumb the depths of the secret incentives of our actions. For when moral value is being considered, the concern is not with the actions, which are seen, but rather with their inner principles, which are not seen.[14]

Reason may command actions that have never before been taken, based on duty that is prior to all experience and "contained as duty in general in the idea of a reason that determines the will by means of a priori grounds."[15] Kant's meaning is overall quite clear: morality is the province of rational beings who are capable of using only their reason to act wholly from duty. Some philosophical assistance might be necessary to accomplish this use of reason and moral actions may have no desirable practical effects, but that is irrelevant because the moral worth of an action is wholly determinable only by its agent.

This preliminary venture into Kant's first two sections of *Grounding for the Metaphysics of Morals* is sufficient to establish the elitism of his moral theory in the necessity for rational calculation of the consistency of one's maxims, the cultivation of reason apart from emotion and interests, and the willingness (or necessity?) to forego happiness in order to have a good will. Although Kant frequently refers to ordinary experience for support of his valorization of a good will, he has made use of "good will" to mean something very different from uncalculated benevolence, which is its ordinary meaning.

If we are going to rely on ordinary intuitions and experience at the outset of moral theory—and I think that Kant is right that we should—the question is whether actions of benevolence done for self-interest or motivated by a sympathetic temperament or a good heart are morally worthless. I would be willing to bet that most people would think less morally, and not more, of a philanthropist who had no feeling for the objects of her charity and merely gave because she had figured out, by reflecting on what would happen if everyone did it, that it was the right thing to do. In the absence of data to support such a wager, suppose that more morally good actions are better than fewer. The sympathetic philanthropist is more likely to keep giving beyond what duty requires, because it is in her nature, whereas the purely dutiful philanthropist, who is only giving because of duty, may justifiably stop giving after what duty requires has been fulfilled. In general, as a practical matter, a person's moral temperament is more reliable than her a priori reasoning skills.

Also, contra Kant, and here returning to Hume, not only do we value good will as a form of temperament, but good will in that sense has greater moral worth than good will as rational calculation in accord with duty. Duty

remains important, from an external point of view and in Kant's own examples, as a subjective prod to action, but it is difficult to see how duty can accomplish anything beyond the bare minima of kindness, help, respect, civility,
and so forth. More good can be furthered in human relationships if people cultivate benevolent emotions toward one another than perform a priori rational
calculations in deliberate disconnection with experience. People can cultivate
such benevolence if they learn more about others, imagine themselves in their
circumstances, examine their own antipathies, and generally make efforts to
'understand' those toward whom they do not feel benevolence. Such practice would be especially relevant to instances of xenophobia, racism, classism,
misogyny, homophobia, and all of the other types of moral malfunction that
create a need for universal and egalitarian ethics. That we prefer the company
of those who behave well out of temperament, that such people are loved
compared to those who behave in the same way out of duty alone, is an important part of human moral life.

Kant's greatest contribution to egalitarianism, which precisely captures
the motivation for cultivating benevolence in the ordinary way, is his version
of the categorical imperative that is usually referred to as "the formula of the
end in itself,"[16] namely: "Act in such a way that you treat humanity, whether
in your own person or in the person of another, always at the same time as an
end and never simply as a means."[17] Kant's reasoning for this formula is that
rational nature is an end in itself because that is how a rational being regards
his own existence. Since every rational being thinks about its own existence in
the same way, this perspective is an objective principle from which "all laws
of the will must be able to be derived."

Suppose that not all who should have moral authority have developed
their rationality to the extent that they can competently reason with Kant's
first, universal-maxim version of the categorical imperative. Suppose further
that all human beings are rational, although not in Kant's sense that requires
detached, abstract reason, but instead, in having an awareness of self, combined
with goal-directed action or behavior. Such a broad description of rationality
would include children, the insane, the cognitively challenged, the unedu-
cated, and perhaps animals as well. Setting aside the rationality of animals—for
which there could be ethical systems with their own requirements—we are
left with an egalitarian and inclusive Kantian regard for human beings that
takes into account the value of their lives to themselves, as individuals.

Kant's religious metaphysics consists in postulating a duty beyond the
limits of our experience, which is our idea of God. This is the duty of religion,
whereby all of our duties are recognized as divine commands. However, we
do not have to be conscious of an idea of God in performing our duty. Instead,
the idea of God is created by us as an incentive for our conduct. He writes: "It

is a duty of man to himself to apply this idea, which offers itself unavoidably to reason, to the moral law within him."[18] If one does not agree with Kant about the a priori form of duty, the need for faith would not be necessary as an incentive for our conduct. Kant's idea of the intrinsic value of every human being thus allows for a purely secular appropriation.

Kant's prohibition against treating others as means is somewhat vague apart from his maxim formulation that translates this idea into a kingdom of ends, each member of which is autonomous in giving the moral law to itself while universally willing it independently of experience. It's as though Kant would draw his audience into synchronous, hidden, reflective abstract cognitive practices. But we don't have to follow him that far away from experience. The recognition of the value of each person's existence, which is more than biological life, is sufficient to generate a perspective of equality that can be shared and objectively observed in action. The equal moral authority of every human subject can be posited in a way that, contra Kant, is directly applicable to the empirical world. This generates an eleventh requirement for an ethics of race:

(11) Everyone should always act in such a way so that the intent and practical effect of the action, so far as one knows, supports every other human being's subjective valuation of his or her own life, or at least does not undermine it, with the possible exception of cases in which persons have acted and shown intent not to obey this principle.

UTILITARIANISM AND DEONTOLOGY COMPARED

When Kant applied his formula of the end in itself to meritorious duty to others, he noted that all have their own happiness as a natural end but that humanity could "subsist" if no one contributed to the happiness of others, provided it was not intentionally impaired. Given "humanity as an end in itself," he required that everyone should "strive as much as he can, to further the ends of others."[19] But, according to Kant, such striving need not result in the happiness of others to be meritorious, and it is not a categorical imperative. Neither is happiness good without qualification, according to Kant. For Bentham and Mill, pleasure or happiness is the ultimate unqualified good and striving for it, both for oneself and others, constitutes the major part of morality, with success in attaining it constituting the rest.

However, the most interesting point of comparison between Kantian deontology and utilitarianism or consequentialism lies in their perspectives on rights. Kant's formula of the end in itself that postulated an intrinsic value in all rational beings, forbidding use of them as means, defines the subjects of rights. However, that seems not to have been Kant's own understanding of the relation between the categorical imperative and rights. Kant holds that "the principle of duty to others" based on their intrinsic worth entails that "a transgressor of the rights of men intends to make use of the persons of others merely as a means, without taking into consideration that, as rational beings, they should always be esteemed at the same time as ends."[20] In a moral sense, obedience to human rights doctrines could be a maxim for Kant, but these would be legal rights. The moral rights of persons to be treated as ends are not necessary to postulate as rights in any fundamental moral sense because they are the effect of the categorical imperative rather than supreme moral principles on their own.

Kant claims in *Perpetual Peace* that insofar as morality is "a collection of absolutely binding laws by which our actions *ought* to be governed, that it belongs to the practical sphere."[21] Concerning the obligation of government in the matter or rights, he wrote:

> The rights of man must be held sacred, however great a sacrifice the ruling power may have to make. There can be no half measures here; it is no use devising hybrid solutions such as a pragmatically conditioned right halfway between right and utility. For all politics must bend the knee before right, although politics may hope in return to arrive, however slowly, at a stage of lasting brilliance.[22]

Without something like God-given natural law or Kant's self-sustaining theoretical moral structure of a kingdom of ends, the nature of moral rights, their normative force, and their very reality is mysterious. If there are universal human rights, then how is it possible that they are violated—legally under governments that do not recognize the rights of their citizens or residents, illegally in societies where legal rights are not enforced, and in legally amorphous situations such as refugee camps, prisons, and conditions of war?

Bentham was well aware of the mystery of moral rights. In *Anarchical Fallacies*, he plied his method of *paraphrasis*, a process of clarification whereby words are analyzed via the translation of a problematic sentence into one that makes sense, to the Declaration of the Rights of Man promulgated by the French National Assembly in 1789.[23] Bentham took strong issue with this document on its grounds of asserting universal rights rather than just the rights of French citizens. His vitriol has three targets: the political concept of human rights, the aboriginal inhabitants of Australia (inadvertently but tellingly), and the French (as compared to the English).

Bentham parses selected articles of the declaration to show first what they empirically imply, which he generally takes to be nonsense perpetrated to inflame the masses against government; he then shows how the right proclaimed in each case has an empirical and historical legal foundation in English society. The most offending articles and Bentham's objections are as follows. Article I: "*Men (all men) are born and remain free, and equal in respect of rights. Social distinctions cannot be founded, but upon common utility.*" Bentham points out that infants are not free, some are born slaves, rights from birth vary depending on social status, and status varies based on social and professional situations, such as madmen and their keepers, masters and apprentices.[24] Article 2: "*The end in view of every political association is the preservation of the natural and imprescriptible rights of man. These rights are liberty, property, security, and resistance to oppression.*" In response to this Bentham famously asserts: "That which has no existence cannot be destroyed—that which cannot be destroyed cannot require anything to preserve it from destruction. *Natural rights* is simple nonsense: natural and imprescriptible rights, rhetorical nonsense—nonsense upon stilts."[25] Bentham accuses the authors of the declaration of intending to incite war against all governments for failing to support fictional rights and claims that there are not even legal rights that are immune from change or repeal as circumstances change. Moreover, there never was a government that originated from a contract; rather, all governments have been founded by force and established by habit. As for the "imprescriptible" rights, unbounded liberty (as liberty is later defined in the declaration) only has meaning as rhetoric against all laws, for every law limits liberty in some way. The claim that every man has a right to property is self-contradictory because it means that everyone has a right to everyone else's property. The right to security thus stated would prevent government from keeping the peace, raising armies, and punishing criminals. Moreover, what are considered rights could be abrogated by future governments, and future citizens will have to decide whether to submit or resist. Bentham takes issue with article 4, which announces unbounded liberty for all, along the same lines. He criticizes article 10 for limiting free speech by stipulating that it not disturb the public order.[26]

Bentham thus insisted that "there are no such things as natural rights." All rights are created by government and are legal rights. The example he gave of the anarchy that he thought the French declaration could provoke was oddly not from the revolution in France, but from what he took to be the conditions of Australian aborigines before 1788:

We know that it is for men to live without government, for we see instances of such a way of life—we see it in many savage nations, or rather races of mankind; for instance, among the savages of New South Wales, whose way of living is so well known to us: no habit of obedience, and hence no government—no government, and thence no laws—no laws, and thence no such things as rights—no security—no property, liberty, as against regular control, the control of laws and government—perfect; but as against all irregular control, the mandates of stronger individuals' none. In this state, at a time earlier than the commencement of history—in this same state, judging from analogy, we, the inhabitants of the part of the globe we call Europe, were; no government, consequently no rights: no rights, consequently no property—no legal security—no legal liberty; security not more than belongs to beasts—forecast and sense of insecurity keener—consequently in point of happiness below the level of the brutal race.[27]

Here is what an official travel website has to say in 2010 about the inhabitants of New South Waales in the time frame relevant to what Bentham wrote.

At the time of British settlement at Sydney Cove it is estimated that 300,000 aboriginal people, speaking around 250 languages inhabited Australia. On arrival, finding no obvious political structure, the Europeans took the land as their own. The Indigenous people were driven out of their homes and many killed. Various new European diseases spread rapidly amongst the indigenous people, killing many. The introduction of feral and domestic animals contributed to the destruction of natural habitats. Fighting wiped out the Aboriginal population in Tasmania and greatly reduced the numbers in the rest of Australia.[28]

We can read the horrors between the lines of this sanitized account; the Australian government's recent efforts to apologize to indigenous groups and make reparations and effect reconciliations are well-known.[29] Bentham's uncharacteristic—and contradictory to what he has said before—reference to a Lockean state of nature is evident in his claim that indigenous non-European groups encountered in colonial projects are on a par with Europeans in prehistory. Morally, Bentham subscribed to something like the fictitious colonialist doctrine identified by Carole Pateman as *terra nullius* (see chapter 6). If Australian aborigines lacked rights, they also lacked security. To ascribe that deprivation to their normal condition of not being English, rather than to the English colonizers' behavior toward them, is similar to how, according to Rousseau, Aristotle mistook the effects of slavery for its cause.[30]

It is further surprising that Bentham is not so much Eurocentric as he is chauvinistic about English tradition compared to French. *Anarchical Fallacies* fulminates with anti-French insult: "shallow and reckless vanity," "the nerve of vanity in a French heart," "legislators turned into turkey cocks," "execrable trash [produced by] the choicest talents of the French nation," "French poisons," and so forth. He especially takes issue with the presumption of the French to insist, in article 16 of the declaration, that all legitimate governments must have constitutions, and he claims for England, where there is a long tradition of legal rights, any legitimate doctrine of rights,

It is in England, rather than in France, that the discovery of the rights of man ought naturally to have its rise: it is we—we English, that have the better *right* to it. It is in the English language that the transition is more natural, than perhaps in most others: at any rate, more so than in the French. . . . *Right*, the substantive *right* is the child of law: from *real* laws come *real* rights; but from *imaginary* laws, from laws of nature, fancied and invented by poets, rhetoricians, and dealers in moral and intellectual poisons, come *imaginary* rights, a bastard brood of monsters, "gorgons and chimaeras dire." And thus it is that from *legal rights*, the offspring of law, and friends of peace, come *anti-legal rights*, the mortal enemies of law, the subverters of government, and the assassins of security.[31]

John Stuart Mill developed a more sophisticated utilitarianism. Mill's distinction between higher and lower pleasures rendered Bentham a philistine, because of his neglect of character development and culture in equating physical pleasure with happiness.[32] However, as Thomas McCarthy has recently pointed out, if he did not share Bentham's distain for the original inhabitants of colonies in the British empire, Mill was politically and morally condescending to them. The lineage of that attitude passes through Bentham's friend James, John's father, who was an administrator and later chief examiner of the East India Company; John was also employed by the East India Company and became chief examiner at the end of his career. James had written about the prolongation of an English government in India: "Even the utmost abuse of European power is better, I am persuaded, than the most temperate exercise of Oriental despotism."[33] John Stuart Mill, in his introductory chapter to *On Liberty*, wrote that the principles he would therein espouse are "meant to apply only to human beings in the maturity of their faculties" and not to "those backward states of society in which the race itself may be considered in its nonage. . . . Despotism is a legitimate mode of government in dealing with barbarians, provided the end be their improvement and the means justified by actually effecting that end."[34] Mill's justification for such paternalism was, he thought, the general principle of utility, which required progress in all human institutions that had stagnated in custom.

Mill did not completely share Bentham's radically reductive legal positivism concerning rights because he set himself the task of showing how what are taken to be rights, in ways that may not always be expressed in law, can be explained in terms of their utility. He provided a utilitarian justification for legal rights such as security and property in chapter 5 of *Utilitarianism*, "Of the Connection of Justice with Utility." Mill's general task there was to show how the idea of justice could be reduced to utility. As a result of the philosophical analysis he undertook, Mill implicitly distinguished between his moral system and the received view of justice. For instance, Herbert Spencer had claimed, as an objection to utilitarianism, that it presupposes that everybody has an equal right to happiness. Mill's reply was, "[that] equal amounts of happiness are equally desirable, whether felt by the same or by different persons" *is* the principle of utility.[35]

Mill's awareness that utilitarianism was a moral doctrine—and as such progressively, critically normative regarding the existing political order—allowed him to acknowledge the existence of rights (as ultimately reducible to utility) as independent of positive law:

> All persons are deemed to have a *right* to equality of treatment, except when some recognized social expediency requires the reverse. And hence all social inequalities which have ceased to be considered expedient, assume the character not of simple inexpediency, but of injustice, and appear so tyrannical, that people are apt to wonder how they ever could have been tolerated; forgetful that they themselves perhaps tolerate other inequalities under an equally mistaken notion of expediency, the correction of which would make that which they approve seem quite as monstrous as what they condemn. The entire history of social improvement has been a series of transitions, by which one custom or institution after another, from being a supposed primary necessity of social existence, has passed into the rank of a universally stigmatized injustice and tyranny. So it has been with the distinctions of slaves and freemen, nobles and serfs, patricians and plebians; and so it will be, and in part already is, with the aristocracies of colour, race, and sex.[36]

Like Bentham, Mill does not think that rights are 'imprescriptible,' but unlike Bentham he is progressively looking ahead to expansions of rights rather than to their possible repeal. In sum, the circumscription of rights to the British by Bentham and the social and political relativity of rights by Mill render both more attentive to mores than to a universal ethics. As a result, neither was prepared to rigorously extend principles of utility to all human beings in their historical times. Before moving on to twentieth-century universal rights doctrine, a twelfth requirement for an ethics of race is suggested by this section.

> (12) An ethics of race ought not to privilege the mores, including the legal system, of any particular nation(s); no one should be excluded from an ethics of race based on national, geographical, or historical contingencies.

INTERNATIONAL RIGHTS DOCTRINES, RACE, AND MORAL EQUALITY

Philosophically, the issue of what human rights are runs deeper than a distinction between ethics and mores. As Bentham was aware, in some nation-states, governments are committed and obligated to guarantee their citizens certain protections that correspond to the rights proclaimed in the French Declaration of the Rights of Man, and those governments fulfill their commitments and obligations. In other parts of the world, rights may be promised by governments, but the governments do not keep their promises or the governments promise less and do less. There are also societies in which human rights are protected without explicit government guarantees and, of course, societies without governments that do or do not protect rights.

We should distinguish between international human rights and universal human rights. International human rights are protected by positive laws and practices within nations on earth. The term 'universal human rights' could mean moral rights applying to all human beings, could refer to a future state in which international human rights exist in every nation, or could be legal rights in international law that are limited to the nations that have endorsed and obey international law. H. L. A. Hart argues that international law is not only, or merely, a system of morality, for the reason that it cannot be reduced to "orders backed up by threats," because there are practices such as etiquette, games, and the fundamental provisions of constitutional law that share this failure in reduction, and none of those practices are moral practices. Nations, in abiding the decisions of international law, including the rulings of international courts that have no legal jurisdiction, may pride themselves on acting morally, but this does not mean that the law(s) they are obeying are moral laws. Furthermore, international law can be legislated and morality cannot.[37]

Another support for Hart's claim that international law is not only, or merely, morality, but a distinct form of law in its own right that resembles municipal or national law, is that the diversities of people who have contributed to international law seem to have done so more in a legalistic way than in an enterprise of constructing an agreed-upon moral code—international law is a matter of negotiation.[38] As a system of law, international law could be criticized, supported, or constructed on moral grounds that were distinct from the international legal system, as well as from the perspective of sovereign national interests. If international law is law, then international human rights are legal human rights, despite their irreducibility to "orders backed up by threats."

Consideration of international human rights doctrine or its documents, in terms of requirements for an ethics of race, specifically 11 and 12, requiring equal moral authority for all human beings irrespective of history or place, is an exercise in moral theory. Requirements 11 and 12, like requirements 1 through 10, are formally race general. Although they are intended to be specifically relevant to human racial history, they do not mention specific races. Race-neutral language would not mention race at all. That has been the predominant language in the history of Western ethics and political philosophy, which, as we have seen, is compatible with oppression and discrimination on the grounds of race. In an ideal world, universal human equality could be proclaimed in race-neutral language, but since that has not worked to create even an awareness of universal human equality, much less its reality, the next liberatory step is race-general language. The use of race-general language in contemporary moral theory preserves the universality of the subject and addresses issues of race in more general terms that pertain to other aspects of human equality as well. That way, the egalitarian issues of race are embedded in a broad foundation and not merely inserted as "special interests," with the potential to relegate an ethics of race to mores. That way, to borrow from Emerson, the chain holding the slave is fastened around the master's neck.

Race-neutral language doesn't mention race. Race-general language mentions race but does not specify which racial identities are at issue. Race-specific language directly refers to concrete racial groups, for instance, African Americans. However, the conceptual terrain is more complicated than neat divisions among race-neutral, race-general, and race-specific language. The use of race-neutral language that is intended to be egalitarian concerning racial difference has dominated the highest official liberatory efforts in American history. Consider the Thirteenth Amendment to the US Constitution:

> SECTION 1. Neither slavery nor involuntary servitude, except as a punishment for crime whereof the party shall have been duly convicted, shall exist within the United States, or any place subject to their jurisdiction.

Although the language here is race-neutral, its intent in historical context was to free African American slaves and abolish racial slavery, so it was also both race-general and race-specific. Consider, now, section 2 of the Voting Rights Act of 1965:

> SEC. 2. No voting qualification or prerequisite to voting, or standard, practice, or procedure shall be imposed or applied by any State or political subdivision to deny or abridge the right of any citizen of the United States to vote on account of race or color.

This is race-general language, but again, its intent was race-specific in a historical context where African Americans had been prevented from voting by literacy and knowledge requirements in the US South. Finally, consider these excerpts from the state of Virginia's Racial Integrity Act of 1924:

> 1. Be it enacted by the General Assembly of Virginia, That the State Registrar of Vital Statistics may as soon as practicable after the taking effect of this act, prepare a form whereon the racial composition of any individual, as Caucasian, negro, Mongolian, American Indian, Asiatic Indian,

Malay, or any mixture thereof, or any other non-Caucasic strains, and if there be any mixture, then the racial composition of the parents and other ancestors, in so far as ascertainable, so as to show in what generation such mixture occurred, may be certified by such individual, which form shall be known as a registration certificate. . . .

2. It shall be a felony for any person wilfully or knowingly to make a registration certificate false as to color or race. The wilful making of a false registration or birth certificate shall be punished by confinement in the penitentiary for one year.

4. No marriage license shall be granted until the clerk or deputy clerk has reasonable assurance that the statements as to color of both man and woman are correct.[39]

This is also race-general language, but its intent is clearly race-specific because only for whites was racial "integrity" or purity a social value. Moreover, US legislation such as this is now recognized as a form of racist oppression, primarily but not exclusively against African Americans.

For the most part, twentieth-century international and universal rights documents have used race-general language (with race-specific examples), even when specific racial injustice is the underlying subject. For example, the United Nations Convention on the Prevention and Punishment of the Crime of Genocide (1948; Entry into Force, 1951), which predated the United Nations Universal Declaration of Human Rights (1948) and was understood to be a response to the Nazi genocide against Jews, used race-general language in article 2: "In the present Convention, genocide means any of the following acts committed with intent to destroy, in whole or in part, a national, ethnical, racial or religious group as such." The UN Universal Declaration of Human Rights also uses race-general language in article 2: "Everyone is entitled to all the rights and freedoms set forth in this Declaration, without distinction of any kind, such as race, color, sex, language, religion, political or other opinion, national or social origin, property, birth or other status."[40]

Race-general language distances legal and judicial bodies from immediate events that may have motivated their actions and preserves the fiction that the legal system(s) of which they are a part has not upheld race-based injustice in the past, as well as the fiction that the law is completely detached from real-life events and concrete people. It also protects the victims of such injustice from public embarrassment if they otherwise have a social status that has not been conditioned by racial injustice against them. However, race-general language has not been a favored method for African American liberatory thinkers ever since W. E. B. Du Bois, for at least two reasons: first, government language of race-general egalitarianism was accompanied by real life antiblack racist beliefs and practices. We have noted how the language of early twentieth-century US state law, which directly affected the everyday life of African Americans, was race-general and compatible with race-specific discrimination against African Americans. But even by the middle of the twentieth century, race-general egalitarian language remained compatible with specific discrimination against African Americans. African Americans did not at the time Du Bois was politically active have a social status that was independent of the racial injustice against them. We will soon see how some of this history came to a point in W. E. B. Du Bois's engagement with the United Nations and its declarations, but first, more background is necessary.

The Western tradition of international law has roots in the ancient world, for example, the *ius gentium*, or law of nations, recognized by Romans for dealing with other nations, and Roman *ius inter gentes*, or body of treaties among nations. There were national human rights proclamations in both the West and China prior to ideas of universal human rights and the existence of modern international law. Twentieth-century international rights doctrines more directly developed from Western nation-based assertions of human rights than from older traditions of international law itself or, for that matter, from non-Western traditions. In his "Grounds for an International Declaration of Human Rights" (1947), Jacques Maritain, the French philosopher (who was also ambassador to the Vatican from 1945 to 1948), speaking on behalf of the United Nations Economic and Social Council (UNESCO) Committee on the Philosophic Principles of the Rights of Man, referred to the British Bill of Rights and the American and French declarations of rights as foundational for the modern Western rights tradition. Maritain points out that these seventeenth- and eighteenth-century rights doctrines focused on political and civil rights within nation-states and that most of them had become part of positive law by the nineteenth century, "incorporated into the constitution or the laws of almost every nation in the world." However, modern progress in science and technology made it possible for the idea of human rights to evolve by including social and economic rights in human rights doctrines. That is the rationale for the United Nations Declaration of Universal Human Rights, which was compiled by the UNESCO Committee based on responses to a questionnaire that was sent to a "select list of the scholars of the world."[41]

The United Nations Declaration of Universal Human Rights did, as Maritain said was appropriate for its time, add a full spectrum of social and economic rights to its reiteration of more established social and political rights. The declaration addresses both rights and freedoms: articles 1 and 2 assert universal human equality to all rights and freedoms, articles 3 through 13 assert individual liberties and rights to life and security, and articles 14 through 21 assert political and civil rights. From article 1 through article 21, there is nothing in the document beyond customary political and civil rights in democratic nation-states, except that the rights are claimed internationally and recognized as universal rights by the fifty nations that originally signed it. Articles 22 through 28, however, proclaim rights to individual development, rewarding employment, education, social security, and community participation. Article 25 proclaims rights of security for the ill, unemployed, aged, and disabled, and special regard for mothers and children. Article 29 states that individuals have duties to their communities, based on their abilities. Article 30 proclaims the validity of all rights and freedoms listed, in that there is to be no implication that they may be violated. The political and civil rights of articles 1 through 21 represent explicit claims against governments, which, as noted, already formally existed in some nation-states. By contrast, it is not clear who is responsible for the fulfillment of the rights listed in articles 21 through 29, particularly article 24, which proclaims everyone's right to rest and leisure, including paid holidays.

The political and civil liberties vouchsafed in articles 1 through 21 already formally existed in the first fifty member states, and the UN had no power to interfere in their sovereignty regarding them. Neither did the UN have a mechanism for enforcing these rights and freedoms in nations that did not formally recognize them. The rights of social and economic equality, particularly the rights to minimal material well-being, are still idealistic goals concerning the three billion people, more than half the world's population, who live on less than $2.50 (USD) a day. Concerning the political and civil rights in articles 1 through 21, Maritain was mistaken in asserting in 1948 that those rights had by then been "incorporated into the constitution or the laws of almost every nation in the world."

Du Bois had been concerned about the colonies of Africa before the UN was established. In 1946 he tried to approach the General Assembly of the UN as a consultant on issues pertaining to Africa. After a series of rebuffs, he sent a petition to the UN in hopes of drawing attention to the 150 million Africans under colonial rule. This petition was supported by a number of organizations, including two regional sections of the NAACP, the National Bar Association, the American Teachers Association, and the Pan-African Federation. The following lines from the petition convey to a contemporary reader what Du Bois himself was up against:

> Progress is hindered by the difficulties which these Negroes have in making known their needs and wants and the opposition that confronts them. In addition, there is the widespread assumption that Negroes lack the intelligence to express their views and can only be represented by imperial governments or by other spokesmen not of their own choosing."[42]

Du Bois further argued for the necessity of development in Africa, toward eventual democratic government. In 1947, the NAACP, through the impetus of Du Bois, sent a petition to the UN Commission on Human Rights, asking it to investigate racial discrimination in the United States. The petition was supported by African nationalists, Caribbean nationalists, India, Pakistan, Egypt, Ethiopia, Belgium, Formosa, and the USSR, and it received widespread press coverage. The petition did not get any further than the UN's Sub-Commission on the Prevention of Discrimination and Protection of Minorities.[43] In sum, the UN did little or nothing for either the African colonies or African Americans at the time of its Declaration of Universal Rights.

There appear to be two alternatives regarding an incorporation of concerns about racism into universal rights doctrines. Either the doctrines are understood to be international, to include specific nations and nongovernment organizations, or else the doctrines are understood to be universal. If the doctrines are universal, it is easier for race-general language to coexist with racial discrimination and oppression because a universal legal doctrine that is not anchored in specific traditions needs no direct relation to those traditions. (This was Bentham's basic point behind his "nonsense on stilts" critique—see above.) If the doctrines are international, it should be easier to address specific racial injustices, such as genocide or racism against specific racial groups, because the doctrines' signatories are already representing specific jurisdictions.

Should an ethics of race be phrased in race-neutral, race-general, or race-specific language? First, as I will elaborate in the conclusion, there is unlikely to be one ethics of race, but if there is one ethics of race, its language should not be race-specific because that would risk overgeneralization from the perspective of one race or misrepresentation of the perspective of others with competing interests. If there is more than one ethics of race, then any one of that number could use race-specific language, subject to the acknowledgment that it was not the only ethics of race. The problem that would then arise is that multiple ethics of race, among which at least one used race-specific language, would create a situation with no common ground on which to decide avowedly race-based conflicts of interests.

Let us return now to Du Bois's struggles with the UN concerning human rights. Did inattention to the ways in which race formed a subtext for how colonialist powers could frame and impose rights doctrines constitute a race-based conflict of interest between nonwhite colonists seeking liberation and white colonists withholding it? If the answer is no, there is no need for race-specific language. But strangely, perhaps, it is not clear that the answer is yes. Although there was undoubtedly racism and antiracism involved, colonialism did not primarily begin, nor was it continued, for racially motivated reasons. Rather, the invention of racial taxonomies and ongoing race prejudice conveniently combined with colonialism—and later on, globalism—to the economic advantage of Euro-American white groups. The problem faced by both Africans and African Americans, in terms of international human rights, was a lack of inclusion of the oppression against them in the *implementation* of egalitarianism. Egalitarianism unimplemented in this way became inegalitarianism. But neither this problem of inegalitarianism nor the racial demographics of the colonies, nor both together, establish that the ills of colonialism were at their core motivated by racism. Both the problem and the demographics could be ad hoc or contingent accompaniments to greed and exploitation for monetary gain. That the nonwhite inhabitants of colonies were crushed by ideologies of racism masking greed and exploitation does not speak directly to fundamental historical causes. However, it is very important to remember that the racist ideologies that began as justifications for colonial exploitation later served to lock that exploitation in place, which they continue to do.

There was from the outset, in the UN Charter, a deference to the sovereign authorities of nation-states, making it difficult to intervene in matters of internal oppression. The UN Charter states in article 2:7 that nothing in the charter would authorize the UN to interfere in domestic matters or require members to submit such matters for settlement by the UN.[44] In the United States, it took ninety-five years for the 1965 Voting Rights Act to 'perfect' the Fifteenth Amendment that had prohibited federal or state governments from infringing on a citizen's right to vote "on account of race, color, or previous condition of servitude."[45] Obviously, the need for the Voting Rights Act was created by antiblack racism, and the US legal system took far too long to address the problem. But it is not clear that had the Fifteenth Amendment specifically referred to African Americans, bogus voting requirements would have been prevented on local levels. The reason it took ninety-five years was that there was not sufficient will to enforce the Fifteenth Amendment for all that time, and powerful interests were served by that laxness. What the civil rights movement accomplished was not so much race-based black legal equality, but its enforcement. Let's return to the third requirement for an ethics of race:

> (3) An ethics of race, as applicable to members of all racial groups, would be egalitarian in terms of race, meaning that racial difference would not be sufficient to constitute different moral treatment, including admission to the realm or class of moral agents or beings who were worthy of the highest moral consideration.

The moral solution to Du Bois's international concerns and the US internal policy concerning antiblack racism would have been to insist on enforcement of existing race-based egalitarian legislation. The legal solution remains a work in progress. In 2011, more than a half century since its formation, the United Nations still suffers from the problem of not being a world government with legal jurisdiction over the entire world or even over its members.

Within the United States, we still suffer from a lack of enforcement of race–general egalitarian legislation, which is at this time only partly motivated by racism, the greater part of it motivated by unscrupulous economic interests that are able to take advantage of a long history of race-based poverty combined with racism. Although, as with colonialism, the lack of enforcement is locked in place by racist ideology and racism. Consider, for example, the financial industry's creation of 'derivatives' based on mortgages solicited from people who were disproportionately poor and nonwhite, before the stock market crash of 2008. Fifty years before, Du Bois was keenly aware of the human destruction caused by unchecked greed. In defending the location of the United Nations in New York, in 1958, he wrote:

> The United Nations had to be located in the United States. Only here could it get world publicity and American publicity, and carry on its battles in the face of and before the eyes of its most vicious enemy, which is the United States. . . . In New York imperialism and capitalism are in control but they are naked and unashamed. There is no camouflage of titled and aristocratic concealment. It shows lying, stealing and murder, open and not denied. Either we conquer it or the world falls.[46]

NOTES

1. Peter Singer, in *The Life You Can Save* (New York: Random House, 2009), 6–7, recounts some of the social, personal, and civic humiliation suffered by the world's extreme poor. Singer cites Deepa Narayan with Raj Patel, Kai Schafft, Anne Rademacher, and Sarah Koch-Schulte, *Voices of the Poor: Can Anyone Hear Us?* (New York: Published for the World Bank by Oxford University Press, 2000).

2. Contemporary discussion about the social minimum, while based on an intuition of universal human dignity, tends not to explicitly start from that foundation. The social minimum and other subjects of distributive justice are relevant to an ethics of race but beyond the scope of this book. For an excellent examination of the literature on this topic up to 2004, see Stuart White's comprehensive review, "Social Minimum," in *Stanford Encyclopedia of Philosophy*, at plato.stanford.edu/entries/social-minimum/ (accessed December 12, 2010).

3. Jean-Jacques Rousseau, *Social Contracts*, in *The Social Contract and the First and Second Discourses*, by Jean-Jacques Rousseau, ed. Susan Dunn (New Haven, CT: Yale University Press, 2002), 158 and 159 (book 1, 4).

4. Rousseau, *Social Contracts*, 161–62, quote from p. 162 (book 1, 4).

5. Rousseau, *Social Contracts*, 176–77 (book 1, 5).

6. See note 2.

7. On Kant's belief in biological races and racism, see Naomi Zack, *Philosophy of Science and Race* (New York: Routledge, 2002), chap. 1, pp. 9–24.

8. Immanuel Kant, *Grounding for the Metaphysics of Morals*, in *Kant's Ethical Philosophy*, trans. James W. Ellington, introduction by Warner A. Wick (Indianapolis, IN: Hackett, 1994), section 1, 7 and 9.

9. David Hume, *A Treatise of Human Nature*, ed. L. A. Selby-Bigge (London: Oxford University Press, 1964), 479 (book 3, part 2, section 1).

10. Kant, *Grounding for the Metaphysics of Morals*, 11–13.

11. Kant, *Grounding for the Metaphysics of Morals*, 13.

12. Kant, *Grounding for the Metaphysics of Morals*, 13.

13. Kant, *Grounding for the Metaphysics of Morals*, 14 and 15.

14. Kant, *Grounding for the Metaphysics of Morals*, 19.

15. Kant, *Grounding for the Metaphysics of Morals*, 20, section 2.

16. Kant, *Grounding for the Metaphysics of Morals*, 36n21, section 2.

17. Kant, *Grounding for the Metaphysics of Morals*, 36n21, section 2.

18. Kant, *The Metaphysics of Morals*, in *Kant's Ethical Philosophy*, trans. James W. Ellington, introduction by Warner A. Wick (Indianapolis, IN: Hackett, 1994), 106–7 (part 2, section 18).

19. Kant, *The Metaphysics of Morals*, 37.

20. Kant, *The Metaphysics of Morals*, 37.

21. Immanuel Kant, *Perpetual Peace*, in *Kant's Ethical Philosophy*, trans. James W. Ellington, introduction by Warner A. Wick (Indianapolis, IN: Hackett, 1994), appendix 1, 116.

22. Kant, *Perpetual Peace*, 125.

23. For a text of the Declaration of the Rights of Man, see "Declaration of the Rights of Man and the Citizen (August 1789)," *History Guide*, at www.historyguide.org/intellect/declaration.html (consulted July 2010).

24. Jeremy Bentham, *Anarchical Fallacies*, 3–5 (lines 100–70), at www.law.georgetown.edu/faculty/lpw/documents/Bentham_Anarchical_Fallacies.pdf (consulted July 2010).

25. Bentham, *Anarchical Fallacies*, 6–11 (lines 230–420).

26. Bentham, *Anarchical Fallacies*, 11–19.

27. See Bentham, *Anarchical Fallacies*, 6 (line 210).

28. See "Australian History," *Australian Explorer*, at www.australianexplorer.com/australian_history.htm (consulted July 2010).

29. See Richard Broome, *Aboriginal Australians: A History since 1788* (Crows Nest, NSW: Allen Unwin, 2010), ch. 14.

30. Bentham's attitude toward indigenous populations is a separate issue from whether or not he supported empire building on utilitarian grounds, because it would be possible to design such governments. For an interpretation that he was skeptical about European imperialism, see Jennifer Pitts, "Legislator of the World? A Rereading of Bentham on Colonies," *Political Theory* 31, no. 2 (April 2003): 200–34.

31. Bentham, *Anarchical Fallacies*, 18–19 (lines 710 and 730).

32. John Stuart Mill, "Bentham," in *Utilitarianism and On Liberty*, by John Stuart Mill, ed. Mary Warnock (Cambridge, MA: Blackwell, 2003), 53–88, also at socserv.mcmaster.ca/econ/ugcm/3ll3/bentham/bentham.

33. Thomas McCarthy, *Race, Empire, and the Idea of Human Development* (Cambridge: Cambridge University Press, 2009), 168.

34. McCarthy, *Race, Empire, and the Idea of Human Development*, 168.

35. J. S. Mill, *Utilitarianism*, in *Utilitarianism, Liberty and Representative Government*, ed. A. D. Lindsay (New York: E. P. Dutton, 1953), 77n1.

36. Mill, *Utilitarianism*, 78–79.

37. H. L. A. Hart, *The Concept of Law* (Oxford: Oxford University Press, 1988), 222–26.

38. On the political processes preceding the adoption of the UN Universal Declaration of Human Rights, see Mary Ann Glendon, *A World Made New: Eleanor Roosevelt and the Universal Declaration of Human Rights* (New York: Random House, 2001).

39. "An Act to Preserve Racial Integrity," at www2.vcdh.virginia.edu/encounter/projects/monacans/Contemporary_Monacans/racial.html (consulted July 2010).

40. Micheline R. Ishay, ed., *The Human Rights Reader* (New York: Routledge, 2007), 484ff. The UN Convention on the Prevention and Punishment of the Crime of Genocide is reprinted on pp. 492–93; the UN Declaration is reprinted on pp. 493–96.

41. See Jacques Maritain, "The Grounds for an International Declaration of Human Rights (1947)," pp. 2–6, in *The Human Rights Reader*, ed. Micheline R. Ishay (New York: Routledge, 2007): 3.

42. Herbert Aptheker, ed., *The Correspondence of W. E. B. Du Bois*, 3 vols. (Amherst, MA: University of Massachusetts Press, 1978), 3: 154–55.

43. For Du Bois's correspondence on this petition, see Aptheker, *The Correspondence of W. E. B. Du Bois*, 3: 153ff.

44. Aptheker, *The Correspondence of W. E. B. Du Bois*, 3: 492.

45. See Craig Newburger, "Voting Rights and African Americans," *The University of Dayton School of Law*, at academic.udayton.edu/race/04needs/98newburg.htm (consulted July 2010).

46. "Letter to Anna Melissa," Brooklyn, N.Y., January 1, 1958, in Aptheker, *The Correspondence of W. E B. Du Bois*, 3: 420.

· 8 ·

Conclusion

Egalitarian Humanism and Requirements for an Ethics of Race

$\mathcal{R}$eturning to the question prompted by Hobbes in calling abstract universal rights "nonsense on stilts," what are rights? Rights pertain to how humans interact, so they are social, and in regulating interactions, rights are normative. Legal rights within nation-states regulate interactions between citizens and government and also among citizens, in both cases backed up by the threat of force. International rights are commitments by governments to recognize and enforce specified rights within their own jurisdictions and possibly in other countries, although the latter is in conflict with claims of sovereignty (which are the rights of governments and people against external intervention).

Are rights, including international legal rights, still rights if they are not enforced? Yes, because of the genesis of rights. First, rights are declared and written up; second, legal authorities agree to recognize them; third, they are "entered into force"; and fourth, they are enforced. So rights must be distinct from their entry into force, as well as their enforcement, if only because an understanding of them precedes their entry into force and enforcement. This still does not tell us what rights are, although it does indicate that they are something like intentions, beliefs, and expectations because they do not 'do' anything on their own in the absence of people acting or not acting in certain ways. During the US civil rights movements of the 1960s, the issues were not to secure voting rights and rights to education and employment as *new* rights for African Americans, but to motivate the enforcement of these national and international rights that they already had. African Americans had been granted those rights, in constitutional amendments, much earlier.

What's strange about an individual having a right to X or a right to not-Y is that the individual's right pertains to what others will or will not do. We could say that whenever an individual has a right, others have duties, either

161

to do or not to do specific things in regard to that individual.[1] The idea of human rights is connected to the idea of human equality. The most striking realization thus far from this inquiry into the history of moral philosophy in search of foundations for an ethics of race is that *egalitarian humanism*, or moral human equality that includes every human being in existence, is a brand new idea, dating from the 1948 United Nations Universal Declaration of Human Rights (UDHR). The idea of human rights as inclusive of all human beings coalesced even later if we consider the human rights of those who are further disadvantaged or relatively lacking in power. The United Nations Declaration of the Rights of Disabled Persons was adopted in 1975 and entered into force in 2008. The Convention on the Elimination of All Forms of Discrimination against Women was adopted in 1979 and entered into force in 1981. The United Nations Convention on the Rights of the Child was adopted in 1989 and entered into force in 1990.[2]

We saw in chapter 7 that the UDHR is best understood as an international, and not a universal, doctrine. As such, it lacks jurisdiction and implementation in nations that have not committed to it, and it lacks enforcement in some nations that have committed to it. Egalitarian humanism is not only new, but it is the next new, new thing if the need for declarations on behalf of the "special" groups—as though they were not already the bearers of *human* rights—is considered. There are several ways to make sense of this: that it was not commonly known before the 1970s that human rights applied to all human beings, including disabled, female, and very young human beings; that the UDHR omitted effective rhetorical stress on the claim that all human beings have the same human rights; that the addition of special rights is not, strictly speaking, a matter of what people know and recognize about rights but a strategy for implementing and enforcing them; that it's expensive to implement rights for women, children, and the disabled, so nations procrastinate in doing so without special prodding; or, the worst case explanation, that members of the special groups have only recently been recognized as fully human.[3]

Distinct consideration of the special groups represented in the UN's additional declarations would not be necessary if the UN's 1948 declaration had world jurisdiction or, lacking that, obligatory moral force to propel its implementation and compliance. As part of implementation and compliance, it would have been understood that the application of human rights doctrine to women, children, and the disabled would require different kinds of practical applications than its application to male adults. Even rights applied to able-bodied male adults require different practices for their application, for example, protecting property rights differs in rural and urban areas. There are, of course, other additional disadvantaged and oppressed groups so far omitted from international/universal rights declarations. Where and whenever an identifiable group of human beings suffers oppression or systematic injustice, they can in principle be identified as the bearers of special rights so as to focus attention on their plight in new ways, insofar as they have been omitted from rights discourse under the name or label that identifies them as an oppressed group.

One group thus far omitted from special UN declarations represents lesbian, gay, bisexual, and transgendered people. At present there appears to be a conflict between those who advocate for their human rights and representatives of the group rights of cultures in which they are oppressed.[4] Here, the moral foundation for legal international human rights is undermined in a struggle between ethics and mores. To be sure, any precise, general distinction between oppressive mores and liberatory ethics is not simple to draw because even the victims of oppression benefit from the stability of culture.

A good part of criticism against the UN in general and its rights statements in particular has involved charges of its Western Euro-American bias, particularly in the instance of women's rights. But, in that case, as Uma Narayan has pointed out, even assuming respect for local tradition and culture, it is not always true that Western practices are not more liberatory than non-Western ones. In Narayan's example, the value of cultural autonomy is often used as an excuse to continue oppressions against women in India, which are intolerable compared to the Westernized liberation of men in the same society.[5] There are many other examples of this conflict between international human rights and cultural group rights, involving women, children, the disabled, the old, the extremely poor, and ethnic and religious minorities. Postcolonial and postmodern critics have strongly criticized human rights doctrine for its hypocritical misuse by imperialist, neocolonialist powers. They observe how people of color in the global South and East (as well as within the North and West) are violently exploited by capitalism under the protection of political imperialists who champion human rights doctrine.[6]

The abuses and misuses of rights doctrine are part of history, which is something different from the doctrine itself, taken theoretically. Still, individualism, in the sense of individuation, so that the human individual is the rights-having unit, is an integral part of rights doctrine. While people originate and live out their lives in communities, tribes, neighborhoods, and collectivities of myriad types, the Kantian subjective self-valuation at the core of human rights doctrine is only temporarily and sporadically erased by dramatic acts of self-sacrifice for the group. As an everyday matter, merging, instead of individuation, continually occurs at the expense of more than half of humanity (in settings where there are no slaves)—women. Women have traditionally sacrificed their autonomy and individual well-being for the sake of their families, and this sacrifice has not been voluntary throughout history. Traditional communities, tribes, neighborhoods, and all of the other collectivities that could serve as moral units alternative to collections of rights-bearing individuals cohere on the basis of some form of internal gender asymmetry in power, work responsibilities, child rearing, family nurturance, and caregiving. Many group rights, arising from local peoples' movements as an alternative to individual rights, may thereby presuppose substantial violations of individual rights. The solution is to force the issue of individual rights, to limit the abuse and misuse of rights doctrine, in ways internal to specific cultures and collectivities. Of course, this is not easy to do because it requires complex negotiations and external resources. The existence, declaration, and recognition of human rights have not yet been sufficient to secure them without additional action or struggle.

RACE AND HUMAN RIGHTS

Concerning black race in the United States, the struggle between ethics (as a basis for legal international rights) and the mores of white dominance has been ongoing since the NAACP's 1947 petition asking the UN to investigate human rights abuses against African Americans died in the Sub-Commission of Prevention of Discrimination and Protection of Minorities (see chapter 7). As noted, it is widely related that this failure was the result of opposition from Eleanor Roosevelt (who was a UNESCO commissioner at the time) and of other US pressures against it, as well as suspicion of support by the USSR in that Cold War environment.[7] However, in 1950 and 1951 UNESCO issued statements on race that stressed the lack of a biological foundation for differences in valued social traits that were associated with racial difference. In 1967 UNESCO revisited its 1950 and 1951 statements to emphasize and expand on the earlier claims, with particular attention to racism. The result was the UNESCO Statement on Race and Racial Prejudice, a very important egalitarian statement on race, which appears in full in the appendix to this chapter. In Article 10, the lack of a biological foundation for racial taxonomies is succinctly related to the reality of racism and its historical and social causes, viz.:

> In order to undermine racism it is not sufficient that biologists should expose its fallacies. It is also necessary that psychologists and sociologists should demonstrate its causes. The social structure is always an important factor.[8]

Prior to the 1967 statement, the UN's International Convention on All Forms of Racial Discrimination had been adopted in 1965 and was entered into force in 1969.[9] As we know, despite these declarations and many others of similarly just intent, ethnic violence and genocide, as well as ordinary hate crimes and institutional racism, have continued to occur in many parts of the world. Race prejudice, or racism, continues to permeate most forms of global disadvantage, particularly that of children.

ETHICS, RIGHTS, AND GLOBAL POVERTY

In 2009, most of the sixteen thousand children who each day died from hunger-related causes lived in the third world. This implies that in a taxonomy of human races, they were not white. But as recipients of humanitarian aid, children suffering from hunger are almost never identified in racial terms. The reasons for that are complicated: bringing attention to their race might alienate rich white sources of aid; talk about race in public is usually interpreted to be talk about racism and many would be reluctant to hear that racism is implicated in the "hunger-related causes" of children's deaths. The ethical problem here lies not with identities of either race or age, but with a failure to effectively implement the social and economic rights set out in articles 21 through 29 of the UN Universal Declaration of Human Rights (see chapter 7). Children suffering from hunger are the recipients of humanitarian aid. Providing humanitarian aid is an imperfect duty in a Kantian sense—everyone is obligated to do something regarding it, but exactly what or how much is undetermined. Indeed, response to all of the economic and social rights listed in articles 21 through 29 are imperfect duties. Any of these duties could be perfected if humanitarian aid were recognized to be a universal moral requirement for inhabitants of rich countries, based on income.[10]

It would not be necessary to have an ethics of race, distinct from race-neutral ethics, if the human rights of individuals and groups were not consistently violated in ways motivated by, and affecting, racial identities. An ethics of race is like a codicil to ethics in general, just as recognition of women, the disabled, and children were codicils to the UDHR. There is much in an ethics of race that overlaps with twentieth-century rights doctrine, and contemporary ethicists have overall been inspired by ideas and ideals of human equality expressed in rights doctrines. However, there are important differences between ethics and rights doctrines. Ethics purports to be closer to what individuals can do, whereas rights, insofar as they are in the last analysis implemented by governments, are more institutional. Once a rights doctrine is proclaimed and specific rights have been declared, all of the important questions turn on implementation and strategies for enforcement. Ethics, by contrast, is more theoretical, more of an ongoing exercise in determining what is good and right, with strategy and implementation relegated to applied ethics, political activism, and politics itself. Ethical principles can be used to prioritize rights, for example, that rights to life are more important than rights to property. Even though fundamental ethical principles, however they arise or wherever they come from, are assertions with or without empirical foundation[11]—some of them even absolute—they remain open to discussion and change, whereas once rights are declared, their legitimacy is considered settled (contra Bentham).

Ethics are prior to rights, not only historically but theoretically. Human rights can come from God, from governments, or from something about human beings. If the source of human rights is human species identity, it is difficult to distinguish between universal human rights and speciesism,[12] and maybe that distinction should be open to question. Nevertheless, modern human rights doctrine seems to be theoretically grounded on Kant's postulation of the intrinsic worth of each moral being, which ties that worth to human subjectivity, in the ultimate value of an individual's life, to that individual (see chapter 7). The idea of intrinsic worth tied to subjective valuation results in the dignity of each human individual. The dignity of each compels respect from all others. Respect for others motivates recognition of their rights, which are necessary conditions for their dignities. Respect and rights recognition are obligatory.

Rights doctrines are thereby deontological because the ethics on which they rest are deontological in the rich sense of duty generated by intrinsic worth, in comparison to duties that are fulfilled without comprehension of their moral foundation or duties that have no moral foundation, such as a duty to follow a dress code. Deontological ethics can also fulfill the requirements of utilitiarianism if everyone actually fulfills their duties. And, insofar as it is an inward subjective practice (which recognizes the subjectivities of others), deontological ethics rests on the virtues of those who practice it. An ethics of race would be deontological in a utopian sense, held as an ideal: everyone is intrinsically valuable; everyone behaves as though everyone is intrinsically valuable; the well-being of the greatest possible number of intrinsically valuable beings will be secured and furthered, with full respect for the intrinsic value of each one.

REQUIREMENTS FOR AN ETHICS OF RACE

The present inquiry has yielded twelve requirements for an ethics of race. Some of these were intuitive, for instance, a presumption of racial equality; others sought to model an ethics of race on assumptions and structures shared by other ethical systems, for example, that *ought* implies *can*; and some of the most interesting requirements, namely 7 through 12, as developed in chapters 5, 6, and 7, arose in critical consideration of key ideas in the history of moral philosophy. The results as developed and first stated over the chapters can now be slightly rephrased and organized as follows, with three egalitarian requirements (I–III), four formal requirements (IV–VII), and five requirements of content (VIII–XII):

Egalitarian Requirements

I. An ethics of race would have as its units human individuals and would assume the intrinsic value and freedom of every human individual. All individuals would have the same human rights and be worthy of respect from one another. It would be morally wrong and, on that basis, legally wrong to violate anyone's rights.

II. An ethics of race, as applicable to members of all racial groups, would be egalitarian in terms of race, meaning that racial difference would not be sufficient to constitute different moral treatment, including admission to the realm or class of moral agents or beings who were worthy of the highest moral consideration.

III. Human equality must include an equality of moral authority. This may require redistribution of material and social resources so that the disadvantaged can be recognized as moral equals by the advantaged.

Formal Requirements

IV. An ethics of race would have to be completely international and include all who were not members of nation-states. Whenever possible, an ethics of race would be more general than its applications to racial difference, racial liberation, or racism. An ethics of race would not mention specific races or racial groups and its language would be race-general.

V. An ethics of race is a mode of discourse and practice and the principles or rules governing both of these, which is independent of politics and political theory. It allows for ethical assessment of laws and government practices, of the state, and of all other social organizations.

VI. An ethics of race must be possible for human beings to practice by applying its principles and constructing virtues related to those principles: *ought* implies *can* in an ethics of race.

VII. In constructing an ethics of race, ideas of unity over groups and individuals, whether physical or spiritual, should be subject to critical empirical examination before acceptance and application: do they represent the interests of all in an egalitarian way? Or do they impose the interests of some on others through fictive "wholes" that are used to mediate the interests of those who are not being fully represented?

Requirements of Content

VIII. Slavery, or the ownership of entire human beings, must be held to be an absolute moral wrong. The moral wrong of slavery would follow from (I) and apply to all individuals, regardless of race. The moral wrong of slavery is more important than any and all protections of property rights, and this wrong extends to control over labor in employment that interferes with autonomy, respect, and well-being.

IX. There should be humanitarian goals of alleviating human suffering, particularly suffering that distinctively accompanies the circumstances of people with disadvantaged racial identities.

X. New governments or revisions of existing governments should not intentionally cause those who are disadvantaged to become worse off, either in terms of material well-being or civil status; if the disadvantaged do become worse off as the result of government founding or revision, those actions should be revised.

XI. Every moral unit, government organization, and social organization should always act in such a way so that the intent and practical effect of the action supports every human being's (subjective) ultimate valuation of his or her own life, with the possible exception of cases in which persons have acted and shown intent not to obey this principle.

XII. An ethics of race ought not to privilege the mores, including the legal system, traditions, and culture of any human organization smaller than the whole of humanity. No one should be excluded from an ethics of race based on national, geographical, or historical contingencies.

HOW MANY ETHICS OF RACE, AND IN WHAT WORDING?

We should now consider whether adequate requirements for an ethics of race could generate one and only one *universal* ethics of race. I think the answer is

No. Race itself is a bogus taxonomy on exactly those biological grounds that it has been falsely assumed to rest for about two hundred years. Race was first developed as an idea in science, followed by its acceptance throughout cultures. The scientific foundation for biological ideas of race has fallen away as the biological sciences have developed, leaving a foundation for race in what can be studied by the social sciences (history, anthropology, sociology, and psychology) and in beliefs in popular culture (i.e., among the populace) itself. It would be tempting on that basis to insist on the removal of racial discourse as a fundamental principle in such a universal ethics. If that principle were universally followed and thoroughly implemented, so that racism were abolished along with the false cognitive components of ideas of race—and only in that case—there would be no need for an ethics of race. But there is little reason to believe that race and racism could be universally eliminated, all at once, or that it will pass away on its own in the foreseeable future. Therefore, insofar as *ought* implies *can*, with the 'ought' in question being existential feasibility rather than logical possibility, a normative statement about the elimination of biologically bogus racial discourse and racism could not be a universal principle. This does not exclude the viability of a contextually circumscribed ethics of race in which race terms were to be eliminated, as in the following examples: situations concerning human skills or requiring pure meritocracy or racial anonymity, where discrimination has previously been explicitly race-based; clinical or scientific contexts where it is known that race terms serve no purpose except as markers for socially created conditions that accompany low racial status[13] (e.g., high-stress environments and high blood pressure for some members of some racial groups); or race-theoretical contexts that are intellectually self-selective.[14] In other contexts, race terms might be ethically necessary for entitlements, affirmation, and integration, where deprivation, neglect, and segregation has 'cleverly' proceeded on the basis of race without explicit mention of race (for example, in environmental racism) or in clinical psychological discourse that addresses the effects of racism.

The use of race-general language in an ethics of race, which does not mention specific races but just generically refers to 'race,' is a wholly separate issue from the question of whether race terms that refer to biological differences ought to be retained or eliminated. The elimination of biologically based racial discourse (i.e., discourse which presumes a biological foundation for human racial taxonomy) is only one example of what could or could not be the subject of an ethics of race. What counts as racism and the justice of how people are permitted to self-identify racially, or are racially identified by others, differs according to place and specific family ties, so racism and racial identity are further subjects.[15] The question of what social or legal racial categories there are to be and whether, for example, in the United States mixed race should be a stand-alone racial category in the case of black and white racial mixture, is another highly contextual issue.[16]

There has been so much variation in racial categories as a taxonomy, in the nature of racism, and in material and psychic resources for correcting racism that we should expect and allow for multiple ethics of race. Nevertheless, for any set of principles to be a valid ethics of race, the assumption that it would have to meet certain general ethical requirements stands as a foundation for race-based justice. Requirement IV, that the language of any specific ethics of race be race-general rather than race-specific (see chapter 7), merits further attention, in conclusion. Pragmatically, the reason for IV is that all of the official liberal documents pertaining to race and racism in the United States and internationally (through the UN) use race-general language (when they do not use race-neutral language), only mentioning specific races as examples justifying the principles they propound (see the UNESCO Statement on Race and Race Prejudice in the appendix to this chapter).

The craft involved in translating race-specific concerns to race-general (and sometimes race-neutral) language involves describing problems faced by specific races and stating remedies for, or preventions of, those problems in general terms, without referring to a specific race. For example, if only blacks are enslaved and suffer from slavery, then the stated remedy makes racial, or any form of, slavery illegal. If black and Hispanic children disproportionately attend poor schools, then the standards for all schools have to be clearly stated, with provisions for their implementation, and such statements need to indicate there is to be no difference based on race. If only, or primarily, undocumented Mexican immigrants are subject to specific searches and seizures that would violate the rights of citizens, then citizens' rights in this regard need to be extended to undocumented immigrants. If there is to be a legal basis for reparations for the descendants of slaves, then parallel to the Fifteenth Amendment, it's not necessary to state the matter any more specifically than this, that the descendants of slaves are entitled to reparations. If whites misuse the ideal of racial egalitarianism in terms of "reverse discrimination," then an ethics of race would hold that where there has been previous discrimination and disadvantage based on race, reactive racism by subordinate groups toward dominant ones is not necessarily racism (although it can be[17]) and that neither is compensatory affirmation of subordinate groups being racist.

Race-general, as well as race-neutral, language has been not only the language of law in attempts to correct racial injustice but the language of ethics or morality—it is in principle "race blind," although its appropriate construction has effects with acute "race vision" in terms of specific racial identities. To use that language to correct for racial injustice requires a special use of syntax to cover particular cases, while the content of the language is based on a common human identity. If specific race-based moral assessments of injustice are to find legal remedies, it is not only strategic to meet the law halfway in language, but it is also just that laws not discriminate for or against specific racial groups as a matter of bare identities (i.e., black, white, mixed, Asian, Native American) in a bogus biological taxonomy. This is not to say anything about people's liberty to preserve cultures and identities associated with social races, although if such preservation is presented normatively, it is a matter of mores, rather than ethics, and as such subject to ethical assessment. Such ethical assessment, on a presumption of egalitarian humanism, is the primary philosophical contribution to the subject of race at this time.

Finally, race-general language is the only way to fully incorporate cosmopolitan egalitarianism and projects of self-creation that diverge from mores into ethical discourse concerning race. In this way, requirement IV makes possible the content specified by XII, to the effect that no particular mores are superior or can be held superior to any others, qua mores. Mores Q may be superior to mores T in ethical terms, but that is another matter. Insofar as some recent forms of cosmopolitanism advocate individual identity creation in directions away from natal mores, or away from one's "tribe,"[18] the foregoing requirements for an ethics of race are compatible with cosmopolitanism. However, as noted in chapter 2, cosmopolitanism alone does not generate either requirements for an ethics of race or a specific ethics of race.

Cosmopolitanism is a way to negotiate differences in mores on the basis of created identities that move away from this or that tribalism. But ethics in the manner discussed here is not a matter of identity but of ideals and principles for action that involve human well-being in important ways. People with spoiled, stagnant, or even deeply tribal identities can still have good ethics, in general and in terms of race.

APPENDIX: UNESCO STATEMENT ON RACE AND RACIAL PREJUDICE

UNESCO Statement on Race and Racial Prejudice, Paris, September 1967[19]

1. 'All men are born free and equal both in dignity and in rights.' This universally proclaimed democratic principle stands in jeopardy wherever political, economic, social and cultural inequalities affect human group relations. A particularly striking obstacle to the recognition of equal dignity for all is racism. Racism continues to haunt the world. As a major social phenomenon it requires the attention of all students of the sciences of man.
2. Racism stultifies the development of those who suffer from it, perverts those who apply it, divides nations within themselves, aggravates international conflict and threatens world peace.

3. Conference of experts meeting in Paris in September 1967, agreed that racist doctrines lack any scientific basis whatsoever. It reaffirmed the propositions adopted by the international meeting held in Moscow in 1964 which was called to re-examine the biological aspects of the statements on race and racial differences issued in 1950 and 1951. In particular, it draws attention to the following points:
   (a) All men living today belong to the same species and descend from the same stock.
   (b) The division of the human species into 'races' is partly conventional and partly arbitrary and does not imply any hierarchy whatsoever. Many anthropologists stress the importance of human variation, but believe that 'racial' divisions have limited scientific interest and may even carry the risk of inviting abusive generalisation.
   (c) Current biological knowledge does not permit us to impute cultural achievements to differences in genetic potential. Differences in the achievements of different peoples should be attributed solely to their cultural history. The peoples of the world today appear to possess equal biological potentialities for attaining any level of civilisation. Racism grossly falsifies the knowledge of human biology.
4. The human problems arising from so-called 'race' relations are social in origin rather than biological. A basic problem is racism, namely, antisocial beliefs and acts which are based on the fallacy that discriminatory intergroup relations are justifiable on biological grounds.
5. Groups commonly evaluate their characteristics in comparison with others. Racism falsely claims that there is a scientific basis for arranging groups hierarchically in terms of psychological and cultural characteristics that are immutable and innate. In this way it seeks to make existing differences appear inviolable as a means of permanently maintaining current relations between groups.
6. Faced with the exposure of the falsity of its biological doctrines, racism finds ever new stratagems for justifying the inequality of groups. It points to the fact that groups do not intermarry, a fact which follows, in part, from the divisions created by racism. It uses this fact to argue the thesis that this absence of intermarriage derives from differences of a biological order. Whenever it fails in its attempts to prove that the source of group differences lies in the biological field, it falls back upon justifications in terms of divine purpose, cultural differences, disparity of educational standards or some other doctrine which would serve to mask its continued racist beliefs. Thus, many of the problems which racism presents in the world today do not arise merely from its open manifestations, but from the activities of those who discriminate on racial grounds but are unwilling to acknowledge it.
7. Racism has historical roots. It has not been a universal phenomenon. Many contemporary societies and cultures show little trace of it. It was not evident for long periods in world history. Many forms of racism have arisen out of the conditions of conquest, out of the justification of Negro slavery and its aftermath of racial inequality in the West, and out of the colonial relationship.

Among other examples is that of antisemitism, which has played a particular role in history, with Jews being the chosen scapegoat to take the blame for problems and crises met by many societies.

8. The anti-colonial revolution of the twentieth century has opened up new possibilities for eliminating the scourge of racism. In some formerly dependent countries, people formerly classified as inferior have for the first time obtained full political rights. Moreover, the participation of formerly dependent nations in international organisations in terms of equality has done much to undermine racism.

9. There are, however, some instances in certain societies in which groups, victims of racialistic practices, have themselves applied doctrines with racist implications in their struggle for freedom. Such an attitude is a secondary phenomenon, a reaction stemming from men's search for an identity which prior racist theory and racialistic practices denied them. Nonetheless, the new forms of racist ideology, resulting from this prior exploitation, have no justification in biology. They are a product of a political struggle and have no scientific foundation.

10. In order to undermine racism it is not sufficient that biologists should expose its fallacies. It is also necessary that psychologists and sociologists should demonstrate its causes. The social structure is always an important factor. However, within the same social structure, there may be great individual variation in racialistic behaviour, associated with the personality of the individuals and their personal circumstances.

11. The committee of experts agreed on the following conclusions about the social causes of race prejudice:

    (a) Social and economic causes of racial prejudice are particularly observed in settler societies wherein are found conditions of great disparity of power and property, in certain urban areas where there have emerged ghettoes in which individuals are deprived of equal access to employment, housing, political participation, education, and the administration of justice, and in many societies where social and economic tasks which are deemed to be contrary to the ethics or beneath the dignity of its members are assigned to a group of different origins who are derided, blamed, and punished for taking on these tasks.

    (b) Individuals with certain personality troubles may be particularly inclined to adopt and manifest racial prejudices. Small groups, associations, and social movements of a certain kind sometimes preserve and transmit racial prejudices. The foundations of the prejudices lie, however, in the economic and social system of a society.

    (c) Racism tends to be cumulative. Discrimination deprives a group of equal treatment and presents that group as a problem. The group then tends to be blamed for its own condition, leading to further elaboration of racist theory.

12. The major techniques for coping with racism involve changing those social situations which give rise to prejudice, preventing the prejudiced from acting in accordance with their beliefs, and combating the false beliefs themselves.

13. It is recognised that the basically important changes in the social structure that may lead to the elimination of racial prejudice may require decisions of a political nature. It is also recognised, however, that certain agencies of enlightenment, such as education and other means of social and economic advancement, mass media, and law can be immediately and effectively mobilised for the elimination of racial prejudice.

14. The school and other instruments for social and economic progress can be one of the most effective agents for the achievement of broadened understanding and the fulfilment of the potentialities of man. They can equally much be used for the perpetuation of discrimination and inequality. It is therefore essential that the resources for education and for social and economic action of all nations be employed in two ways:

    (a) The schools should ensure that their curricula contain scientific understandings about race and human unity, and that invidious distinctions about peoples are not made in texts and classrooms.

    (b) (i) Because the skills to be gained in formal and vocational education become increasingly important with the processes of technological development, the resources of the schools and other resources should be fully available to all parts of the population with neither restriction nor discrimination.

    (ii) Furthermore, in cases where, for historical reasons, certain groups have a lower average education and economic standing, it is the responsibility of the society to take corrective measures. These measures should ensure, so far as possible, that the limitations of poor environments are not passed on to the children. In view of the importance of teachers in any educational programme, special attention should be given to their training. Teachers should be made conscious of the degree to which they reflect the prejudices which may be current in their society. They should be encouraged to avoid these prejudices.

15. Governmental units and other organisations concerned should give special attention to improving the housing situations and work opportunities available to victims of racism. This will not only counteract the effects of racism, but in itself can be a positive way of modifying racist attitudes and behaviour.

16. The media of mass communication are increasingly important in promoting knowledge and understanding, but their exact potentiality is not fully known. Continuing research into the social utilisation of the media is needed in order to assess their influence in relation to formation of attitudes and behavioural patterns in the field of race prejudice and race discrimination. Because the mass media reach vast numbers of people at different educational and social levels, their role in encouraging or combating race prejudice can be crucial. Those who work in these media should maintain a positive approach to the promotion of understanding between groups and populations. Representation of peoples in stereotypes and holding them up to ridicule should be avoided. Attachment to news reports of racial designations which are not germane to the accounts should also be avoided.

17. Law is among the most important means of ensuring equality between in-dividuals and one of the most effective means of fighting racism. The Universal Declaration of Human Rights of 10 December 1948 and the related international agreements and conventions which have taken effect subsequently can contribute effectively, on both the national and international level, to the fight against any injustice of racist origin. National legislation is a means of effectively outlawing racist propaganda and acts based upon racial discrimination. Moreover, the policy expressed in such legislation must bind not only the courts and judges charged with its enforcement, but also all agencies of government of whatever level or whatever character. It is not claimed that legislation can immediately eliminate prejudice. Nevertheless, by being a means of protecting the victims of acts based upon prejudice, and by setting a moral example backed by the dignity of the courts, it can, in the long run, even change attitudes.

18. Ethnic groups which represent the object of some form of discrimination are sometimes accepted and tolerated by dominating groups at the cost of their having to abandon completely their cultural identity. It should be stressed that the effort of these ethnic groups to preserve their cultural values should be encouraged. They will thus be better able to contribute to the enrichment of the total culture of humanity.

19. Racial prejudice and discrimination in the world today arise from historical and social phenomena and falsely claim the sanction of science. It is, therefore, the responsibility of all biological and social scientists, philosophers, and others working in related disciplines, to ensure that the results of their research are not misused by those who wish to propagate racial prejudice and encourage discrimination.

This statement was prepared by a committee of experts on race and racial prejudice which met at Unesco House, Paris, from 18 to 26 September 1967. The following experts took part in the committee's work:

Professor Muddathir Abdel Rahim, University of Khartoum (Sudan)
Professor Georges Balandier, Université de Paris (France)
Professor Celio de Oliveira Borja, University of Guanabara (Brazil)
Professor Lloyd Braithwaite, University of the West Indies (Jamaica)
Professor Leonard Broom, University of Texas (United States)
Professor G. F. Debetz, Institute of Ethnography, Moscow (USSR)
Professor J. Djordjevic, University of Belgrade (Yugoslavia)
Dean Clarence Clyde Fergusm, Howard University (United States)
Dr. Dharam P. Ghai, University College (Kenya)
Professor Louis Guttman, Hebrew University (Israel)
Professor Jean Hiernaux, Université Libre de Bruxelles (Belgium)
Professor A. Kloskowska, University of Lodz (Poland)

Judge Kéba M'Baye, President of the Supreme Court (Senegal)
Professor John Rex, University of Durham (United Kingdom)
Professor Mariano R. Solveira, University of Havana (Cuba)
Professor Hisashi Suzuki, University of Tokyo (Japan)
Dr. Romila Thapar, University of Delhi (India)
Professor C. H. Waddington, University of Edinburgh (United Kingdom)

NOTES

1. Some writers have divided rights into claim rights and liberty rights based on the distinction between action and restraint. See Peter Jones, *Rights* (Basingstoke: Macmillan, 1994).

2. All of these declarations are reprinted in Micheline R. Ishay, ed., *The Human Rights Reader* (New York: Routledge, 2007), 526ff.

3. Under international law the doctrine of the *persistent objector* holds that if a state persistently objects to an international law as it becomes customary, the state cannot be held to the law unless the law becomes a *peremptory norm*. For an argument against this doctrine see Holning Lau, "Rethinking the Persistent Objector Doctrine in International Human Rights Law," *Chicago Journal of International Law*, July 1, 2005, at www.allbusiness.com/legal/international-law/884010-1.html (consulted July 2010).

4. On this issue and the connection between movements in support of identities and political rights, see Carl F. Stychin, "Same-Sex Sexualities and the Globalization of Human Rights Discourse," *McGill Law Journal* 49 (2004): 951–68.

5. Uma Narayan, "Contesting Cultures: 'Westernization,' Respect for Cultures, and Third-World Feminists," in *The Second Wave: A Reader in Feminist Theory*, ed. Linda Nicholson (New York: Routledge, 1997), 396–414.

6. See, for an example of such criticism and further sources, Randall Williams, *The Divided World: Human Rights and Its Violence* (Minneapolis: University of Minnesota Press, 2010).

7. See "African Americans—The United Nations Petition," in *Encyclopedia of the New American Nation*, at www.americanforeignrelations.com/A-D/African-Americans-The-united-nations-petition.html (consulted July 2010).

8. See appendix to this chapter; the 1967 UNESCO Statement on Race and Racial Prejudice is also available at www.honestthinking.org/en/unesco/UNESCO.1967.Statement_on_Race.htm (consulted July 2010).

9. The UN's International Convention on All Forms of Racial Discrimination is available at www2.ohchr.org/english/law/cerd.htm (consulted July 2010).

10. See Peter Singer's compelling exhortation along these lines in *The Life You Can Save: Acting Now to End World Poverty* (New York: Random House, 2009).

11. Marc Hauser suggests that one foundation could be a shared evolutionary history that has resulted in a certain degree of normative "hard wiring," which could be consciously and deliberately changed to the extent that it has resulted in preferences

for one's own tribal/racial/ethnic group. Hauser notes that insofar as the in-group preference is unconscious, its correction would be difficult for the Rawlsian individual who makes normative political judgments behind a veil of ignorance. See Marc D. Hauser, *Moral Minds: The Nature of Right and Wrong* (New York: Harper Perennial, 2007), 111–114.

12. For a succinct defense of human speciesism and arguments against it, see Bernard Williams, "The Human Prejudice," and "Reply by Peter Singer," in *Peter Singer under Fire: The Moral Iconoclast Faces His Critics*, ed. Jeffrey A. Schaler (Chicago and La Salle, IL: Open Court, 2009), 77–102.

13. For a thorough discussion of the misuses of social ideas of race in medical clinical practice and public health, see Adolph Reed Jr., "Making Sense of Race, I: The Ideology of Race, the Biology of Human Variation, and the Problem of Medical and Public Health Research," in *The Journal of Race and Policy* 1, no. 1 (Spring/Summer 2005): 11–42. For a succinct account with sources of how BiDil was/is not a "black heart drug," see Nell Irvin Painter, *The History of White People* (New York: Norton, 2010), 393–94.

14. See Joshua Glasgow, *A Theory of Race* (New York: Routledge, 2009), 2–6 passim; Naomi Zack, *Philosophy of Science and Race* (New York: Routledge, 2002), ch. 7.

15. Naomi Zack, *Thinking about Race* (Belmont, CA: Wadsworth, 2005), 20–29.

16. See Naomi Zack, "The Fluid Symbol of Mixed Race," *Hypatia* 25, no. 4 (2010): 875–90. Naomi Zack, "American Mixed Race: Theoretical and Legal Issues," *Harvard BlackLetter Law Journal* 17 (Spring 2001): 33–46; Naomi Zack, "Mixed Black and White Race and Public Policy," *Hypatia* 10, no. 1 (Winter 1995): 120–32.

17. Shirley Sherrod, an African American USDA official, was fired, with approval by the NAACP, on grounds of racism for remarks she made about a white farmer. Then the media and others looked at the full context of her remarks and apologies were forthcoming. See Karen Tumulty and Ed O'Keefe, "Fired USDA Official Receives Apologies from White House, Vilsack," *Washington Post*, July 22, 2010, at www .washingtonpost.com/wp-dyn/content/article/2010/07/21/AR2010072103871.html (consulted March 2011).

18. See Jason D. Hill, *Beyond Blood Identities: Posthumanity in the Twenty-First Century* (Lanham, MD: Rowman and Littlefield, 2009).

19. The 1967 UNESCO Statement on Race and Racial Prejudice is available at www.honestthinking.org/en/unesco/UNESCO.1967.Statement_on_Race.htm (consulted July 2010).

Select Bibliography

WEBSITES CONSULTED FROM APRIL TO JULY 2010

Australian Aboriginal History. www.australianexplorer.com/australian_history.htm
George W. Bush, Speeches. www.usa-patriotism.com/speeches/gwbush_911.htm
Declaration of the Rights of Man. www.historyguide.org/intellect/declaration.html
Free the Slaves. www.freetheslaves.com
Fugitive Slave Law (1850). www.usconstitution.net/fslave.html
United Nations, Documents. www.un.org/en/documents/index.shtml
UNESCO 1967 Statement on Race and Racial Predjudice. www.honestthinking.org/en/unesco/UNESCO.1967.Statement_on_Race.htm
United Nations International Convention on All Forms of Racial Discrimination. www2.ohchr.org/english/law/cerd.htm
United Nations Petition for African Americans, *Encyclopedia of the New American Nation*. www.americanforeignrelations.com/A-D/African-Americans-The-united-nations-petition.html

BOOKS AND ARTICLES

Appiah, Kwame Anthony. *Cosmopolitanism: Ethics in a World of Strangers*. New York: W. W. Norton, 2006.
———. "What's Wrong with Slavery." In *Buying Freedom: The Ethics and Economics of Slave Redemption*, ed. Kwame Anthony Appiah and Martin Bunzl. Princeton, NJ: Princeton University Press, 2007.
Aptheker, Herbert, ed. *The Correspondence of W. E. B. Du Bois*. 3 vols. Amherst, MA: University of Massachusetts Press, 1973–1978.
Aquinas, Saint Thomas. *On Law, Morality, and Politics*. Ed. William P. Baumgarth and Richard J. Regan, S.J. Indianapolis, IN: Hackett, 1988.

Aristotle. *Nichomachean Ethics*. Trans. Terrence Irwin. Indianapolis, IN: Hackett, 1985.
———. *Rhetoric*. In *Basic Works of Aristotle*, ed. Richard McKeon, trans. W. D. Ross. New York: Random House, 1941.

Aubrey, John. *Brief Lives, Chiefly of Contemporaries, set down by John Aubrey, between the years 1669 and 1696*. Ed. Andrew Clark. 2 vols. Oxford: Clarendon Press, January 1898, Facsimile available at books.google.com (consulted June 2010).

Augustine. *Confessions: Books I–XIII*. Trans. F. J. Sheed. Indianapolis, IN: Hackett, 1993.

Bair, Asatar P. *Prison Labor in the United States: An Economic Analysis*. New York: Routledge, 2008.

Bentham, Jeremy. *Anarchical Fallacies*. Ed. William Atkins Edmunson. Cambridge: Cambridge University Press, 1998.

Berger, Joseph. *The World in a City: Traveling the Globe through the Neighborhoods of the New New York*. New York: Random House, 2007.

Boas, Franz. "Race Problems in America." *Science* 29 (1909): 839–49.

Broome, Richard. *Aboriginal Australians: A History since 1788*. Crows Nest, NSW: Allen Unwin, 2010.

Buber, Martin. "The Question to the Single One." In *The Writings of Martin Buber*, ed. Will Herberg. New York: World Publishing, 1956.

———. "The Two Foci of the Jewish Soul." In *The Writings of Martin Buber*, ed. Will Herberg. New York: World Publishing, 1956.

Cicero, Marcus Tullius. *On Obligations (De Officiis)*. Ed. and trans. P. G. Walsh. Oxford: Oxford University Press, 2000.

———. *Orations of Marcus Tullius Cicero*. Trans. C. D. Yonge, London: George Bell and Sons, 1891.

Coles, Robert. *The Moral Life of Children*. New York: Grove Atlantic, 1986.

Cornford, Francis Macdonald. *Before and After Socrates*. New York: Cambridge University Press, 2007 [1932].

Corwin, Edward S. *The "Higher Law" Background of American Constitutional Law*. Ithaca, NY: Cornell University Press, 1955. Reprinted from the 1928 edition, reprinted from *Harvard Law Review* 42 (1928–1929): 149–85.

Darnton, Robert. "A Bourgeois Puts His World in Order: The City as a Text." In *The Great Cat Massacre and Other Episodes in French Cultural History*. New York: Vintage Books, 1985.

Den Boer, W. *Private Morality in Greece and Rome: Some Historical Aspects*. Leiden, The Netherlands: E. J. Brill, 1979.

Descartes, Rene. *Meditations on First Philosophy*. In *The Philosophical Writings of Descartes*, ed. John Cottingham, Robert Stroothoff, and Dugald Murdoch. 3 vols. Cambridge: Cambridge University Press, 1984. Vol. 2.

Dillon, John, and Lloyd P. Gerson, eds. *Neoplatonic Philosophy: Introductory Readings*. Indianapolis, IN: Hackett, 2004.

Drescher, Seymour. *Abolition: A History of Slavery and Antislavery*. Cambridge: Cambridge University Press, 2009.

Du Bois, W. E. B. "The Conservation of Races." Reprinted in *The Idea of Race*, ed. Robert Bernasconi and Tommy L. Lott, 108–117. Indianapolis, IN: Hackett, 2000.

Edwards, Paul, ed. *The Encyclopedia of Philosophy*. 8 vols. New York: Macmillan, 1967.

Emerson, Ralph Waldo. "Compensation" (185). In *Journals and Miscellaneous Notebooks of Ralph Waldo Emerson*, ed. H. Orth, 6: 215. Cambridge, MA: Harvard University Press, 1966.

Eze, Emmanuel Chukwudi, ed. *Race and the Enlightenment: A Reader*. Cambridge, MA: Blackwell, 1997.

Finley, M. I. *Ancient Slavery and Modern Ideology*. New York: Penguin, 1980.

Furley, David J. "Antiophon's Case against Justice." In *The Sophists and Their Legacy: Proceedings of the Fourth International Colloquium on Ancient Philosophy Held in Cooperation with rojektgruppe altertumswissenschaften Der Thyssen stiftung at Bad Homburg, 19th August–1st September, 1978*, ed. G. B. Kerferd, 81–91. Wiesbaden: Franz Steiner Verlag GMBH, 1981.

Gierke, Otto. *Natural Law and the Theory of Society 1500–1800*. Trans. Ernest Barker. London: Cambridge University Press, 1934.

———. *Political Theories of the Middle Ages*. Trans. Frederic William Mairland. Boston: Beacon, 1958.

Glasgow, Joshua. *A Theory of Race*. New York: Routledge, 2009.

Glick, Leonard B. "Types Distinct from Our Own: Franz Boas on Jewish Identity and Assimilation." *American Anthropologist* 82 (1982): 545–65.

Hauser, Marc. *Moral Minds: The Nature of Right and Wrong*. New York: Harper Perennial, 2007.

Heer, Friedrich. *The Medieval World*. Trans. Janet Sondheimer. New York: New American Library, 1961.

Hart, H. L. A. *The Concept of Law*. Oxford: Oxford University Press, 1991.

Hayek, F. A. "The Legal and Political Philosophy of David Hume." In *Hume*, ed. C. V. Chappell. New York: Doubleday, 1966.

Hill, Jason D. *Becoming a Cosmopolitan: What It Means to Be a Human Being in the New Millennium*. Lanham, MD: Rowman and Littlefield, 2000.

———. *Beyond Blood Identities: Posthumanity in the Twenty-First Century*. Lanham, MD: Rowman and Littlefield, 2009.

Hobbes, Thomas. *De Cive*. Ed. Bernard Gert. Indianapolis, IN: Hackett, 1991.

———. *Leviathan*. Ed. Edwin Curley. Indianapolis, IN: Hackett, 1994.

Hume, David. "Of Commerce." In *Essays Moral, Political, and Literary*, ed. Stuart D. Warner and Donald W. Livingston, 220–21 (essay 7). Indianapolis, IN: Hackett, 1994.

———. *A Treatise of Human Nature*. Ed. L. A. Selby-Bigge. London: Oxford University Press, 1964 [1888].

Ishay, Micheline R., ed. *The Human Rights Reader*. New York: Routledge, 2007.

Jacob, Mary C. *The Enlightenment: A Brief History with Documents*. Boston: Bedford/ St. Martin's, 2001.

John of Salisbury. *Policraticus*. Ed. Cary J. Nederman. Cambridge: Cambridge University Press, 1990.

Jones, Peter. *Rights*. Basingstoke: Macmillan, 1994.

Justinian. *The Digest of Justinian*. Trans. Charles Henry Monro. Cambridge: Cambridge at the University Press, 1904. Available online at www.archive.org (consulted May 2010).

Kant, Immanuel. *Grounding for the Metaphysics of Morals.* In *Kant's Ethical Philosophy,* trans. James W. Ellington, ed. Warner A. Wick. Indianapolis, IN: Hackett, 1994.

———. *The Metaphysics of Morals.* In *Kant's Ethical Philosophy,* trans. James W. Ellington, ed. Warner A. Wick. Indianapolis, IN: Hackett, 1994.

———. *Perpetual Peace.* In *Kant's Ethical Philosophy,* trans. James W. Ellington, ed. Warner A. Wick. Indianapolis, IN: Hackett, 1994.

LaBelle, Deborah. "Ensuring Human Rights for All: Realizing Human Rights for Prisoners." In *Bringing Human Rights Home: Portraits of the Movement,* ed. Cynthia Soohoo, Catherine Albisa, and Martha F. Davis. 3 vols. Santa Barbara, CA: Praeger, 2007. Vol. 1.

Laëtius, Diogenes. *Lives and Opinions of Eminent Philosophers.* Trans. C. D. Yong. London: Henry G. Bohn, 1853.

Lang, Berel. "Metaphysical Racism (Or: Biological Warfare by Other Means)." In *RACE/SEX: Their Sameness, Difference and Interplay,* ed. Naomi Zack, 17–28. New York: Routledge, 1997.

Lau, Holning. "Rethinking the Persistent Objector Doctrine in International Human Rights Law." *Chicago Journal of International Law,* July 1, 2005, at www.allbusiness.com/legal/international-law/884010-1.html (consulted July 2010).

Levy, Richard S., ed. *Antisemitism: An Historical Encyclopedia of Prejudice and Persecution.* Santa Barbara, CA: ABC-CLIO, 2005.

Locke, John. *A Letter concerning Toleration.* Latin and English texts revised and edited by Mario Montuori. The Hague: Martinus Nijhoff, 1963.

———. *Further Considerations concerning Raising the Value of Money Wherein Mr. Lowndes's Arguments for it concerning an Essay for the Amendment of the Silver Coins, are particularly Examined, 1865.* In *Locke on Money,* by John Locke, ed. Patrick Hyde Kelly. Oxford: Oxford Clarendon Press, 1991.

———. *Some Considerations of the Consequences of the Lowering of Interest and Raising the Value of Money.* In *Locke on Money,* by John Locke, ed. Patrick Hyde Kelly. Oxford: Oxford Clarendon Press, 1991.

———. *Two Treatises of Government.* Ed. Peter Laslett. Cambridge: Cambridge University Press, 1991.

Lorde, Audre. "The Master's Tools Will Never Dismantle the Master's House." In *This Bridge Called My Back: Writings by Radical Women of Color,* ed. Cherríe Moraga and Gloria Anzaldúa, 94–101. New York: Kitchen Sink Press, 1983.

MacIntyre, Alasdair. *After Virtue.* Notre Dame, IN: University of Notre Dame Press, 1984.

McCarthy, Thomas. *Race, Empire, and the Idea of Human Development.* Cambridge: Cambridge University Press, 2009.

McDowell, Gary L. "Coke, Corwin and the Constitution: The 'Higher Law Background' Reconsidered." Review of *Corwin on the Constitution* by Richard Loss. *Law and Social Inquiry* 14, no. 3 (Summer 1989): 603–14.

Maritain, Jacques. "The Grounds for an International Declaration of Human Rights (1947)." In *The Human Rights Reader,* ed. Micheline R. Ishay, 2–6. New York: Routledge, 2007.

Melzer, Milton. *Slavery: A World History.* 2 vols. New York: Da Capo Press, 1993.

Michaels, Walter Ben. *Our America: Nativism, Modernism, and Pluralism*. Charlotte, NC: Duke University Press, 1995.

Mill, John Stuart. "Bentham." In *Utilitarianism and On Liberty*, by John Stuart Mill, ed. Mary Warnock, 53–88. Cambridge, MA: Blackwell, 2003. Also available online at socserv.mcmaster.ca/econ/ugcm/3ll3/bentham/bentham.

———. *Utilitarianism*. In *Utilitarianism, Liberty and Representative Government*, ed. A. D. Lindsay. New York: E. P. Dutton, 1953.

Morrow, Glenn R. "The Murder of Slaves in Attic Law." *Classical Philology* 32, no. 3 (July 1937).

———. *Plato's Law of Slavery*. New York: Arno Press, 1976.

Narayan, Uma. "Contesting Cultures: 'Westernization,' Respect for Cultures, and Third-World Feminists." In *The Second Wave: A Reader in Feminist Theory*, ed. Linda Nicholson, 396–414. New York: Routledge, 1997.

Noonan, John T., Jr. "Development in Moral Doctrine." *Theological Studies* 54 (December 1993): 662–78.

Norwood, Hermond. "Fountain Hughes Interview." June 11, 1949. Baltimore, Maryland. WPA project. Available at xroads.virginia.edu/~hyper/wpa/hughes1.html (consulted March 2010).

Nussbaum, Martha. "Kant and Cosmopolitanism." In *Perpetual Peace*, ed. James Bohman and Matthias Lutz-Bachmann, 25–58. Cambridge, MA: MIT Press, 1997.

———. "Patriotism and Cosmopolitanism." *Boston Review* 19, no. 5 (1994). At www.soci.niu.edu/phildept/Kapitan/Nussbaum1.html.

Oboria, Leslye Amede. "Bridges and Barricades: Rethinking Polemics and Intransigence in the Campaign against Female Circumcision." In *Global Critical Race Feminism: An International Reader*, ed. Adrien Katherine Wing. New York: New York University Press, 2000.

O'Brien, Conor Cruise. "Rousseau, Robespierre, Burke, Jefferson, and the French Revolution." In *The Social Contract and the First and Second Discourses*, by Jean-Jacques Rousseau, ed. Susan Dunn, 301–15. New Haven, CT: Yale University Press, 2002.

Okin, Susan Moller. "Philosopher Queens and Private Wives: Plato on Women and the Family." In *Feminist Interpretations and Political Philosophy*, ed. Carole Pateman and Mary Lyndon Shanley. University Park: Pennsylvania State University Press, 1991.

Painter, Nell Irvin. *The History of White People*. New York: Norton, 2010.

Pateman, Carole, and Charles W. Mills. *Contract and Domination*. Malden, MA: Polity Press, 2007.

Pitts, Jennifer. "Legislator of the World? A Rereading of Bentham on Colonies." *Political Theory* 31, no. 2 (April 2003): 200–34.

Plato. *Apology*. Trans. Hugh Tredennick. In *Collected Dialogues*, ed. Edith Hamilton and Huntington Cairns. New York: Random House, 1964.

———. *Crito*. Trans. Hugh Tredennick. In *Collected Dialogues*, ed. Edith Hamilton and Huntington Cairns. New York: Random House, 1964.

———. *Euthyphro*. Trans. Lane Cooper. In *Collected Dialogues*, ed. Edith Hamilton and Huntington Cairns. New York: Random House, 1964.

———. *Gorgias*. Trans. W. D. Woodhead. In *Collected Dialogues*, ed. Edith Hamilton and Huntington Cairns. New York: Random House, 1964.

———. *Phaedo*. Trans. G. M. A. Grube. In *The Trial and Death of Socrates*, by Plato. Indianapolis, IN: Hackett, 1975.

———. *Protagoras*. Trans. W. K. C. Guthrie. In *Collected Dialogues*, ed. Edith Hamilton and Huntington Cairns. New York: Random House, 1964.

———. *Republic*. Trans. Francis Cornford. London: Oxford University Press, 1945.

———. *Republic*. Trans. Paul Shorey. In *Collected Dialogues*, ed. Edith Hamilton and Huntington Cairns. New York: Random House, 1964.

Plotinus. *Enneads*. In *Neoplatonic Philosophy: Introductory Readings*, ed. John Dillon and Lloyd P. Gerson. Indianapolis, IN: Hackett, 2004.

Porphyry. *On the Life of Plotinus and the Arrangement of His Work*. Trans. Stephen McKenna. Sequim, WA: Holmes Publishing, 2001.

Proclus. *Platonic Theology*. In *Neoplatonic Philosophy: Introductory Readings*, ed. John Dillon and Lloyd P. Gerson. Indianapolis, IN: Hackett, 2004.

Rawls, John. *A Theory of Justice*. Cambridge, MA: Harvard University Press, 1971.

Reed, Adolph, Jr. "Making Sense of Race, I: The Ideology of Race, the Biology of Human Variation, and the Problem of Medical and Public Health Research." *Journal of Race and Policy* 1, no. 1 (Spring/Summer 2005): 11–42.

Rousseau, Jean-Jacques. *The Social Contract and the First and Second Discourses*. Ed. Susan Dunn. New Haven, CT: Yale University Press, 2002.

Sartre, Jean-Paul. *Anti-Semite and Jew*. Trans. George J. Becker. New York: Schocken Books, 1946.

———. "Existentialism Is a Humanism." Trans. Bernard Frechtman. Reprinted in *Existentialism and Human Emotions*. New York: Philosophical Library and Carol Publishing, 1985. Available online at www.marxists.org/reference/archive/sartre/works/exist/sartre.htm.

Singer, Peter. *The Life You Can Save: Acting Now to End World Poverty*. New York: Random House, 2009.

Stocker, Michael. "The Schizophrenia of Modern Ethical Theories." *Journal of Philosophy* 73, no. 14 (August 1978): 453–66.

Stychin, Carl F. "Same-Sex Sexualities and the Globalization of Human Rights Discourse." *McGill Law Journal* 49 (2004): 951–68.

Terence. "The Self-Tormentor (Heautontimorumenos)," trans. Palmer Bovie. In *Terence: The Comedies: (Complete Roman Drama in Translation)*, ed. Palmer Bovie, trans. Constance Carrier and Douglas Parker. Baltimore, MD: Johns Hopkins University Press, 1992.

Untersteiner, Mario. *The Sophists*. Trans. Kathleen Freeman. New York: Philosophical Library, 1954.

Vishneski, John. "What the Court Decided in Dred Scott v. Sandford." *American Journal of Legal History* 32, no. 4 (1988): 373–90.

Walters, John. "The Commons and Their Mental Worlds." In *The Oxford Illustrated History of Tudor and Stuart*, ed. John Stephen Morrill. Cambridge: Oxford University Press, 1990.

Westermann, William Linn. *The Slave Systems of Greek and Roman Antiquity*. Philadelphia: American Philosophical Society, 1955.

Wiedemann, Thomas. *Greek and Roman Slavery*. Baltimore, MD: Johns Hopkins University Press, 1981.

Wergeland, Agnes Mathilde. *Slavery in Germanic Society during the Middle Ages*. Chicago: University of Chicago Press, 1916.

Williams, Bernard. "The Human Prejudice" and "Reply by Peter Singer." In *Peter Singer under Fire: The Moral Iconoclast Faces His Critics*, ed. Jeffrey A. Schaler, 77–102. Chicago: Open Court, 2009.

Wilshire, Susan Ford. *Greece, Rome, and the Bill of Rights*. Norman: University of Oklahoma Press, 1992.

Wood, Neal. *Cicero's Social and Political Thought*. Berkeley: University of California Press, 1988.

Young, Iris M. "The Ideal of Community and the Politics of Difference." In *Feminism/Postmodernism*, ed. Linda J. Nicholson, 300–24. New York: Routledge, 1990

Zack, Naomi. "American Mixed Race: Theoretical and Legal Issues." *Harvard Black-Letter Law Journal* 17 (Spring 2001): 33–46.

———. *Bachelors of Science: Seventeenth Century Identity, Then and Now*. Philadelphia: Temple University Press, 1996.

———. Review of *Contract and Domination*, by Carole Pateman and Charles Mills. *Ethnic and Racial Studies* 32, no. 8 (November 2008): 1506–7.

———. "Ethnicity, Race, and the Importance of Gender." In *Race or Ethnicity?: On Black and Latino Identity*, ed. Jorge Gracia, 101–22. Ithaca, NY: Cornell University Press, 2007.

———. "The Fluid Symbol of Mixed Race." *Hypatia* (25th Anniversary Issue) 25, no. 4 (2010): 875–90.

———. "Lockean Money, Globalism and Indigenism," In *Civilization and Oppression*, ed. Catherine Wilson. *Canadian Journal of Philosophy* 25 (1999): 31–53.

———. "Mixed Black and White Race and Public Policy." *Hypatia* 10, no. 1 (Winter 1995): 120–32.

———. *Philosophy of Science and Race*. New York: Routledge, 2002.

Index

acceptance of difference in cosmopolitanism, 27
action, reasons for, 33–34
African American philosophy, global concerns of, 32
African Americans, denial of moral respect for, 138
Alcidamas of Elaea, 57–59
Amelius (Amerius), Plotinus' student, 110n44
anachronism about race, 2–3
Anarchical Fallacies, 146–49
andropoda (man-footed beings), Greek word for slaves, 73
anomie, urban, 35
anonymity, 34
Antiphon the Sophist, 56–57
Anti-Semite and Jew, 35–36
anti-Semitism: French, 35–36; medieval, 103
Appiah, Kwame Anthony, 28, 31, 39, 72–73
applied ethics as individual virtues, in *Republic*, 8–10
Aquinas, Thomas, on slavery, 93–94
Aristotle: happiness, 13; invention of ethics, 11–16; man as political animal, 1, 11, 12, 17–18; mean in virtues, 15; slavery 3, 58, 78–79; universal law, 58–60; virtues for rulers, 11–16

atheism in Sartrean existentialism, 44n28
Australian aborigines described by Bentham, 147–48
axiology, 68

bad faith, 36
Baudelaire, Charles, 43n20
Becoming a Cosmopolitan: What it means to be a human being in the new millennium, 38
Bentham, Jeremy: English chauvinism of, 148; paraphasis, method of, 146; on rights, 146–47, 149
Beyond Blood Identities: Posthumanity in the Twenty-First Century, 36–37
black essences, ideas of, 83
black mores, perception of racism in, 29–31
black racial identity and US slavery, 71; as hereditary mechanism for slavery, 83
Boas, Franz, 24, 40–41n2
Boer, W. D., 75
Bridges, Ruby, xi
Buber, Martin, 91–92

categorical imperative and intrinsic worth formulation, 144–45

187

About the Author

Naomi Zack received her Ph.D. in philosophy from Columbia University, has taught at the University at Albany, SUNY, and has been professor of philosophy at the University of Oregon since 2001. Zack's most recent books are *Ethics for Disaster* (2009, pb. 2010) and *The Handy Philosophy Answer Book* (2010). Her other books include *Race and Mixed Race* (1993), *Bachelors of Science* (1996), *Philosophy of Science and Race* (2002), *Inclusive Feminism* (2005), and the short textbook *Thinking about Race* (2006). She is presently working on a book about African American entertainment and freedom. She can be reached at nzack@uoregon.edu.

Naomi Zack is also the executive producer and founder of Philosophical Installations, a website of streaming videos of academic philosophers performing outside the classroom: philinstall.uoregon.edu.